Yale Historical Publications, Miscellany, 118

THE POLITICS OF PROPAGANDA
THE OFFICE OF WAR INFORMATION
1942–1945

Allan M. Winkler

New Haven and London   Yale University Press

1978

Designed by John O. C. McCrillis
and set in Baskerville type.
Printed in the United States of America by
The Haddon Craftsmen, Inc., Scranton, Pennsylvania.

Published in Great Britain, Europe, Africa, and
Asia (except Japan) by Yale University Press,
Ltd., London. Distributed in Latin America by
Kaiman & Polon, Inc., New York City; in
Australia and New Zealand by Book & Film
Services, Artarmon, N.S.W., Australia; and in
Japan by Harper & Row, Publishers, Tokyo
Office.

Library of Congress Cataloging in Publication Data

Winkler, Allan M   1945–
    The politics of propaganda.
    (Yale historical publications: Miscellany, 118)
    Bibliography: p.
    Includes index.
    1. World War, 1939–1945—Propaganda. 2. United
States. Office of War Information. 3. Propaganda,
American. I. Title. II. Series.
D810.P7U8   940.54'886'73   77–21746
ISBN 0–300–02148–8

For
Alberta, Jenny, and David

Contents

Acknowledgments

In studying American propaganda in World War II, I received willing aid from a large number of people. I would like to thank all the archivists and librarians who helped find the materials for my work. I am grateful, too, to Joseph M. Goldsen and the Yale University Concilium on International and Area Studies, to Bruce M. Russett and the Yale University Council on International Relations, and to the A. Whitney Griswold Faculty Research Fund at Yale University for the grants that provided assistance for research. Most of all I appreciate the help I received while writing. Many people read either all or part of the manuscript in some form and offered a variety of useful suggestions. For their aid I am grateful to Richard N. Chapman, George Cunningham, Donna L. Dubinsky, Andrew Fisher, Miles Fletcher, Nagayo Homma, John Houseman, Herman Kahn, Mark Lytle, Gaddis Smith, and C. Vann Woodward. Richard W. Fox, John W. Jeffries, Richard L. McCormick, Richard Polenberg, and Michael S. Sherry have my thanks for their particularly penetrating critiques. My father, Henry R. Winkler, also an historian, has long provided me with an example of how to study history, and in this project he was especially helpful. He read all of an early version, and his comments improved the manuscript. To my sister, Karen J. Winkler, I am similarly grateful. Drawing on her background in history and journalism, she aided at a crucial time by helping me rethink many of the important questions and decide how to rearrange the material into a final draft. I would like to offer a special word of thanks to John Morton Blum, who first interested me in twentieth-century America and then helped me define my study. He read numerous drafts promptly and patiently and gave me the benefit of his own sense of the period as well as his sense of expression. I appreciate the typing done by Claudia Jensen and Beverly Cedarbaum, and the assistance of Lynn Walterick of the Yale University Press and all the others who helped bring the manuscript to its final form. Finally, I would like to thank my wife, Alberta, for giving her warm support, and our children, Jenny and David, for aiding in their own little ways.

Prologue

Six months after the United States entered World War II, the federal government launched a major propaganda program to assist in fighting the war. The Office of War Information, established by executive order in June 1942, was the dominant agency in that campaign. From the start, the propaganda organization had a vision of the role it could play. It wanted to take an active part in winning the war and in laying the foundations for a better postwar world. To that end, OWI sought to communicate American aims in the struggle at hand and at the same time tried to convey to audiences at home and abroad the ideals that could give rise to a peaceful, democratic world, just as the Committee on Public Information had attempted to do in World War I twenty-five years before. For all the hopeful expectations, those tasks proved more formidable than the leaders of OWI had ever imagined. Disputes with congressmen, military officials, and various members of Franklin Delano Roosevelt's administration hampered their efforts for much of the war. And while the disputes themselves were troubling, they also reflected the deeper problems the propaganda organization could not escape.

OWI found itself in an awkward position from the very beginning. The first difficulties stemmed from the public fears of propaganda that emerged soon after World War I, lingered on for decades, and never really died away. Those fears generated carping criticisms, both inside and out of the government, that were often unfounded but still hampered the effective functioning of the agency. More serious troubles came from the growing disagreements OWI encountered over American aims in the war. All too soon the propaganda leaders realized that their view of the struggle was considerably more ambitious than that of the policy makers in Washington whose lead they had to follow. Liberal propagandists accepted at face value the democratic pro-

nouncements of the Roosevelt administration, only to discover
that the ultimate commitment was far more ambiguous than they
had believed. That discovery, and the slow and painful adjust-
ments it entailed, provided the framework within which American
propaganda finally emerged. Amid the conflict and controversy,
the suspicion and distrust that surrounded OWI, the early idealistic vision gave way to a more accurate reflection of the dominant
view of the war, as the propagandists reluctantly learned to accommodate themselves to realities they could not avoid.

Propaganda had initially fared better in World War I, when
large-scale political persuasion had come of age. Although the
use of propaganda by warring states was as old as human mem-
ory, technological advances in the late nineteenth and early twentieth centuries opened up vast new possibilities. With world-wide
communication now easily possible, the major powers all established programs to gain support from their own peoples and
from the rest of the world, and to drive wedges between the
powers they were fighting. Techniques varied widely. The British
established separate organizations to deal with home information
and enemy propaganda. The Germans allowed each governmental department to issue propaganda statements and then attempted to coordinate those messages and announcements at
press conferences held several times a week. The French, too,
maintained a fragmented administration, with propaganda responsibilities in the hands of established governmental units.[1]

The most systematic centralization of propaganda came in the
United States, where the Committee on Public Information,
headed by the contentious journalist George Creel, assumed all
responsibility. Created by executive order in April 1917, one
week after the United States entered the struggle, the CPI was
designed to be run by a committee that included the secretaries
of war, navy, and state, but the committee held only one meeting
and Creel never convened it again. Enjoying the confidence and
support of President Woodrow Wilson, Creel as sole head pursued his aims with a single-minded intensity.[2]

Creel's organization sought first to unite American public
opinion behind the war. By posters, pamphlets, and even volun-

tary speakers who invaded movie houses during intermissions, the CPI attempted to combat opposition to the war and to persuade Americans that sacrifices were necessary if democracy was to survive. Creel's efforts also went beyond American shores. He was convinced that he was involved in a "fight for the mind of mankind." To the rest of the world he emphasized America's vast resources and proclaimed inevitable victory. Through all means at his disposal he announced that Woodrow Wilson's Fourteen Points would usher in a new world order. Creel was sincere. Though he viewed his task as "the world's greatest adventure in advertising," he believed America's cause was just. If he could present America's unassailable aims clearly and simply he could overcome all opposition.[3]

Creel accomplished his task too well. As his agency sought to arouse America, it stirred up hatred of all things German. Portrayed as barbaric Huns, Germans appeared intent on conquering the world for their own selfish ends. German spies, the CPI hinted, were everywhere. Anyone voicing the least sympathy for anything German might well be a traitor in disguise. The CPI did spark support for the war, but it also helped stir up the hysteria that led unthinking Americans to rename sauerkraut "liberty cabbage" and hamburger "Salisbury steak." At the same time, it generated unrealistic hopes for a better world. The CPI had sold the war with religious fervor, as "a Crusade not merely to re-win the tomb of Christ, but to bring back to earth the rule of right, the peace, goodwill to men and gentleness he taught." When Wilson's hopes for a peace of reconciliation were eroded at the peace conference at Versailles and in the subsequent debate over ratification at home, Americans were left with the sharp contrast between unfulfilled dreams and the realities of world politics. And so in the following decades the Creel Committee was remembered in a bitter way. Creel's penchant for overstatement and acrimonious argument left some ill feelings. But the propaganda itself was viewed as too boisterous, too exuberant for a world that had hardly been made safe for democracy. Creel had oversold his product. Propaganda became a scapegoat in the postwar period of disillusion.[4]

As Americans became increasingly aware of propaganda, many began to feel uneasy about its implications. They viewed it with a morbid fascination, studied and wrote about it, and began to fear its possible consequences. Propaganda to some seemed to have an unlimited force—the power to capture men's hearts and to bypass their rational processes. Good propaganda was so subtle that people might not even be aware they were being taken in. Under those circumstances democracy itself seemed endangered, for the mythical marketplace of ideas could no longer be truly competitive if ideas could be so easily manipulated. The rise of Germany's Nazi regime, which made extensive use of propaganda, gave further cause for alarm.[5]

Propaganda suffered too from the arguments of isolationists in the 1930s. As some Americans retreated from political involvement with the outside world and began to consider their entrance into the Great War a mistake, they could draw on scholarly accounts that argued that the United States had been duped by propagandists into entering the war. James Duane Squires's *British Propaganda at Home and in the United States, From 1914 to 1917,* published in 1935, and H. C. Peterson's *Propaganda for War: The Campaign against American Neutrality, 1914–1917,* published in 1939, both claimed that Britain had engaged in a successful campaign to shape American perceptions about the war. Those studies fanned isolationist sentiment and exacerbated suspicions of propaganda.[6]

Propaganda also fared poorly from associations with critical attitudes that accompanied the remarkable growth of advertising in the years following World War I. As the volume of expenditures rose astronomically and advertising became an integral part of the American economy, criticisms began to mount. The truth sometimes seemed lost in the drive to sell new goods. Worse, audiences were being encouraged, even pressured, to buy products they neither wanted nor needed as advertisers sold their own conception of the Good Life in an effort to make consumer demand match America's ever increasing production. Critics resented the ways the techniques of mass persuasion were used,

and their arguments colored attitudes about similarly manipulative propaganda.[7]

Americans, in short, had serious reservations about propaganda even before World War II made another government venture into the field seem likely. Although social scientists at the
end of the 1930s shifted position and started to argue that there
were limits to the effectiveness of political persuasion, the less
attractive connotations of propaganda remained. Ordinary
Americans, wary still, continued to shy away from the very term,
and the president of the United States shared their suspicions. A
member of Wilson's administration in World War I, Roosevelt
remembered the hate and hysteria generated by Creel's Committee on Public Information. He was wary from the start of any
similar program. Sensitive to public opinion, persuasive in his
own way, he had no intention of allowing a formal government
bureau the same latitude the CPI had enjoyed. His reservations
and those of the people behind him had important effects on all
further American efforts to use propaganda in the national interest. The legacy of suspicion could not be denied.[8]

The more serious limitations on American propaganda came
from the ambiguity over basic American aims in the war. Rhetoric
and reality did not always correspond. Victory was, without question, the essential concern of American policy makers during the
struggle. Yet the Allies had deliberately and aggressively proclaimed that World War II had a larger meaning. Even before
Pearl Harbor, in his message to Congress on January 6, 1941,
Roosevelt had spoken of the "four essential human freedoms"—
freedom of speech and expression, freedom of worship, freedom
from want, freedom from fear. In the summer of that year, in the
Atlantic Charter, he and British Prime Minister Winston Churchill had laid out their conception of the postwar world, in which
the self-determination of nations, equal trading rights for all, and
a system of general security would prevail. Those declarations
gave a sense of mission to the war, and as the United States
entered the conflict at the end of 1941, its leaders used the
slogans to underscore the fundamental American aims.[9]

The early participants in the American propaganda campaign were dedicated to those democratic ideals. Most were passionate interventionists who had sought American entrance into the war long before the attack at Pearl Harbor. They saw the war as a real war of liberation. For them, it was a battle between the forces of fascism and the forces of democracy—a conflict that could be won only by the triumph of their vision. Through propaganda, they wanted to communicate what they considered the basic American values of freedom and democracy to friends and foes alike in all corners of the earth. They took the Four Freedoms and the Atlantic Charter seriously and used the slogans to shape their messages about the war. A brave new world was possible, and victory would help bring it about.

The propaganda leaders articulated that vision as they spoke to audiences both at home and abroad. To the outside world they transmitted their hopes and expectations of a free and open postwar order. To citizens within the borders of the United States they conveyed the same vision in a less proselytizing way. Fearful of taking too strong a line in a democratic society, they concentrated on presenting the "facts" about the war, with the confident expectation that the public, when properly informed, would fully endorse their view.

But OWI soon found that it lacked support at the top for its picture of the war. Unlike Woodrow Wilson, who showed a stubborn dedication to his ideals, Franklin Roosevelt took a more flexible view of the struggle in which he was engaged. The president had a vision of the postwar world and of America's role in it, but he hesitated to move beyond vague generalities about his plans. Reluctant to make firm commitments, he preferred to concentrate on winning the war. While Roosevelt had proclaimed the liberal, democratic war aims, and while those aims gave substance to the struggle, as the fighting wore on the propaganda leaders became increasingly aware that the president, and the State, War, and Navy Departments, were willing to compromise those aims in the interests of a quick end to the struggle. Victory often appeared to be not just a necessary aim, but an end in itself. And as expediency triumphed, the views of the propagandists, although nominally those of the rest of the government, seemed out of place in the broader framework of the military effort.

American propaganda, generated largely by the Office of War Information, developed within the limits of strictures it could not avoid. Amid the public squabbles so characteristic of wartime Washington, OWI found itself permanently cast in a circumscribed role. As its once idealistic pronouncements gave way to battlefield messages meant to encourage surrender and pictures of America that were frequently trite, above all noncontroversial, the propaganda finally began to reflect the country's dominant view of the struggle. The propaganda revealed what the nation considered important as it strove to reconcile its basic values and the requirements of war, even as it demonstrated the limitations of the American vision itself.

1 The Origins of OWI

The growth of the American propaganda effort reflected the growth of the nation's larger effort in World War II. The information program developed to explain the defense program even before the United States entered the war. Although Americans avoided active military participation in the European struggle that started in September 1939, they nonetheless watched what was going on and expanded their own preparations to ward off attack. The Roosevelt administration oversaw the rapid increase in military spending and at the same time began to take at first tentative, then more aggressive, steps to assist the underdog Allies. In response to those moves, other interested Americans began to consider once again how they might explain both their productive accomplishments and their aims in the war to audiences at home and abroad. Interventionists in particular, eager to persuade both the public and the president that the destiny of the United States lay in joining the fight against fascism, pressed hard for the establishment of information channels that would alert audiences to the nature of the stakes involved. They knew they had to approach propaganda with caution, for George Creel's shadow was still a source of concern, yet they also realized they had to find some way to interpret for others the enormous changes that were taking place. As the first limited information efforts gave way to more extensive ones, those liberal and articulate interventionists who had a vision of their nation's responsibility in the war came to play an increasingly important role in shaping American propaganda. They were not the first, nor were they the last, to make their influence felt, but by the time the Japanese attack on Pearl Harbor brought the United States into the war, they had determined the basic directions the information program would take.

No one American possessed the powers of German Propaganda Minister Joseph Goebbels. Germany's rigid centralization of authority was alien to the American way, and even more unlikely after George Creel's experiences in World War I. But as participation in the next war seemed more and more likely, and as the United States proceeded cautiously towards establishing its own information network, two men played an especially important part. Archibald MacLeish and Robert Emmet Sherwood, both literary figures of note, both dedicated antifascists, helped map out the course of American propaganda in the early days of the war. Both had come slowly and painfully to recognize the need for involvement, and in so doing had developed strong feelings about the struggle and firm convictions about the role propaganda could play. Their own careers had taught them the importance of words and expressions in human affairs. They now began to use their considerable talents to shape the information program and thereby to transmit their convictions to the nation and to the world.

Archibald MacLeish was anxious to help other Americans understand their vested interest in the outcome of the war. He had watched with horror the growth of fascism in Europe and had come to realize that the regimentation and brutalization he saw in Germany and Italy threatened the values he held most dear. Conquest in Europe would change Western society in ways he found profoundly disturbing. Passionately committed to the survival of democracy in an unstable world, he knew he had to take some action and hoped to use the information program to point out the dangers he saw.

MacLeish brought assorted gifts to the task at hand. Widely recognized as a poet of the first rank, he also had practical expertise in government and business affairs. In a varied career he had long shown a talent and versatility that led others to view him with a genuine respect. After a successful undergraduate experience at Yale College, where he was a member of the football and swimming teams, wrote poetry, and was elected to Phi Beta Kappa, he served in World War I, then completed studies at the Harvard Law School. Cited for his legal promise, over the next few years he taught law and then began private practice with a distinguished firm in Boston. But in 1923 he put that start behind him and left for France to devote himself fully to the world of poetry.[1]

In his five years abroad, and even after his return home, MacLeish concentrated on his art and remained conspicuously aloof from political crusades. As his own work progressed, he became increasingly concerned with defining for himself and for others his own view of the creative role. The poet, he declared, was an artist who observed the world around him and articulated the images he saw. But always the commitment was to art and not to social or political ends, for "the artist is not and never can be an instrument of society." That position brought him into conflict in the early 1930s with Marxists, whom he criticized for subordinating art to revolutionary belief. And despite their rejoinders in the arguments that ensued, he continued to insist that the artist had to be independent, that poetry and politics did not mix.[2]

Yet MacLeish had not divorced himself entirely from the outside world. From 1930 to 1938, while continuing to write poetry, he served as an editor of *Fortune* magazine and contributed a variety of pieces to the publication. His work at *Fortune* alerted him to the problems in the world outside. He saw the ravages of the Depression and came to understand that the economic collapse could undermine the stability of the nation he loved. He also watched the ominous events unfolding in Europe and in the face of those developments found his poetic detachment harder and harder to maintain.[3]

MacLeish recognized the dangers posed by Adolf Hitler and his ever-growing following abroad. That understanding led him finally to change his earlier views about his own art and about the responsibilities of the creative members of society. Where he had earlier focused on literary themes, and on the need for the independent artist to explore for himself the life of the mind, now he began to call attention to current affairs and to demand that other poets, artists, and intellectuals affirm their own roots and traditions in the face of the outside peril. For, as he wrote in one of his strongest statements, "What matters now is the defense of culture—the defense truly, and in the most literal terms, of civilization as men have known it for the last two thousand years." Working largely in prose, MacLeish expressed his own belief that men should behave according to the dictates of reason to meet the dangers that threatened the world they knew. Active even before the European war broke out in 1939, he increased his efforts with the fall of France in 1940 and had become a strong spokesman for democracy and for American commitment to the cause at hand by the time the United States entered the war in 1941.[4]

MacLeish lashed out incessantly at the evil of fascism. That dictatorial system, he argued in his lyrical way, grew out of the chaos created by World War I and the subsequent upheaval of the 1930s. "Fascism," he wrote, "is capitalism's revenge upon itself: an old and dying king eaten by the children his own crimes conceived." Fascism was brutal and irrational; it appealed to the worst in mankind. It was "in its essence a revolt of man against himself—a revolt of stunted, half-formed, darkened men against a human world beyond their reach and most of all against the human world of reason and intelligence and sense." While the poet recognized the insidious attraction fascism might hold for those down and out, that meant only that the fascist revolution was "a revolution of the defeated, a revolution of the dispossessed." Indeed, "Caliban in the miserable and besotted swamp is the symbol of this revolution."[5]

Against that devastating portrait, MacLeish put forth the vision of democracy he had been struggling to define. Though the vision was vague and the outlines were occasionally blurred, the spirit was clear. In 1939 he declared, "We mean by democracy a society in which the dignity of man is of first importance, a society in which everything else must be subject to, and must support, the dignity of man." In such a setting, self-respect was possible, as was a corresponding respect for individual diversity in all its forms. Going further, MacLeish stressed that democracy represented more than the material advantages America enjoyed. It had rather to do with a "man's belief in liberty of mind and spirit, and his willingness to sacrifice his comforts and his earnings for its sake." Men could never take the system for granted, "for democracy is never a thing done. Democracy is always something that a nation must be doing." But the rewards of the way of life were clear. As MacLeish concluded in one of his passionate statements, "Democracy in action is a cause for which the stones themselves will fight."[6]

MacLeish had become a conscious spokesman for the position he embraced. Well aware of what he was doing, he hoped he could follow the example of Lincoln, who "reduced the violence and confusion of his time to the essential moral issue," and thereby persuade Americans seventy-five years later of the importance of the struggle they were not going to be able to avoid. Both as private citizen and, after his appointment in 1939 as Librarian of Congress, as government official, MacLeish preached his cause in speeches and articles directed at audiences throughout the country. Even after the United States entered the war, he sensed the importance of keeping the public informed. "The principal battleground of this war," he said on one occasion, "is not the South Pacific. It is not the Middle East. It is not England, or Norway, or the Russian Steppes. It is American opinion." For without American opinion firmly behind the war, victory was not at all sure to be won. Yet even while he sought to ensure adequate support for the necessary fighting, he tried to spark support too for the kind of war he hoped was possible, not a soldiers' war in support of the status quo, but a people's war to affirm for the rest of the world the principles of democracy wherever fascism reared its ugly head.[7]

That vision of possibility guided MacLeish's efforts, but he understood, too, as he became formally involved in the propaganda program, that a democracy had to be careful about the manipulation of opinion. Unlike a dictatorship, it could not baldly tell its people what to think. Rather, the poet declared, "The government of a democracy, by virtue of its existence as a democratic government, has a very different function in relation to the making of opinion. It is the government's function to see to it that the people have the facts before them—the facts on which opinions can be formed." Democratic propaganda had to be based on the "strategy of truth," which involved giving out the honest facts about the struggle, and then trusting the people to make up their own minds in the right way.[8]

MacLeish could endorse that strategy because his own intense faith in man's reason convinced him that informed men would make what he considered to be appropriate decisions. And so he dedicated himself to informing the people and then pleading with them to let their hearts and minds draw the necessary conclusions. Using the literary gifts that had earlier gained him a Pulitzer Prize, he argued his case with dignity and integrity as he sought to define the war for all men as a necessary struggle for a better world.

Playwright Robert Sherwood shared most of MacLeish's convictions. Equally passionate, equally committed, and in time even more involved with propaganda, he too understood the stakes involved in the war that would not go away. He shared the poet's revulsion for fascism and his dedication to democracy. And like MacLeish he devoted himself to warning others of the threat to their very way of life.

Sherwood was in a good position to make his views heard. By the time World War II broke out in Europe, his theatrical success had established him as a figure of note. A writer for most of his life, he was accustomed to addressing the public. After an academically uninspired stay at Harvard that was mercifully cut short by service in World War I, he had worked as a journalist, editor, and movie critic before beginning to write the plays that eventually won three Pulitzer Prizes in five years. Now he had a following who enjoyed his plays and listened to what he said.[9]

At first glance Sherwood appeared to be an unlikely publicist for anything. The gaunt, six foot seven inch playwright looked, according to a former secretary, "like a walking coffin." Shy and with a mournful, granite-like face, he could be witty, though *The Saturday Review of Literature* noted after the war that "Mr. Sherwood is reported, with some exaggeration, to talk about ten words a minute." He also took his time in making up his mind on questions that were important to him. But once he did, he moved forward without stopping. A man of strong opinions, he did all he could to persuade others of his convictions, and he used his talent to express in words the feelings that could move an audience to support his views.[10]

On the question of the war he had agonized at length. Like others of his generation, his experience with combat had been a wretched one. He had been eager to fight in World War I, and when rejected by American military authorities because he was too tall and thin, he joined the prestigious, kilted Canadian Black Watch. Gassed and wounded overseas, he fervently denounced war after the Treaty of Versailles and for the next two decades repeated arguments about avoiding war, challenged the idea of a big navy, and favored disarmament. His first play, *The Road to Rome*, which appeared in 1927, was a comic antiwar statement that stemmed from Sherwood's disillusionment with the peace. Even as Europe began to experience the turmoil that inexorably led to war, Sherwood held back. In the preface to the published version of *Idiot's Delight*, which opened in 1936, he defined war as a futile exercise that accomplished nothing. "I believe that the world is populated largely by decent people," he wrote, "and decent people don't want war. Nor do they make war. They fight and die, to be sure—but that is because they have been deluded by their exploiters, who are members of the indecent minority." If only the decent people would stand aloof, by that very act they could prevent future wars from being fought.[11]

Yet Sherwood himself could not stand aloof. His hatred of what he saw happening in Europe would not permit it. In March 1938, after the Nazi absorption of Austria, he confided to his diary, "Oh God, how I hope to live to see the day when those unspeakable barbaric bastards get their punishment." He began to realize that war was indeed coming, that it could not be stopped, and that perhaps "the sooner it comes, the better." But he still was not ready to endorse American entrance into such a conflict. Then came the British capitulation to Hitler at Munich in September which disturbed him deeply and led him to question his earlier views. To columnist Walter Winchell, Sherwood wrote in October of his opposition to "the total isolation idea" which was pushed by as narrow-minded and backward a minority as the Anti-Saloon League. Not yet an ardent interventionist, he was on his way.[12]

Sherwood's work at the time helped him as he struggled to make up his mind. A new play, *Abe Lincoln in Illinois*, reflected his indecision even as it helped him come to terms with what he had to do. In the episodic drama which spanned thirty years of Lincoln's life, Sherwood was concerned most with the politician's growth as he overcame the doubts and fears that plagued him. Slowly Lincoln moved from a live-and-let-live attitude toward slavery to a recognition of its evils and an acceptance, even at the cost of war, of the need "to state and restate the fundamental virtues of our democracy, which have made us great, and which can make us greater." Lincoln's views on slavery were, in another form, Sherwood's views on dictatorship. The hatred of war, the reluctance to fight, were the same, but for both men the possibilities of democracy in the end prevented them from standing back, and both recognized that there was a moment when it was indeed necessary to fight. By the time the play opened in the fall of 1938, Sherwood was ready to follow Lincoln's example and face the issues at hand.[13]

Sherwood did just that. He now publicly branded Hitler a maniac and in his "Report of the President of the Dramatists' Guild" in 1939 he echoed Archibald MacLeish in urging writers to use their talents to oppose aggression. The Russian invasion of Finland led Sherwood to take his own advice. *There Shall Be No Night*, which gained him a third Pulitzer Prize in 1941, was a tremendously popular play which appealed to men's consciences to act to preserve human freedom and dignity. It was a deadly serious work that appealed to people who were concerned about the chaos in the world around them. Kaarlo Valkonen, the central figure, was a Finnish neurologist, a Nobel Prize winner, who saw war coming but regarded force as a poor substitute for the power of reason. Before long, however, he recognized the threat to freedom and resolved to join the fight. Through the characters Sherwood voiced his own now firm convictions. Gosden, a British pacifist, at one point acknowledged the reasons for not fighting and then declared, "But—the time comes when you've bloody

well got to fight—and you might just as well go cheerfully." But
the real justification came through the words of Kaarlo Valkonen
on his way to war:

> Listen! What you hear now—this terrible sound that fills the
> earth—it is the death rattle. One may say easily and dramati-
> cally that it is the death rattle of civilization. But—I choose
> to believe differently. I believe it is the long deferred death
> rattle of the primordial beast. We have within ourselves the
> power to conquer bestiality, not with our muscles and our
> swords, but with the power of the light that is in our minds.
> What a thrilling challenge this is to all Science! To play its
> part in the ultimate triumph of evolution. To help speed the
> day when man becomes genuinely human, instead of the
> synthetic creature—part bogus angel, part actual brute—
> that he has imagined himself in the dark past—[14]

For Sherwood the war now appeared as the same struggle
between the forces of good and the forces of evil that MacLeish
had perceived. And Sherwood too began to describe the menace
of fascism even as he glorified the democratic way. The contrast
between the systems was stark: "The Nazis have established the
world's most thorough despotism, trampling over the decayed
body of liberty to achieve authority; we still strive to perfect the
world's finest democracy." The dictatorships throughout the
world denied the dignity of man that for Sherwood was of crucial
importance. Devoted to what he called "true Democracy and true
Christianity," he turned to scriptural passages to illustrate what
he held most dear. Quoting the first chapter of the Book of
Genesis—"So God created man in his own image, in the image
of God created he him; male and female created he them. . . . And
God saw every thing that he had made, and, behold, it was very
good"—Sherwood declared that "In these old scriptural words
is the fundamental conception of the dignity, the essential virtue
of individual man." And, he went on, "this is the substance of the
democratic faith: the faith whose divine light guided the people
of Israel out of bondage; the faith which flamed in eternal splen-
dor in Athens in the Golden Age of Pericles; the faith which

shone forth in the star over Bethlehem, in Judea."[15]

If Sherwood's vision, like MacLeish's, was occasionally vague, its thrust was similarly and unmistakably clear. Sherwood trumpeted his vision, not only in *There Shall Be No Night*, but increasingly in speeches, articles, and public appearances as well. Like MacLeish, who turned from poetry to prose to make his meaning clear, Sherwood sought out new audiences to warn of the dangers he saw. In May 1940, he joined William Allen White's Committee to Defend America by Aiding the Allies, for which his greatest contribution came two weeks later as he wrote the full page "STOP HITLER NOW" advertisement that appeared simultaneously in newspapers in over one hundred cities. The advertisement stated the committee's point of view in support of sending guns, planes, and other supplies to the Allies, and at one point it also included Sherwood's more extreme view. The Nazis would not wait for America to defend herself, the playwright declared. "Anyone who argues that they will wait is either an imbecile or a traitor." An article in *The Reader's Digest* in September 1940 again urged Americans to "Rush All Possible Aid to Britain!" And another essay in the *Ladies' Home Journal* in August 1941 told readers that "The Front Line Is in Our Hearts" as it pleaded with them to remember what the war was all about.[16]

At the same time Sherwood was working as a speech writer for President Roosevelt. That task had started during the 1940 campaign when presidential adviser Harry Hopkins, whom Sherwood had met two years before, opened the way to the White House. A Republican in his early years, Sherwood had supported the Democrats and Roosevelt for most of the last decade, and now he entered into a very special relationship that he would continue to cherish long after Roosevelt's death. Sherwood developed a tremendous enthusiasm for the president, and saw in him the hope for a better world. As Roosevelt inched toward war, Sherwood supported him and helped write the words that persuaded Americans that the course they were taking was the right one. Even as he became immersed in other government activities during the war years, the playwright remained on call to the White House at all times.[17]

In all of his efforts Sherwood proceeded with an intensity that reflected his aggressive belief in the rightness of his cause. The truth was unquestionably on the American side, and if only it could reach around the world, it could help end the war on a hopeful note. "To all victims of oppression who may hear us," he told an audience in the fall of 1942, "to all lovers of freedom everywhere, we Americans express the substance of our democratic faith—that the truth is mighty and shall prevail—the truth shall set you free." Sherwood recognized the importance of the powers of communication. His own sensitivity to language and ability to express human feelings and sentiments, when coupled with his belief in the cause, led him to propaganda as a means of making his views heard.[18]

Both Sherwood and MacLeish had a general sense of what an information program should do. Picking up on the first halting ventures to explain American policy as the United States became inexorably involved in the European war, they tried to use propaganda to achieve what they considered the important ends in the struggle. Working on their own projects, in their own ways, together they helped set the tone and define the aims of the propaganda program as it started to get off the ground.

MacLeish, who was more concerned with domestic matters, with the impact of the war on the American people, wanted to establish an open and honest information network that could work with the press and other media portraying the war, but which could also project more than the sometimes stereotyped popular accounts. The real aim was to persuade the American public, by the straightforward presentation of the facts of war, that the outcome of the struggle was of the utmost importance to everyone at home. Propaganda could help portray the war's sober and high-minded meaning, the aspect that mattered so much to MacLeish. Sherwood, more interested in overseas propaganda, favored the same forthright approach, which, with a dedicated reliance on the truth about the war, could persuade foreign audiences that a democratic society that had nothing to hide would inevitably triumph. For Sherwood, as for MacLeish, the candid facts about the United States and about its opponents would reveal both the evil of fascism and the virtue of democracy, and demonstrate the obvious outcome. In the broad framework that both poet and playwright defined, the truth was of the first importance, for it reflected the very commitment of the democratic way in what both insisted was an ideological war.

If Sherwood and MacLeish knew in general terms what they wanted to do with American propaganda, they had no doubt about what they wanted to avoid. Fighting against fascism, they were insistent that their efforts bear as little resemblance as possible to those of the fascists. They had to avoid the ruthless methods, however successful, of their Nazi counterpart, Joseph Goebbels.

The German minister of propaganda had long supported the National Socialist movement, had accompanied Adolf Hitler in the rise to power, and had, by the time the war began, established an almost total control over the radio, press, and other means of expression in the Nazi state. Goebbels was single-minded in his approach, for he saw propaganda as a means of control over an entire way of life. Dedicated to his fuehrer's dreams of conquest, he adhered to Hitler's own precepts in swaying people to the cause. Hitler had declared earlier in *Mein Kampf* that since "the great masses' capacity to absorb is very limited, their understanding small, and their forgetfulness is great, . . . any effective propaganda must be confined to a very few points, and must use these as slogans until the very last man cannot help knowing what is meant." Goebbels adopted that view of audience and technique and proceeded accordingly. He directed that all German propaganda appeal to the instincts and emotions, and not to the rational processes, of the people he was trying to reach. He also followed his master's example by using the credible lie, which by continuous repetition in time took on the force of fact. The truth, for Goebbels, was not important, for propaganda, he declared, had "nothing at all to do with truth." Rather, the real aim was success. In pursuit of that aim Goebbels had without question achieved the results he sought. Propaganda had helped create fear in foreign listeners as Germany prepared to attack, while meanwhile the messages that inundated the home front persuaded audiences there that victory was near. People did believe what they saw and heard. William L. Shirer, then a journalist in Germany, later observed that he himself "was to experience how easily one is taken in by a lying and censored press in a totalitarian state," for despite his own outside sources of information, "a steady diet over the years of falsifications and distortions made a certain impression on one's mind and often misled it." The German example, despite its ominous successes, had no attraction for Sherwood and MacLeish, who remained convinced that the truth would triumph in the end.[19]

Sherwood, MacLeish, and others interested in propaganda still had to hammer out the details of how the American program would operate, and that process proved long and hard. From the start the obstacles seemed immense, and one of the largest was the president of the United States. Franklin Roosevelt, a master publicist in his own right, was reluctant to establish formal publicity channels. Furthermore, he remembered the CPI in World War I and hesitated to open the way to similar extremes. Roosevelt's reservations ensured that the first attempts to establish any propaganda network would be halting and hesitant. And once the process was underway, the president's idiosyncratic organizational preferences further hindered the development of a coordinated system. Roosevelt was notorious for creating agencies with little regard for clear lines of authority. If one was not functioning smoothly, his response was often to create another. If that approach may have caused confusion, Roosevelt was undisturbed, for he once commented, "There is something to be said . . . for having a little conflict between agencies. A little rivalry is stimulating, you know. It keeps everybody going to prove that he is a better fellow than the next man." Roosevelt's method allowed him to procrastinate when he chose, to watch his subordinates thrash out the details of an issue, and then to intervene only when he felt the time was right, with the ultimate power of decision in his own hands. But the method, however calculated, still caused the effort to establish a coherent information program to proceed with a series of false starts and tentative steps.[20]

Although the Roosevelt administration had established a few formal channels to publicize what the New Deal was doing, they had played but a limited role in the 1930s. The approach and then outbreak of war, however, led to the creation of a number of other organizations that could start to explain what the United States was doing by way of response. Those worked in a variety of ways, some more effectively than others, yet all suffered from the fact that they had to share the mandate they had received from FDR.[21]

The first of the new organizations, and the one least oriented to defense work, was the Office of Government Reports, which at the start had no responsibilities for explaining the reactions to the war. Established in September 1939 as the successor to the public information programs of the New Deal years, the OGR was to serve as a clearinghouse for both general and specific requests for material from the government. The agency was to provide the public with information about the activities of various government agencies and also to keep the administration aware of how the public responded to national and governmental problems. Innocuous as those responsibilities seemed, the OGR, under the direction of presidential assistant Lowell Mellett, soon faced mounting criticisms from hostile Republican legislators who feared that it would become a propaganda machine for the Roosevelt administration. Congress failed to recognize the agency formally for two years, and the press attacked the erection of its new $600,000 structure on Pennsylvania Avenue as "Mellett's Madhouse." In its effort to pass on to the public all available information about government activities, the OGR did in time inevitably touch on defense related matters, but it never became the propaganda organization its critics seemed to fear.[22]

More successful was the Division of Information of the Office of Emergency Management. The defense effort had led to the creation of a number of new production and supply agencies, each with its own story to tell. To forestall competition among those organizations, the Division of Information, established in March 1941, was to serve as the chief source of information about the government's defense activities. Directed by former Scripps-

Howard editor Robert Horton, the DOI coordinated materials
relating to the OEM and issued information the administration
wished the public to have. Even so, there were snags. The division's releases sometimes conflicted with those of organizations
like the Army and Navy, and Horton's bluntness proved a liabil-
ity. Because of the president's reluctance to assign central information work to Horton, the division remained a small operation.[23]

Meanwhile the president found that he had to respond to pressures from supporters who were worried about American morale.
He himself hoped that the story of the war itself, fully and accu-
rately told, would win his constituents to the cause, but he
nonetheless acceded to demands that he do something more. In
the spring of 1941 he permitted a Treasury campaign initiated by
Henry Morgenthau, Jr., "to use *bonds* to sell the *war.*" And in May
of that year he reluctantly agreed to set up an Office of Civilian
Defense to deal with civilian protection, national morale, and
public opinion as well. Under Fiorello La Guardia, the colorful
mayor of New York, the information part of the program never
emerged as the originators had hoped, while the morale measures taken aroused such intense opposition from critics of the
administration that the OCD was not as effective as it might have
been.[24]

By the fall of 1941 Roosevelt realized that he had to try something new. At the urging of advisers who wanted to generate
support for a more active American role in the war, the president
now embraced a policy of giving the public the presumably un-
garnished facts about the war and the American response to it—
facts that would ideally speak for themselves and permit enlight-
ened decisions by an informed citizenry. Typically, the new
Office of Facts and Figures, established in October 1941 from a
branch in La Guardia's agency, did not replace any of the existing
agencies. Roosevelt had simply superimposed a new organization
upon the old framework. To coordinate the presentation of
materials relating to national defense, the OFF was to ascertain
those subjects about which the American public needed to be
better informed, and then formulate plans that could be carried

out by the executive agencies themselves. Though it was not intended to be a real propaganda agency, the OFF was, Roosevelt indicated, "to facilitate a widespread and accurate understanding of the status and progress of the national defense effort . . . and activities of the Government."[25]

Heading the new agency was Archibald MacLeish. With his own firm convictions about the struggle against fascism, the poet now had access to a public forum for his views. An active interventionist who saw his agency's task as one of stimulating support for the war the United States was sooner or later going to have to fight, he was nonetheless determined to observe the limits imposed by his own "strategy of truth." The Office of Facts and Figures, he announced, would "not use bally-hoo methods," for "a democratic government is more concerned with the provision of information to the people than it is with the communication of dreams and aspirations. . . . The duty of government is to provide a basis for judgment; and when it goes beyond that, it goes beyond the prime scope of its duty." To that end, he asserted fervently if perhaps naively, OFF would deal only with accurate facts and figures, which he promised would be "neither perverted nor colored."[26]

Despite his good intentions, the Office of Facts and Figures met with a mixed response from the very beginning. The *New York Herald Tribune* slyly assessed the new agency in an editorial entitled "Here's Where We Get OFF": "OFF is just going to superimpose its own 'well organized facts' upon the splendid confusion, interpret the interpreters, redigest those who now digest the digesters, explain what those who explain what the explainers of the explanations mean, and co-ordinate the co-ordinators of those appointed to co-ordinate the co-ordinations of the co-ordinated." The press, hostile to the idea of a central information clearinghouse from the start, came to view OFF as a collection of dreamy experts-on-everything. Soon there appeared references to the new agency as the "Office of Fun and Frolic."[27]

Often the criticisms were justified. While the OFF did provide hard data to the press and radio, that material had to be screened to ensure that it did not reveal too much about production schedules or shortages or military deployment plans. Despite its recruitment of able publicists, people like well-known writer Malcolm Cowley and Pulitzer Prize-winning historian Henry Pringle, its early publications were disappointing and dull. The agency also proved unable to handle its primary assignment of coordinating war information. While the OFF could recommend certain courses of action to other agencies, it had no authority to enforce its recommendations. If on minor issues it was occasionally successful, on major questions it might "call the signals," as an article in *Harper's* observed, "but the players ran where they pleased with the ball."[28]

The president, again in characteristic fashion, often appeared to ignore the Office of Facts and Figures. Bypassing his information agency, he issued material directly to the press. The most significant instance occurred after the Japanese attack on Pearl Harbor. MacLeish knew no more than what he had heard on the radio, and the president, in his press conference of December 9, 1941, finally told the public of the problems it would now face. OFF might thereafter attempt to secure the release of information about the attack and subsequent events, but it found itself up against the War and Navy Departments which insisted on maintaining a controlled silence.[29]

OFF's difficulties were abundantly clear to MacLeish, who could see no solution within the existing framework. In February 1942 he wrote to Budget Director Harold D. Smith about the need to reorganize the information network. OFF should be liquidated, he argued, and its place should be taken by a stronger organization that would have adequate authority over both foreign and domestic functions. MacLeish himself, after head-on debates with the press and conflicts with other government agencies, was ready to step down. For the head of his proposed domestic branch he recommended the appointment of someone with experience in various parts of journalism. "I hardly need to add, in case it has any relevance," he told Smith, "that I am NOT the man for that job."[30]

MacLeish's difficulties, though, revealed only half the picture, for the problems involving domestic information paralleled those in the field of foreign propaganda. There a variety of independent efforts evolved because the State Department was reluctant to become involved in the area of overseas information. When war broke out in Europe, the department was unwilling or unable to respond effectively to the propaganda released by the Axis powers. That propaganda, as it was directed to Latin America in an attempt to split the hemisphere, pictured the United States as grasping and imperialistic, but the federal government lacked the facilities even to determine the details of the Axis message.[31]

The State Department therefore accepted Nelson Rockefeller's appointment as Coordinator of Inter-American Affairs in August 1940. Grandson of the great oil magnate, Rockefeller had followed him naturally into the world of business. Working with a Standard Oil subsidiary in Venezuela in the 1930s, he became interested in Latin America, and that interest led him into government service dealing with the region. As Coordinator of Inter-American Affairs, Rockefeller enjoyed State Department support as he sought to promote good hemispheric relations and thereby to counteract the Nazi propaganda. After American entry into the war, the CIAA continued to work actively to persuade Latin America that defense of the hemisphere depended on the solidarity of the region. With radio, press, and motion picture activities part of the broader cultural and commercial operations program, the CIAA was effective, but messages went out only in one direction.[32]

Another approach came from the efforts of Colonel William G. Donovan. "Wild Bill" Donovan was an energetic figure who had fought in World War I, worked as a Wall Street lawyer, and served as a high-ranking official in the Department of Justice in Calvin Coolidge's administration. A Republican who enjoyed the confidence of the president, he was eager to see American involvement in the European war. Starting on a fact-finding mission for the Navy Department in late 1940 to assess the risks of protecting the Atlantic lifeline, he returned home after several months and twenty-five thousand miles to report to the president his belief that, given the threat of war, the United States needed

a unified intelligence-gathering agency, one that could engage in
unorthodox missions and counter Axis propaganda.[33]

And so in July 1941 Roosevelt appointed Donovan to head a
new Office of the Coordinator of Information. In that capacity
Donovan was to collect and analyze material dealing with national security, to make such information available to the president, and to carry out any related activities requested by the
president. Responsibilities were not precisely defined, for Donovan had operations in mind that could not be spelled out in full.[34]

From the beginning Donovan's mission was shrouded in mys-
tery. Cryptically he undertook to collect strategic intelligence
materials throughout the world. To accomplish that task he engaged in espionage and subversion through secret agents behind
battle lines and in other locations affected by the war. In part
because of the confidential nature of his work, in part because of
his own aggressive personality, Donovan soon aroused the suspicion or antagonism of people working around him. The State
Department resented the free-wheeling activities which con-
trasted with its slow diplomatic procedures. In the early days, the
department was reluctant to cooperate too closely with an agency
whose undercover activities might compromise American neutrality. At the same time military personnel had little use for
Donovan, despite his reserve rank. War Department officials
criticized the new agency as a "fly-by-night civilian outfit headed
up by a wild man who was trying to horn in on the war." The FBI
feared that he would try to conduct espionage within the United
States. Nelson Rockefeller, always jealous of incursions into his
territory, sought to exclude Donovan from Latin America.[35]

On top of all those troubles, Donovan had to deal with still
another information agency, which, though nominally under his
control, had notions of its own. The idea of a Foreign Information Service had come from Robert Sherwood, who persuaded
the president that such an organization could play an important
role in telling the rest of the world about the aims and objectives
of the American government and the American people. In response to that suggestion, Roosevelt set up the FIS in August
1941 in the Office of the COI where Donovan had ultimate re-

sponsibility, though most decisions were left in Sherwood's hands.[36]

Sherwood gathered around him men who shared his views. Journalists, writers, broadcasters, and others, most of whom were prewar interventionists who believed that words and ideas could be used to fight fascism, joined the new organization. Men like James P. Warburg, a banker and one-time adviser to Roosevelt, and Joseph Barnes, former *New York Herald Tribune* correspondent in Moscow and Berlin, were among the first principals. Motion picture producer John Houseman soon came into the new organization, as did such literary figures as Thornton Wilder and Stephen Vincent Benét.[37]

Largely through radio—the newly founded "Voice of America"—the group spread the gospel of democracy throughout the world. Working on the basis of Sherwood's statement that "truth is the only effective basis for American foreign information," the FIS based its programs on truthful news, but still managed to cast its message in favorable terms. The selection and arrangement of news releases emphasized America's productive capacity, and after Pearl Harbor they stressed the strength that would bring an end to the war. When there were no Allied victories to report, the FIS used the story of American preparations to argue that the tide had already turned against the Axis forces. At the same time it juxtaposed stories about fascist treatment of occupied areas with the pledges of the Four Freedoms and the Atlantic Charter to underscore the virtues of the Allied cause. Sherwood believed "that all U.S. information to the world should be considered as though it were a continuous speech by the President," and Roosevelt became his symbol for American idealism and dedication to a lasting peace.[38]

Optimistic and enthusiastic from the start, Sherwood and his assistants soon found themselves involved in a growing dispute with COI head Donovan. The colonel, chiefly interested in secret activity, was impressed by German propaganda and saw Sherwood's program as a front. He wanted to use propaganda specifically as a weapon of war. It needed to have, he wrote to Roosevelt, "a judicious mixture of rumor and deception . . . to foster disunity and confusion in support of military operations." Sherwood, on the other hand, insisted on holding to his version of the truth, for he feared that American credibility would be impaired by the use of outright lies. He insisted on civilian control rather than the military orientation that Donovan preferred. Accordingly he moved toward the position that foreign information activities should not even be centered in the same organization that conducted secret espionage.[39]

Personal difficulties exacerbated the split. Sherwood's strong loyalties made him resentful of Donovan's increasing closeness to Roosevelt. He was suspicious of the Republican who he felt was unsympathetic to New Deal objectives. And he found himself in disagreement with Donovan's conservative position on Argentina and Spain. In a memorandum to the president, Sherwood wrote: "It is all right to have rabid anti-New Dealers or even Roosevelt haters in the military establishment or in the OPM, but I don't think it appropriate to have them participating in an effort which must be expressive of the President's own philosophy." Donovan, always strong-minded, felt a similar antipathy toward those who disagreed with him.[40]

Meanwhile the FIS was having administrative troubles too, as the organization, in the words of one member, "like Topsy, just 'growed' out of nothing." Some of the problems related to internal functioning, others to relations with groups outside. Sherwood and his staff, independent and creative, often distrusted the policies and procedures of the slow-moving State Department. The members of FIS had frequent difficulty getting authoritative statements on policy to serve as guides for programs, and incurred a reciprocal hostility from diplomatic officials who felt the information organization really wanted to make policy and not simply to use it.[41]

By early 1942 the whole information program was in trouble. On the foreign front, America's entrance into the war after the attack on Pearl Harbor led to demands for a stronger propaganda effort, but the directions it should take were unclear. Still, some change seemed necessary. Earlier Sherwood had told Donovan, "We cannot afford to lose invaluable time through childish bickerings, puny jealousies or backstairs intrigue," yet in the prevailing setup those diversions seemed unavoidable. On the domestic front the situation was worse. Americans wanted to know what was happening but military restrictions kept the public less informed than before. Agencies either fought with one another or made duplicate presentations of what material was available. The OFF, which had promised to coordinate the field, had been discredited. Even the press began to favor some central agency. One observer remarked of the chaos: "It all seemed to boil down to three bitter complaints: first, that there was too much information; second, that there wasn't enough of it; and third, that in any event it was confusing and inconsistent."[42]

To deal with the situation, the Bureau of the Budget, in February 1942, asked Milton S. Eisenhower to make a survey of war information needs. Dwight D. Eisenhower's youngest brother, who had been raised and educated in Kansas, had entered government service in the 1920s. He had first worked for the State Department as a vice-consul in Edinburgh, then returned to the United States to enter the Department of Agriculture, where he served as director of information from 1928 to 1941. A Republican by preference, he was nonetheless on good terms with FDR, whom he liked and respected. After more than a decade and a half as a civil servant, Eisenhower was a respected administrator in Washington, and one who, on the basis of his work with press and radio relations, was fully familiar with the information field. Within weeks he returned his recommendations. While he found the current conditions unsatisfactory, his cautious nature led him to recommend against a centralized service like the earlier Creel Committee. He felt that better liaison could ensure the necessary control. Noting that foreign and domestic work should be coordinated, he nonetheless felt that those functions need not be housed in the same agency.[43]

At the same time the Bureau of the Budget drew up a proposed draft of an executive order "Consolidating Certain Information Functions of the Government into an Office of War Information." That order provided for consolidation into one central agency of most domestic information activities with the FIS and information functions of Nelson Rockefeller's Latin American organization. Taking Eisenhower's report and the proposals of his own organization, Budget Director Smith, in a letter to Roosevelt, pointed out that all information facilities need not be concentrated in a single agency, but that some centralized government control was necessary. He submitted the proposed executive order as a solution.[44]

The president hesitated. Rockefeller meanwhile insisted that his CIAA remain out of the proposed Office of War Information, with the claim that information activities were an integral part of his total program. Undersecretary of State Sumner Welles, interested in Latin America and friendly with the president, supported Rockefeller, and asserted that since the CIAA was working in close harmony with the State Department, it should not be disturbed by transfer or consolidation. No compromise could be worked out. After two months of haggling, despite the opposition of Hopkins, Smith, and speech writer Samuel Rosenman, Roosevelt agreed to allow Rockefeller to retain his independent status.[45]

Similarly Donovan opposed inclusion of the Foreign Information Service in the new agency. He insisted that propaganda was a weapon of war and that tying together foreign and domestic functions would compromise security and hinder the effectiveness of psychological warfare. Proponents of the new plan responded that overseas and domestic tasks were intimately related and that both should be guided by the strategy of truth. Sherwood, partly as a result of his philosophical and personal difficulties with Donovan, was eager to bring the FIS into the OWI, but Donovan remained undaunted. He was encouraged by Rockefeller's success in remaining out of the new organization and even tried to buy time by suggesting to the president a three month delay to see if the domestic integration worked well. Despite the support of the Joint Chiefs of Staff, Donovan was unsuccessful. Roosevelt listened to Sherwood and accepted the argument that all propaganda, domestic and foreign, should be placed under one roof. Relinquishing his propaganda arm, Donovan was to retain control over the secret activities in which he had been engaged as head of a new Office of Strategic Services. He had responsibility for subversion while the contemplated OWI had authority over foreign information. Psychological warfare, which in time became so important, was neither defined nor discussed.[46]

With most problems solved, the executive order seemed ready for signing. But though the structure and directive of the new Office of War Information now seemed in order, Roosevelt still seemed reluctant. When Smith advised that action should be taken before the end of the fiscal year, the president finally acted. Yet in typical fashion he insisted on the selection of the director who would carry out the terms of the executive order before he signed it. Only after Elmer Davis, journalist, author, and extraordinarily popular radio commentator, agreed to head the new organization, did Roosevelt, in an executive order signed on June 13, 1942, formally create the Office of War Information.[47]

Davis was welcome in all quarters. The fifty-one-year-old Hoosier with the white hair, black brows, and dark eyes behind horn-rimmed glasses inspired confidence and seemed to be the perfect man to bring order out of the information mess. The press was pleased, for Davis had long before established himself as a journalist of the first rank. *Time* magazine called him "clear-headed, sensible . . . one of the best newsmen in the business," while Norman Cousins in *The Saturday Review of Literature* pointed to the "fundamental clarity in his thinking," and *The New Republic* hailed him as "a liberal respected by conservatives," a man of broad appeal. Archibald MacLeish echoed administration sentiment when he called Davis "a grand choice," and the public was perhaps most pleased of all, for Davis's nightly newscasts had gained him a national reputation for accuracy, integrity, and simple good sense.[48]

By the time the war intervened, Davis had already had a successful and satisfying career. After graduating from Franklin College in Indiana, he had gone to England as a Rhodes Scholar, where, in Edward R. Murrow's phrase, he "survived two years of Oxford with accent and outlook unimpaired," and then returned to the United States to make his way in the field of journalism.

He worked first for *Adventure* magazine, then moved in 1914 to the *New York Times,* where he served as a reporter, then editorial writer. He was on board Henry Ford's Peace Ship during World War I for the newspaper, and later covered the 1922 Washington Arms Conference. After ten years he left the *Times* to work as a free-lance writer and published a steady and profitable stream of novels, stories, essays, and reviews.[49]

But his real reputation came from his role as a radio announcer. He had broadcast occasionally for CBS in the early 1930s and had even filled in for H. V. Kaltenborn when the commentator was away during the summer of 1937. Then in August 1939, as war threatened, Kaltenborn was again in Europe and CBS needed somebody to work on a regular basis. Davis made the most of the opportunity and quickly attracted a large following. His flat, even voice with the slight nasal tone somehow seemed to convey honesty and common sense. His clear, direct delivery and dry humor soon gave him a nightly audience of twelve and a half million people and prompted fellow broadcaster Murrow to praise him for the best "fair, tough minded, interesting talking" he had heard. Americans appreciated Davis, for he was, indeed, as one journalist noted, "solid American to the core—the sort of American that belongs to the heart of the country."[50]

In his professional capacity Davis was a perceptive observer of the national scene. He followed politics closely and chose his positions with care. He was a member of the American Labor Party in New York until communist elements gained the upper hand. Dubious about FDR prior to the first inaugural, he later lost his doubts, although he gave him but lukewarm support in the quest for a third term. Yet he always respected the president and was willing to work on his behalf, even though he did not share Sherwood's almost unquestioning admiration.[51]

Nor did he share the intense convictions of either Sherwood or MacLeish in the face of the coming world war. He too saw the fascist threat and wrote about it, but his work was more analytical and less impassioned than that of the poet or the playwright. He had read *Mein Kampf,* understood what Hitler was after, and argued in 1938 that "so long as that man lives he is the principal fact in world politics." Yet while he observed the sadism and enslavement that marked the Nazi regime, and wanted to warn his fellow citizens of what he saw, he was at first less willing to demand an American response. In 1938 he declared that the United States should remain aloof, for "twenty years ago we went on a crusade which would have made sense if we had got what we wanted; but we failed to find the Holy Grail, and the experience ought to have cured us of our inclination to go grailing." A year later he was still arguing that "in a world of force we ought to look out for our own interests." Once the war was under way, he conceded that an Allied victory was preferable, but he still wanted the United States to avoid involvement, for to his mind, there was unfinished business at home, and there was also reason to doubt that the United States could do much good. "To sit tight," he wrote in April 1940, "to keep the record clear, to keep out of this war so long as it—and its clear and immediate implications—keeps out of us; to do any fighting that we may be forced to do for the protection of American interests, but only to the extent that those interests may require—that seems to me a sane national policy." A month later the Nazi blitzkrieg changed his mind, but while he now accepted the need for sending economic and financial aid to the Allies, not until December 1941 did he publicly favor sending an army overseas.[52]

Nor did Davis gravitate on his own toward propaganda work. While Sherwood and MacLeish had been led by their convictions to try to arouse the nation, Davis concentrated on reporting the war clearly and concisely in his nightly broadcasts to his regular listeners. But as the United States muddled through the first months of involvement in the war, Davis recognized the confusion in the government's information program and the effect it was having on the effort to mobilize support for the war. Complaining publicly over the air about the chaos, he deplored the constant conflict among the numerous agencies. "Under one head, with real power, they might get somewhere . . . ," he said.

"Objection has been made that it might be hard to pick the man to head them. But almost anybody would be better than half a dozen heads."[53]

Soon after, humorist E. B. White picked up that comment in "The Talk of the Town" column in *The New Yorker*. Davis, White observed, was right in his criticisms and Davis should be the man in charge. Davis himself wrote to Harry Hopkins suggesting Edward R. Murrow, William L. Shirer, or Rex Stout, in that order, as new administrator. When it came time to make the actual selection, however, the president wanted the radio commentator "with the funny voice. Elmer—Elmer something."[54]

So Elmer Davis became head of the finally coordinated American information network. While he had at first been reluctant to accept the position and had finally done so only out of a sense of duty in wartime, now, as he prepared to leave New York, he was determined to make the best of the situation, to do all he could to advance the national cause. "As soon as they give me a chair to sit on in Washington," he told reporters, "I'll go to work."[55]

Davis would need more than a chair to deal with the huge job that lay ahead of him. All kinds of tasks required immediate attention. He was to "formulate and carry out, through the use of press, radio, motion picture, and other facilities, information programs designed to facilitate the development of an informed and intelligent understanding, at home and abroad, of the status and progress of the war effort and of the war policies, activities, and aims of the Government." He was to coordinate the related activities of all federal departments to ensure that audiences at home and abroad remained constantly well informed.[56]

His mandate seemed broad, as *The Saturday Review of Literature* observed in remarking that the new office would "be more than merely a coordinating super-agency." That was an illusion. As usual, the president had resisted creating too powerful an organization. The executive order had carefully avoided setting up another Creel Committee. The OWI was not to be a central agency that would assume all information functions. It had some consolidating control, but individual federal departments still had their own information units, and the Office of War Information was empowered only to coordinate the various activities. While it could suggest that certain items be released or withheld, it had no authority over officials in other agencies who refused to cooperate.[57]

The president's order, by combining several different predecessor agencies, also gave the new OWI a number of potentially conflicting functions. It was to provide truthful information to the American public, and meanwhile to develop campaigns—like those on behalf of bond-buying or salvage—to secure certain actions by that public. At the same time it was to provide truthful information to overseas audiences, but that material had to be slanted for the purposes of propaganda. Davis sometimes "felt like a man who had married a wartime widow and was trying to raise her children by all her previous husbands."[58]

Most troublesome was the executive order's ambiguity on the question of how much the American public was entitled to know. The opening lines did recognize the right "to be truthfully informed about the common war effort," but the order said nothing about how questions of national security would affect the release of material. Military officials who sought to keep the enemy in ignorance about their maneuvers bridled at the thought of frank disclosure of losses or weaknesses which they felt would compromise their position, and the State Department was equally sensitive. George Creel understood the situation from the very beginning. Soon after Davis took office he wrote, "I am more sorry than I can say that your control over Army, Navy and State is not real in any sense of the word. I know admirals and generals, also Sumner Welles, and while you may think you have established an arrangement that will permit a free flow of news, just wait until an issue arises." Creel was right.[59]

For all the public support he received as he entered office, Davis faced those problems without the preparation or experience that might have stood him in good stead. He was a likable man, an earnest and able man, but he lacked the aggressiveness of the seasoned bureaucrat intent on getting his way in Washington. His work as a newsman gave him the background he needed to deal with the press, but it did not steel him to handle the conflicts and squabbles that arose in a large organization. He was no administrator, he freely acknowledged. Indeed, he told the president that he was unused to having anyone other than a part-time secretary work for him. Now he had imposing problems to solve, and as he soon discovered, he did not really have the support of the president in working towards a solution. George Creel had earlier succeeded because of his access to the White House, but Davis had not known Roosevelt personally before he came to Washington and had no reason to expect an intimate relationship. Only mildly interested in a formal propaganda organization from the start, the president had acted to consolidate the information services in response to the criticisms that had become too loud, but now he had no intention of going out of his way to protect the new agency. Davis was on his own.[60]

Davis's response was to compromise, to seek harmony wherever possible in his dealings with his own subordinates as well as with his counterparts elsewhere in Washington. Uneasy with contention, he stood firm when it was absolutely essential, but generally remained open to change and ready to back off. George Creel understood the situation. Soon after Davis took office, Creel wrote that he "seemed to perceive a tendency to make the best of things as you have found them. Such a course is possible when things are fairly good, but when things are downright *bad*, nothing is more fatal than an amiable effort to make the best of them." Perhaps, given the suspicions of propaganda and the skepticism with which other officials in Washington viewed it, Davis had no choice but to back off, but that response led him to come off second best in the Washington tug-of-war and colored the course of American propaganda.[61]

During the course of the war, in an effort to ensure that his agency survived, Davis oversaw a shift in direction from the earliest start. Basically in sympathy with the aims of the liberal and creative individuals who came into OWI from its assorted predecessors, Davis at first allowed them free rein to espouse their hopeful vision of the war, to portray it as a fight to the finish between fascism and democracy. Indeed, when he signed on as head of OWI he himself subscribed to their notion of a people's war. But for him the idealistic hope was less intense than the practical reality of his position. With his newsman's instincts, his first concern was to get the news out as fully and faithfully as he could, and when the visionary views of his staff came into conflict with the more utilitarian notions of the policy makers in the war, Davis proved willing to temper the approach that many of his colleagues contended was what gave real meaning to the struggle. Under Davis the agency and its propaganda changed in time to become more closely attuned to the real American aims in the war.[62]

2   Propaganda at Home

The first struggles over the shape of American propaganda occurred in the Domestic Branch of the new Office of War Information. There talented men joined the organization because they shared Archibald MacLeish's perception of an ideological battle between the forces of good and evil. They sought almost at once to determine how far they could go in laying out the issues honestly and openly in the face of the demands of war. Starting out with high hopes, they soon discovered that they could not go very far at all in pursuing their own ends. Encountering opposition at every turn, they became aware of how differently others in the administration viewed the war and how those other views affected the propaganda they wished to produce. Their experience in the Domestic Branch in a rocky first year provided a good test of the limits of American propaganda, and one which reflected what might be attempted and what might be allowed in the organization at large.

The struggles that ensued revolved around the tough questions concerning the nature of propaganda in a democratic society at war. Men of good will had long disagreed about how manipulative a government might be in a supposedly free setting. In time of peace the issues could be debated at length, but in time of war they became more troublesome. While a measure of national unity seemed necessary to support the war effort, the very pursuit of that unity might compromise the values of diversity and independence on which the society was based. With World War II already underway, officials both in and out of the organization felt the pressure of time as they sought to determine the way a propaganda system might unfold. There were, to be sure, questions about whether there was any place at all for an information branch at home, but since OWI had been established with a Domestic Branch as part of its format, for the moment, that matter had been resolved. Now the question was how such a branch might proceed. Should it, for example, work on its own to interpret the fundamental issues of war and peace for the public at home? Or should it follow the administration's lead in interpreting the war, if indeed there was a lead to be followed? Should it play a manipulative role in trying to arouse a lethargic people to support a war deemed necessary by the nation's leaders? Or should it simply serve as an information channel, a glorified press bureau whose releases had as little embellishment as possible? There were no easy answers to those questions, for there were disagreements at all levels of government, both outside the organization as well as within.[1]

Elmer Davis's top aides soon found that they, too, disagreed. Meeting daily as the Board of War Information to determine propaganda policy, the group was made up of capable men of different convictions. Some of the more liberal voices from the pre-OWI days were again heard in the new organization. Archibald MacLeish was involved as assistant director in charge of the Policy Development Branch, while Robert Sherwood headed the Overseas Branch. But there were now others whose ideological views were less intense and whose sense of purpose pointed them in a different direction. The more cautious Milton Eisenhower had agreed to be associate director of OWI when Davis had insisted on an experienced administrator to help run the agency and Eisenhower had been only too ready to leave the War Relocation Authority after serving a short stint there. And Gardner Cowles, Jr., the moderate Midwestern newspaper publisher, was now involved as director of the Domestic Branch.[2]

Cowles, like Eisenhower, had moved in different circles from the more outspoken leaders of OWI. After a Harvard education that included editing the *Crimson,* he returned to Des Moines, Iowa, where he soon moved up to the top editorial position at a family-owned newspaper. In time he became associate publisher as well, and also helped the family acquire another newspaper monopoly in Minneapolis and a chain of radio stations throughout the Midwest. In early 1937 the thirty-four-year-old Cowles and his brother established *Look* magazine—a popular interest,

pictorial journal that quickly enjoyed tremendous success. His
experience with the communications and business worlds left
Cowles with strong convictions about the publications he ran and
the public he served. Relying on some of George Gallup's earliest
polls, he worked hard to adjust format to meet his readers' demands. Most newspapers, he argued, were "too pompous and
ponderous." Where Sherwood and MacLeish both believed that
the American public was rational and reasonable and with the
proper evidence at hand would make informed decisions, Cowles
argued rather that "the public, generally speaking, won't read
long columns of type in any newspaper or magazine explaining
heavy-weight, important public problems." His own success with
pictorial techniques led him to favor a more diluted form of
argument. Cowles differed too with some of the other propaganda leaders in his political inclinations. A liberal Republican
who had helped start the Willkie boom in 1940, he generally
backed Roosevelt's international policies, but differed with him
sharply on domestic matters. While the partisan politics of the
OWI leaders never intruded directly on the functioning of the
agency, their broader preferences still left a mark on the decisions made.[3]

The top leadership was therefore split from the start. MacLeish
in particular, with Sherwood's support, played the major part in
demanding that the agency assume a forceful role in guiding
American aims for the future, while Eisenhower, and later
Cowles, claimed in response that such an aggressive posture was
out of place. Elmer Davis found himself unhappily caught in the
middle where he discovered that he had to make the first of many
compromises if his organization was going to survive.

MacLeish touched off the dispute in a Rede Lecture at Cambridge University on July 30, 1942. Speaking on "American
Opinion and the War," he declared that although angry Americans hesitated after Pearl Harbor to question the real meaning of
the war, they were now ready to consider what kind of victory
they sought. There was "a forward thrusting and overflowing of
human hope and human will which must be given channel or it
will dig a channel for itself." As people tried to understand the

war they were fighting, he wrote in a "Basic Policy Statement on
OWI Objectives" three weeks later, the government had an obli-
gation to help them.[4]

The battle was joined in three months time when the Board of
War Information began to consider OWI's role in stimulating
interest in the postwar world. Repeating his basic point, Mac-
Leish wrote that now was the time for Americans to decide just
what they were fighting for. OWI should help them resist "the
soldiers who say 'Let's wait to decide what we are going to do
about our victory until we have won it' . . . [and] the political
leaders (of sorts) who say that there is nothing to decide—that
all we have to do is to stop everything we're doing and the world
will return to normalcy." OWI should also do more. It should
take the responsibility for putting the main issues before the
people of the country and should advance the significant solutions and try to stimulate discussion of them. MacLeish acknowledged that others might disagree. "If OWI takes a position on
issues as bitterly controversial as those here involved it will be
attacked as OFF was attacked," he wrote. "I submit, however,
that if OWI is not prepared to take a position on these fundamental issues it may suffer in other and more fatal though less painful
ways."[5]

Sherwood agreed "with Mr. MacLeish's assumptions, his conclusions and his recommendations," and Cowles at that point
evidently approved the proposition in general terms. "Go with
God," Davis scribbled at the bottom of MacLeish's memorandum. But Eisenhower was dubious. He accepted OWI's responsibility for encouraging the widest possible discussion of the forthcoming peace, but he insisted on a policy of objectivity that would
refrain from endorsing one particular blueprint. The crux of the
matter was his belief that the OWI "should continue to be
thought of primarily as an *information* agency." Several days after
his first response to MacLeish he underscored his position. OWI
had a responsibility to encourage "post-war planning" but it was
a circumscribed one. More important, "I must insist that our job
is to promote an understanding of policy, not to make policy."[6]

MacLeish noted their "very strong difference of opinion" on

the fundamental matter. "The basic question," he wrote, "is whether OWI is to be a mere issuing mechanism for the government departments. I gather it is your position that it should be. On that I disagree with you emphatically." When the matter reached Davis, he backed down from his former position. Earlier he had given MacLeish general approval to pursue his plans for the agency, but now the controversy among the members of the staff persuaded him that his office could not go that far. OWI's first step should be to approach the State Department's planners, he decided. "Thereafter I am convinced we should function as an information agency, setting forth the proposals of authoritative persons or agencies, but *not* adopting an OWI policy as to what might . . . be done."[7]

There the matter rested for the time being. OWI never did embark on the course MacLeish had recommended, for Eisenhower was right in his observation that the agency had no mandate for such broad activities. On a number of occasions in the summer and fall of 1942 MacLeish had indicated to Davis that he felt he was not functioning effectively and ought to leave the organization. In the midst of the debate over OWI's role he had written to Eisenhower that he had "little interest in trying to work for an agency which was nothing but an issuing mechanism." Though the definition of responsibilities that emerged was not that narrow, MacLeish was disappointed at the direction the agency was taking. Feeling less useful than he had hoped he might be, he quietly resigned at the end of January to devote more time to his duties at the Library of Congress.[8]

MacLeish's departure was his acknowledgment that the propaganda program would not serve the purpose he had long envisioned. He had hoped that OWI might lay out the issues of the war in serious terms as a way of persuading the people at home that they should support the struggle. Even within the agency itself he had lost out in the first major confrontation. And though many in OWI still shared his views, they had an even slimmer chance than before of gaining a hearing as they faced the powerful outside forces with whom they had to work.

Cordell Hull was one of the first stumbling blocks. The courtly

Southern secretary of state, seventy years old when the United States entered the war, had unshakable confidence in his own ideas, which he proclaimed with a self-righteous zeal in his slow and lisping way. Throughout a long and distinguished career in Democratic politics in both houses of Congress, fiscal policy had been Hull's chief passion, and he had concentrated first on taxation, then on the tariff. After his appointment to head the State Department in 1933, he continued to fight for lower tariffs and freer trade to promote international peace and prosperity. Preoccupied with his own aims, he was less aggressive in strengthening the State Department to meet the rush of world events. Diplomatic procedures remained slow, for Hull approved of the status quo in the department and was generally comfortable with the lethargic pace his predecessors had established. As the political situation deteriorated in Europe and the Far East, Hull spoke out in the interests of peace, without ever really accepting the need for war until the war had all but arrived.[9]

Hull frequently voiced American policy, but he did not always play a key role in making it. Henry Stimson, his predecessor in the Department of State, perceived as he left office that Roosevelt planned for all practical purposes to be his own secretary of state, and that situation held for the remainder of his presidency, particularly once the war began. Hull, sensitive to criticisms and slights, was normally able to cope with that state of affairs, yet he occasionally became upset. "The President runs foreign affairs," he complained to Treasury Secretary Henry Morgenthau, Jr., in 1943. "I don't know what's going on."[10]

In part because of that curious relationship, Hull guarded jealously what remained of his domain. Cautious by nature, he was not particularly interested in functions that lay beyond the traditional scope of the State Department, but he was reluctant to allow other organizations to intervene in anything that touched on foreign affairs. Independent efforts bothered him, and he therefore moved to control them in whatever ways he could.[11]

From the beginning Hull was uncomfortable with OWI. He and his staff had found the early propaganda agencies careless and irresponsible. Now, given the carry-over of personnel, they had no reason to believe that the bureaucratic reorganization would make much difference. The Foreign Information Service, reconstituted as the Overseas Branch of the new agency, did not seem to diplomatic officials to take adequate security precautions and sometimes allegedly used confidential material for inappropriate purposes. Furthermore, the State Department did not have a good view of what was going on, for the FIS had been established in New York, partly because that was a key center for broadcasting, but primarily because Sherwood and his associates had deliberately wanted to avoid contact with any potentially unsympathetic groups in Washington. The fact that aliens worked for OWI also irritated the State Department. Although they were not numerous—at the end of 1943, of the 2,885 employees in the Overseas Branch, 493 were aliens, of whom 343 had applied for citizenship—they were not, as Sherwood observed, "100 per cent dyed-in-the-wool Americans." And while they performed important language services, some of them, uprooted by the fighting, did have, in Davis's words, "passionate political convictions" that led them to speak out on the war. The State Department, dignified and staid, had no use for the excesses of the refugees. Finally, Hull and his assistants felt that the entire propaganda organization seemed to be going off on a tack of its own. Many broadcasts, Assistant Secretary of State Breckinridge Long noted in his diary, "follow a policy widely divergent from the official foreign policy and from time to time make trouble for us abroad." With some truth the State Department felt that the more liberal propaganda wing really wanted to make policy and not simply use it. The State Department, from the top on down, was ill-disposed to view any part of the new organization with sympathy. OWI constituted a threat that the department intended to meet head on.[12]

OWI faced similar troubles from the military services. Secretary of War Henry L. Stimson, seventy-four years old at the time of Pearl Harbor, was intent on winning the war and gave military necessity precedence over everything else. A distinguished lawyer in private life, secretary of war under Taft, secretary of state under Hoover, and now once again at the head of the War Department, Stimson concentrated all his energy on his last major task in public service. He could, as Felix Frankfurter once observed, focus on one thing like an old victrola needle caught in a single record groove. Now, a Republican in a Democratic administration, he subordinated both personal and party considerations to the task at hand. The old man could be harsh and abrupt with his subordinates, could exhibit a somewhat chill manner to the public, and yet by his own grim devotion to what he perceived was his duty, he could still inspire a sense of confidence, even affection, among those who worked with him and who knew him well. Recognizing in the 1930s the threat that fascism posed, he followed his sense of public responsibility and spoke out in favor of "an affirmative foreign policy for this government." His ideological convictions in defense of democracy were every bit as strong as those of the aggressive staffers in OWI. But Stimson was secretary of war, responsible for whipping a flabby department into fighting shape and impatient with programs that he feared might complicate his work. Suspicious of civilians who might interfere with strategic operations or compromise security regulations, Stimson saw the war as a military engagement that the Army and Navy could best fight. He viewed OWI and the newfangled propaganda techniques as only peripheral to that effort.[13]

High-ranking Navy officials took Stimson's side. At the head of the department was Frank Knox, a Rough Rider in the Spanish-American War, later a prominent newspaperman, and then the Republican candidate for the vice-presidency in 1936. Knox, like Stimson, had joined Roosevelt's Cabinet in 1940 so that the nation could face the impending struggle with a show of unity. Because of his newspaper ties, it at first appeared that the secretary of the navy might be receptive to the problems and needs of the new information services. Starting as a reporter, he had bought and run papers in Michigan and New Hampshire, then had become general manager for all twenty-seven Hearst papers before taking over as editor and publisher of the influential *Chicago Daily News.* Yet while he understood the demands of the press, his new position had its own requirements. Although he could be easygoing and friendly in private, he had to plead the cause of a temperamental Navy about which he knew little. Well aware, as he told friends in 1942, that "any layman would be a damn fool to get himself mixed up in the professional business of trying to fight a naval war," he understood what he had to do: "My job is to find out what the top admirals want to put across, talk it over with them and then do my damnedest to see that the job gets done as economically and efficiently as possible."[14]

The admirals knew what they wanted. Admiral Ernest J. King, chief of naval operations and commander-in-chief of the United States Fleet and perhaps the most powerful officer the Navy had ever known, had fixed notions about the way the Navy should fight the war. After the disaster at Pearl Harbor he had reputedly commented to colleagues that when leaders found themselves in trouble, "they always send for the sons of bitches" and he was the one sent for to revive the fighting fleet. King could be brutal and harsh, forthright and grim. Devoted to the Navy, he had a sense of naval tradition that he intended to maintain untarnished. In fighting the war, he had little use for embellishments that he felt only got in the way. Orders should be simple, with adjectives left out; information should stay classified; and naval officers should remain as tight-lipped as he was, even in the face of public demands to know what was going on. Admiral King did agree with Davis's conclusion that "propaganda can only be effective if it is guided by military intelligence and synchronized with military operations," but always the emphasis was on the military and not on the propaganda organization.[15]

Given the personalities involved, it was no wonder that American information leaders came into constant conflict with the other departments prosecuting the war. The top staffers may have decided earlier, to the chagrin of the most aggressive men in their midst, to give a more circumscribed focus to their work. But even in taking a more limited approach to the possibilities of propaganda in war, they found themselves overwhelmed by external constraints.

The question of the release of news, so important to newsman Elmer Davis, became the first source of serious contention. Davis had come to Washington to "see that the American people are truthfully informed," for he felt that in a democratic society the people were entitled to full knowledge if they were expected to fight well. But he felt with some truth that the military services in particular were unnecessarily hiding their losses and had not considered the need to keep the people informed. He hoped to persuade his top-ranking colleagues to relax their restrictions.[16]

Davis ran into more resistance than he had anticipated. The secretary of state, mindful of the trouble between his department and the Foreign Information Service, reacted adversely to Davis's first attempts to establish what news came within OWI's domain. Hull wrote in July 1942 that he assumed from the executive order that war information activities did "not include information relating to the foreign policy of the United States over which this Department . . . has exclusive jurisdiction." That view, Davis responded, "would appear tenable only on the hypothesis that our foreign policy has no relation to the war." Thereafter OWI continued to claim a mandate to see that pertinent material relating to foreign policy was made public, while the State Department, still in disagreement, proposed that "the Secretary of State shall have the exclusive right and duty to determine what information shall be made public relating to the international relations and foreign policies of the United States, and the manner in which it shall be made public." Though OWI rejected the proposal, the State Department followed only those suggestions of OWI of which it approved. "On the whole," Davis later wrote, "the Department cooperated with OWI only when and insofar as it chose."[17]

The military branches were even less responsive. When Davis first reached Washington, he called on Secretary of War Stimson. Preoccupied with larger matters, Stimson recorded in his diary that he was "rather disappointed" with Davis, whom he called "a typical newspaper man." He had no sympathy for Davis's contention that the Army and Navy were withholding information that the people ought to have. Instead he lectured Davis on the difficulties of getting news about a modern naval battle and he underscored the need for military secrecy. "Pretty good reasons, military and diplomatic," Davis wrote; "still all in all I got the polite brush-off." To the press Stimson proved somewhat less polite. When, soon after Davis's appointment, a reporter asked him whether Davis would have the authority to supervise military communiqués, Stimson responded stiffly, "Is Mr. Davis an educated military officer?"[18]

Davis was not, and his first efforts to secure news for the public were probably doomed from the start. Barely two weeks after he took office, the FBI announced the capture of eight Nazi saboteurs who landed from German submarines along the East coast. The Justice and War Departments claimed that any publicity would compromise counterespionage activities of the FBI, and the president appointed a military commission to try the saboteurs behind closed doors. The secrecy surrounding the case irritated the press. When Brigadier General Frank R. McCoy, who headed the tribunal, refused to arrange for the release of any news about the trial, Davis sent Henry Paynter, a veteran newspaperman, to the opening session to see if some arrangements might be worked out. Paynter waited for an hour in a War Department anteroom. McCoy finally sent a message through a minor officer: "The General does not wish to see the gentleman. The gentleman need not wait."[19]

Davis and Stimson went to the White House to settle the issue. Roosevelt, with characteristic deference to military demands, refused Davis's request that three representatives from the press agencies be admitted to the proceedings. In the end, the sole result was an agreement for McCoy to issue a brief daily communiqué about the trial's proceedings that OWI could publish through its newsroom. Though the communiqués said little, there was not much Davis could do.[20]

The trial of the saboteurs did not affect military operations, but the War Department had indicated that it still held the upper hand in determining what news might be released. With the basic question settled for the moment, Stimson invited Davis to dinner to discuss the issue of publicity during the war—from the military perspective. Now he found Davis "fair-minded and cooperative." The head of OWI knew that his organization had taken a beating.

He also knew that there would be other more significant issues involving questions of military security, and if he hoped to get anywhere he had to keep his channels open.[21]

Davis kept after the Army, with moderate success. When news released by military authorities in theaters of action was either inadequate or misleading, OWI worked through the chain of command, however long that took, to secure the necessary clarification. Stimson himself eventually proved helpful by reviewing military operations at his own weekly news conferences. His prompt admission of defeat at the Kasserine Pass in North Africa in February 1943, for example, helped restore public confidence in war information. Slowly the Army gave more assistance, but always on its own terms.[22]

The OWI experienced greater difficulties with the Navy. Ever since the Japanese attack on Pearl Harbor the American public suspected that the United States Navy was trying to hide its losses. Occasional news from Japanese broadcasts or from journalists or politicians just returned from the Pacific theater of the war merely enhanced suspicions that the Navy was not revealing the damage it was suffering. As public indignation grew even more intense when the Navy finally admitted months after the May 1942 battle of the Coral Sea the extent of the losses there, Davis resolved to see what he could do.[23]

Although in his first meeting with Secretary Knox Davis concluded that he got no more "than .0001 of a millimeter ahead," Ernest King was the major problem. Davis later said that he "always suspected that Admiral King's idea of War Information was that there should be just *one* communiqué. Some morning we would announce that the war was over and that we won it." Still he respected King's capabilities and their long argument of October 1942, he told his wife, was "acrimonious yet somehow remained friendly." Under pressure from Roosevelt and Secretary Knox, who wanted to quiet rumors that bad news was being withheld until after the congressional elections, Admiral King ultimately gave ground.[24]

The Navy moved to clear up the backlog of unreported sinkings. On October 13, 1942, it acknowledged the heavy losses off

Savo Island, near Guadalcanal, which had occurred over two months earlier. But then the criticisms that the news had been withheld too long grew sharper when word arrived the next day of the victory at Cape Esperance. The public suspected on the basis of past experience that the bad news was reserved until there was good news with which to balance it. Still the disclosures continued and by October 28 Davis was able to declare that all American sinkings to date had been reported. Then came the news that the U.S. aircraft carrier *Hornet* had been lost a short while before in the fighting off the Santa Cruz Islands. King wanted to hold back an official report until it could be determined whether or not the Japanese knew of the sinking, but Davis vigorously disagreed. The elections were only a few days away, and to withhold the news until they were over would be to encourage charges of playing politics. He told Knox and Roosevelt that the only way to quiet the rumors was to tell the full story. They agreed and the sinking was reported.[25]

Though Davis wrote to his wife that the incident made him almost mad enough to resign, he restrained himself for the first of many times from making a public outburst. He pointed out somewhat lamely that when the Navy had told him that all sinkings were revealed the carrier had only been damaged and had some chance of reaching port. Recognizing how the demands of military necessity circumscribed his own role, he confided to his wife, "Nor can I afford to defend myself . . . by anything that might undermine confidence in King: for his job is to fight the war and as I said the other night, he should not be judged by his shortcomings in any other capacity." Davis was exercising the basic common sense that inspired the confidence of millions of Americans. Yet the compromises he had to make weakened his position.[26]

With the tide of war turning in the Pacific, OWI's relations with the Navy gradually improved. The battles of the Coral Sea and Midway in mid-1942 had partially stopped the Japanese, and then the campaigns in Papua, in southeastern New Guinea, and in Guadalcanal, both in the latter part of the year, halted the enemy offensive. As Davis pointedly observed: "There is no temptation

to hold back bad news when there is no bad news to hold back."
Admiral Chester Nimitz organized an effective Public Relations
Office, and beginning with the attack on Tarawa in November
1943, the public received prompt and full accounts.[27]

For all the minor breakthroughs, Davis had not succeeded in
what he regarded as his central task. Even though by the end of
1942 a relationship had evolved whereby Davis met regularly
with Hull, Knox, and Stimson at the close of their regular Tuesday afternoon conference, the OWI head got only what the others were willing to give. He was disappointed and his colleagues
were disappointed, and so too were liberal observers like Bernard DeVoto who complained later in the war that "it is cynical
[of American leaders] to make speeches about the basic freedoms
of our way of life, naming a free press among them, and then
permit the Army and Navy to prevent OWI from serving the
function assigned to it." Davis no doubt agreed, but as long as
he intended to remain in Washington, there was little he could
do.[28]

If OWI fared poorly in its dealings with the three most important departments of government, it also took a beating from
other equally aggressive organizations. Recognizing that its mission went beyond securing news about the fighting, OWI set out
to uncover background material that could help people understand the news from the front as well as the activities at home that
sustained the military effort. That function seemed necessary at
the start of the war, for throughout the country there was public
confusion about the various wartime activities of the government. Few people understood the plans for dealing with vital
materials, in part because the plans themselves were uncertain,
especially as they pertained to labor and rubber shortages. Public
officials contradicted one another repeatedly. One woman from
Schenectady, New York, demanded better coordination of information in a letter to Roosevelt. "We are tougher than you think,"
she wrote, "we can take a lot if we only know where we stand."[29]

Davis agreed and was again disappointed as agencies simply
refused to cooperate. The Office of War Information could coordinate information but was not allowed to interfere in the policy

disputes which had disrupted the situation in the first place. Frequently it found its mild efforts to encourage agreement bitterly resented. The War Manpower Commission, organized in April 1942 and headed by Paul V. McNutt, tangled with Congress over how much compulsion could be used to direct people to war-related jobs. Workers, fearful of a job freeze or the cancellation of deferments, were anxious to know what was happening as the quarrel dragged on and on and other groups entered the controversy. But OWI could neither resolve nor analyze publicly the important questions at stake. Its task was to explain policy, and it could simply try, Davis pointed out, "to persuade the agencies that they have got to do something which we can make intelligible."[30]

So it was with rubber. The Japanese had cut off the supplies of crude rubber and left the United States with serious shortages. In May 1942, Roosevelt announced that he favored nationwide gasoline rationing to limit driving and conserve the rubber in automobile tires. An outraged public, which could see plenty of gasoline everywhere except on the East coast where rationing had already been imposed, refused to believe that the step was necessary, or to understand that the necessity arose in part from the need for petroleum in the manufacture of artificial rubber. Government agencies fed the confusion by offering alternative suggestions and raising hopes that the drastic measures could be avoided. A firm voice was needed to end contradictions in the press and to stop the rumors, but other agencies refused to allow OWI to play that role. Even its quiet efforts to explain the situation brought trouble. A story in April 1943 about the continuing shortage of automobile tires, based on a report of Rubber Director William M. Jeffers to the president several months before, angered Jeffers. He first tried to kill the story, then announced he needed no help. "I can get along very well on the rubber program without Mr. Davis," he said.[31]

At the same time OWI was coming into conflict with members of the press. Many newsmen had hailed Davis's appointment to head the new organization in mid-1942, for they viewed him as one of their own. But there were those like columnist Ernest K.

Lindley who complained soon after the agency was created about the very effort on the part of the government to tell a simple coherent story about what was going on. "On the whole," Lindley wrote, "it is better that the public should be confused temporarily than that opposing viewpoints should be muffled or suppressed." Men of that persuasion would probably have agreed with Walter Lippmann's statement that "the theory of a free press is that the truth will emerge from free reporting and free discussion, not that it will be presented perfectly in any one account."[32]

As time went on, and as the agency did not live up to its early promises to ferret out the news the reporters sought, the criticisms began to mount. More and more the newsmen and correspondents clung to their own prerogatives and challenged the organization that they now claimed only intruded on territory already staked out. Many were aware of what had happened in World War I, when George Creel's staff had guided what news could be printed and what should be withheld and had provided in addition canned releases to fill the papers with officially sanctioned news. Many too were having their own difficulties with the president and allowed those problems to color their feelings about the assorted parts of his administration. Roosevelt, so receptive and accessible when he first took office, was much more guarded during the war. His often unexplained absences and his efforts to guide press coverage led columnist Raymond Clapper to complain that he was taking "the whole technique of a controlled press far beyond anything we have experienced in this country." Newsmen who felt their primary allegiance was to the people at large were increasingly ill-disposed, on the basis of past and present experience, to cooperate with what some viewed as the president's publicity bureau—an agency that seemed either unnecessary or unhelpful or both.[33]

In the face of all that antagonism, OWI found itself increasingly constrained. So much of what the agency had first tried to do had failed to bring results. Only marginally successful in freeing the flow of news, hardly able to coordinate the wartime stories that so often seemed to conflict, the information leaders knew that any contribution they could make would have to take another form. As a result they gave more and more of their attention to programs, already underway, aimed at generating support for the war.

Some sort of effort seemed necessary indeed, for Americans appeared unclear about the broader purposes of the struggle in which they were engaged. In the first months after Pearl Harbor, it seemed obvious that the United States was fighting in self-defense. By the middle of 1942 public opinion analyst Jerome Bruner found that significant numbers of people were not as sure why they were involved. In July, 30 percent of those responding to the question, "Do you feel that you have a clear idea of what this war is all about—that is, what are we fighting for?", answered negatively, while in December the number had risen to 35 percent. Other polls in the fall of 1942 showed that approximately a third of the people interviewed were willing to accept a separate peace with Germany, and even after the announcement of the policy of unconditional surrender at the Casablanca conference in early 1943, the percentage remained almost as high. Other surveys too indicated significant public mistrust of America's allies. OWI clearly had its work cut out for it if it was to educate the public about the war.[34]

But the task was a delicate one, for the Roosevelt administration itself had not been wholly clear about the purposes of the war. Although he had conveyed his ultimate ends in his announcement of the Four Freedoms and in his proclamation of the Atlantic Charter, the president had not spelled out the immediate aims of the struggle. Partly because of the resulting ambiguity, partly because of their own convictions, the top OWI staffers had decided early on not to sell any one particular version of the war, and that decision still held. Now they clearly had to do something, and that need only brought to the surface the tensions still prevalent in the Domestic Branch of the organization. Some members, particularly those who had followed MacLeish, wanted to stimulate support by conveying the sober and serious facts about the war, to deluge the public with reasoned explanations of the important questions at hand. Others, especially those with ties to the media outside, hoped to use their connections on behalf of exhortation, to appeal to the hearts, if not the minds, of the public at large. No one approach was settled on at the start. Rather, various groups within the organization proceeded as they saw fit and turned out the materials they hoped would bring results. And their individual efforts only heightened the tensions that seemed increasingly difficult to avoid.

Many of the more creative members of OWI, the writers in particular, wanted to use their talents to educate the American public about the issues of the war. Back in the days of OFF, Archibald MacLeish had established a writers' section, and most of the personnel—Henry Pringle and others—moved on to OWI when the June 1942 reorganization took place. Although they found themselves more isolated in the new and larger agency, they still hoped to continue what they had already started. Believing deeply in the war, they wanted to convey the evil of fascism, the insidious way it had infected enemy populations, and the desperate need to destroy all traces of the disease. They wanted, too, to contrast American values to those of the fascists, and thereby to show the stake that every American had in the outcome of the struggle, as a way of justifying the sacrifice and personal expense involved in winning the war. They subscribed to Davis's assertion in his first year in office that "we are not yet more than ankle deep in war" and even when the momentum began to favor the Allies, they wanted the public to know that ships and planes were still being destroyed and that bitter battles were still leaving behind maimed men.[35]

Through the Bureau of Publications and Graphics the writers put out a number of items for the public at large. There were serious pamphlets like *The Unconquered People,* which showed Europe resisting, *Divide and Conquer,* which outlined Hitler's tactics, and *The Thousand Million,* which carried brief stories about the various United Nations. Those materials were straightforward enough and managed to convey the serious nature of the struggle. But the writers also wanted to use their talents to help people at home understand the need for sacrifices and disruptions that contributed to the larger cause.[36]

One pamphlet, entitled *How to Raise $16 Billion,* confronted the
ticklish question of taxation. It discussed reasonably dispassionately the need to raise more money to fight the war and described
the arguments for and against greater income taxes, sales taxes,
and the Ruml plan to forgive 1942 taxes as a preliminary to
withholding at the source.[37]

Battle Stations for All, a long piece of 123 pages prepared under
the direction of Samuel Lubell, dealt with the problem of inflation. The battle at home, the pamphlet said at the start, "is chiefly
a struggle to control living costs and prevent inflation," for
"when prices skyrocket, the burdens of war fall unevenly and
unfairly, morale is drained and the nation divided against itself."
The president himself had urged everyone to do whatever was
necessary to keep the economic system secure, and the pamphlet
therefore outlined what might be done. Acknowledging that
some aspects of the program were controversial, the booklet
defended rationing, increased taxation, and the war bond drive,
and gave full support to price control, rent control, and the
policies aimed at, in the words of one chapter title, "Taking the
Profit out of War." The war's burdens should be shared demo-
cratically, the writers argued, by the policies the administration
was working out.[38]

Still another publication addressed America's blacks. *Negroes
and the War* began with an essay by black publicist Chandler Owen
which stressed the "stake the Negro has in America—[and] just
what he has to lose under Hitler." Owen quoted *Mein Kampf* to
point out just what a German victory would mean and told readers that in the United States, despite a slow start, blacks had
"come a long way in the last fifty years, if slowly. There is still a
long way to go before equality is attained, but the pace is faster,
and never faster than now." The pamphlet then went on, in
words and pictures, to show blacks in all kinds of jobs, as soldiers
and civilians, in war work and other employment as well. It
showed black schools and churches, and pictured blacks at home
in both rural and urban settings. Jesse Owens appeared, as did
Marian Anderson and Joe Louis, to depict the accomplishments
of the race. Lavish and expensive, the pamphlet was meant to

quell the justifiable doubts of many blacks about the commitment of the administration to their cause.[39] Idealists in OWI understood those doubts, yet hoped and trusted that they could be overcome in the interests of the larger struggle.

The writers therefore did all they could to convey the serious side of the war. But others in OWI were equally involved in trying to maintain the morale of the public they served. Many had been active before the war in the motion picture and radio industries and now sought to use their talents with nonwritten communication to reach the nation.

Movies, so popular with the public, offered an obvious way of informing the people about the war. Approximately eighty million Americans each week attended films, and the sixteen thousand theaters throughout the country could accommodate eleven million at any given time. The president himself, soon after Pearl Harbor, called the motion picture "one of our most effective media in informing and entertaining our citizens" and declared that it could make "a very useful contribution" to the whole war effort. Movies could clarify complex problems for people who were less inclined to read newspapers and other written materials, and the seductive qualities of the screen could help generate the support the nation needed.[40]

And so OWI's Bureau of Motion Pictures, under the direction of Lowell Mellett, set out to try to influence the audience outside. Responsible for serving as a point of contact with the Hollywood industry, the bureau also distributed films put out by assorted agencies and produced as well a number of its own for commercial release and for nontheatrical distribution. Most of its own efforts had a self-explanatory, didactic quality evident in titles like *Manpower, Fuel Conservation, Food for Fighters,* or *Doctors at War. War Town* told how Mobile, Alabama, dealt with housing and health problems brought on by the war. *Troop Train,* suggested by the Office of Defense Transportation, explained how an armed division was transported by rail. And *Salvage* showed what happened to the materials the public was so desperately being urged to save.[41]

Those ventures, which took the same approach as the literary

efforts of the writers, were but a part of the motion picture program, for Hollywood had long been making movies on its own,
and OWI realized that it had to achieve some sort of coordination
with the industry. That prospect proved more difficult to attain
than expected, for the film capital had for years held a self-
centered notion of its own importance. The industry did set up
a War Activities Committee after Pearl Harbor that became
OWI's point of contact, but the relationship was never more than
one-sided, for Hollywood jealously resisted anything approach-
ing censorship and even considered OWI's advisory role too
heavy-handed. The motion picture magnates, long dedicated to
entertaining the American public according to well-worn but
popular formulas, set out to convey the social and philosophical
problems of the war in their own mundane way.[42]

Those in OWI who watched Hollywood were not particularly
happy with what they saw. Archibald MacLeish, while still with
the organization, had called popular films "escapist and delu-
sive" and had asserted that Hollywood had "a primary and ines-
capable responsibility" for what he felt was the nation's failure to
deal with the important issues of the war. Even Elmer Davis
claimed in the first year that "Hollywood is letting its imagination
carry it away." Those criticisms emerged even more pointedly in
the regular assessments of OWI's Bureau of Intelligence which
watched the effects of all kinds of programs on American
morale.[43]

Basically the critics in the propaganda organization argued that
Hollywood's movies provided a deceptive picture of the war. In
most films the United Nations fought against invasion and enslavement, but there was little indication of what they were
fighting for. The critics, stressing the principles of the Atlantic
Charter, wanted to project a concern for law and justice and the
dignity of human beings, but failed to find what they sought in
the movies. They were disturbed by a film like *Tarzan Triumphs*,
starring Johnny Weissmuller, which showed "Nadzies" suffering
defeat, but hardly seemed to take the war seriously. Worse were
the light musicals like *Star Spangled Rhythm* or *The Yanks are Com-*

ing, which used the war as background but showed little or no sensitivity to the larger issues.[44]

Films about the home front in the first couple of years of the war were hardly more inspiring. Skeptics in OWI claimed that too many showed the United States as a nation full of gangsters and thugs, and that those criminals were brought to justice, not by the bungling police, but by private detectives who coincidentally happened to appear on the scene. One critic who had watched Hollywood carefully declared, too, at the end of the war, that films like *Blondie for Victory, Dixie Dugan,* and *Air-Raid Wardens* tended to make fun of serious civilian activities and therefore undermined not merely the effort to raise morale but the volunteer program as well.[45]

In the same way those in OWI watching the movies objected to Hollywood's treatment of the enemy. Too often the forces fighting the United States appeared in stereotyped form. Germans spoke in guttural accents and went around saying "Heil Hitler" to show their devotion to the cause. Japanese came across even more poorly, as cruel, ruthless, unscrupulous fighters who seldom observed the rules of civilized warfare. Even worse, in Hollywood's version of the war, the enemy seldom looked like a genuine threat to basic institutions. Rather he was simply a gun-toting soldier to be met with similar force. Any hints at ideological confrontation soon degenerated into physical blows. A movie like *Stand By for Action,* with Charles Laughton among others, was a typical battle picture, where armed strength was all that mattered.[46]

There were, to be sure, some acceptable films that came out of Hollywood, and OWI commended *The Moon Is Down, Hangmen Also Die,* and a number of other movies in 1943 for their interpretations of the issues of the war. But always the Bureau of Motion Pictures, ostensibly assigned to oversee the film effort, functioned as a passive observer, for Hollywood would allow no further interference. With its own resources limited at best, the bureau had no choice but to comply. The messages that emerged from films proved radically different from those that came from the written word.[47]

Different too were the messages that came from radio. Radio was ready-made for propaganda, for with sixty million receivers scattered throughout the nation, 90 percent of the American people could be easily reached in their own homes. OWI's Domestic Radio Bureau therefore set out to play its part in gearing the public for war. Again, however, as with the motion picture efforts, an established industry ended up playing a large part in the arrangements worked out, although OWI enjoyed a better relationship and more important role with the radio leaders than it had ever had with the Hollywood impresarios.[48]

Recognizing the strength of the industry, those in OWI interested in radio resolved to work with the broadcast heads as much as possible. Bureau Chief William B. Lewis wanted not to disrupt the standard and successful patterns of broadcasting, but to superimpose wartime necessities on the established system. Audiences had to be maintained if radio was to be a successful weapon of war. Early in the war, when there seemed to be too much haphazard war-related activity on the airwaves, radio personnel, first from OFF, then from OWI, worked out a network allocation plan to balance the contributions and range of topics covered across the spectrum. The propaganda office got the various stations to agree to contribute air time on a regular basis for government-sponsored radio messages, and that setup worked well for the duration of the war.[49]

But OWI's radio officials did even more. They received the appropriate messages from various agencies and channeled them to programs like "The Lone Ranger" and "Terry and the Pirates" at the proper times. They worked out a series of one-minute transcriptions about the war effort to be plugged by all radio stations in an intensive campaign and then approached prominent personalities like H. V. Kaltenborn, Raymond Gram Swing, Lowell Thomas, and William L. Shirer, among others, to make the recordings. And they saw to it that popular shows incorporated war-related themes into their story lines.[50]

To that end Jack Benny, on the "Victory Parade" on August 23,

1942, went through several routines that dealt with the war effort. In one, Mary Livingston spoke of her uncle on a diet who lost twenty-three pounds in several days by eating nothing but soup. Benny as straight man, with the comment "Nothing but soup? . . . Say, he musta had a lot of will-power," set her up for the punch line: "No, my Aunt gave his teeth to the Rubber-drive." In another sequence, Rochester asked to borrow Benny's car for an important engagement with his girl. Benny's response was that he had to save the rubber on the tires, and despite Rochester's retort, "Boss, there ain't no more rubber on the wheels of that car than there is on the Chatanooga Choo-choo," Benny's argument held. But then humor aside, in a final routine Benny told his audience that *"This is a total war!"* and went on in a very serious vein to urge listeners to do their part and to buy the war bonds the government was selling: "WHEN WE BUY THOSE BONDS, REMEMBER WE'RE NOT DOING THE *GOVERN-MENT* A FAVOR. *WE'RE* THE GOVERNMENT! THIS IS *MY* WAR, AND *YOUR* WAR! SO LET'S GET ROLLING . . . HARD AND FAST."[51]

So too did Fibber McGee and Molly do a whole routine related to the war effort on February 16, 1943, when they received a government circular asking for workers with special skills, for tack welders, flanging press operators, plate hangers, and others. After fooling around and trying to figure out just what those people did, they became serious for a moment, as Fibber said, "LADIES AND GENTLEMEN, NO FOOLING, THE GOVERN-MENT *DOES* NEED SKILLED WORKERS IN THE LINES WE'VE BEEN TALKING ABOUT. . . . IF YOU CAN DO ANY OF THESE THINGS, AND AREN'T IN WAR PRODUCTION WORK AT THIS TIME, DO YOUR COUNTRY A GOOD TURN AND REPORT TO YOUR NEAREST U.S. EMPLOY-MENT SERVICE OFFICE." To which Molly could only add, "DON'T FORGET . . . IT'S YOUR SONS OF TOIL THAT'LL HELP PUT THOSE NAZIS UNDER TONS OF SOIL!"[52]

Radio really did assist the war effort, in many different ways. OWI officials helped push for the spot announcements and the serious discussions, the comedy hours and the dramas that were occasionally maudlin and trite. The regular programs went on, but the networks did prove able to integrate the new offerings into their schedules. OWI's Radio Bureau took advantage of the cooperative relationship and made some efforts to communicate soberly the issues of the war, but at the same time devoted even more time to the campaigns and cajolery that were deemed important for the home front at war.[53]

The latter activity, however, was more strictly the province of still another branch of OWI—the Bureau of Campaigns. And members of that office, drawn largely from advertising, had their own ideas about arousing the American people. As they worked through various media in behalf of the purchase of bonds, the collection of salvage, the conservation of fuel, the sharing of meat, and similar programs, they engaged in frankly promotional activities. Behind their approach was a view of the American people distinctly different from that of others in the organization, particularly that of the writers who followed MacLeish. Where the writers sought to inform a public that they considered intelligent enough to use good judgment if only properly informed, the advertising executives saw the American people as hesitant customers who had to be persuaded by gut-level appeals. A booklet, produced by the bureau and directed at merchants and others involved in the campaign to raise and share food, underscored the necessity of appealing to basic self-interest. It pointed out the need to "remind people of the pleasure and deliciousness and health benefits of having all the dewy-fresh vegetables they want." It emphasized that "this positive approach, which quickly answers the instinctive human question 'What is there in it for me?' seems to be the *surest* way to get people to take action." Similarly a booklet entitled *Conserve* advised people involved in the various campaigns not to stress "the general, national, patriotic 'why' " but rather "the *personal, private* 'why.' " Liberal author Malcolm Cowley decried that method which could be used "to sell anything, good, bad, or indifferent" and which was "based on distrust and contempt for the people." Bernard DeVoto complained later that some radio announcements were "so phony and so hoked up that they stink violently." Overall, he wrote,

"there has been too God-damned much exhortation and denun-
ciation, too God-damned much cleverness, . . . and too God-
damned little straight talking over the table at an adult public."
But the campaigns continued, for they were well-run, and the
result was, according to Bruce Catton, then a young journalist
and war agency official, "a steady absorption, by OWI, of the
sales-promotion ideas and techniques."[54]

The submerged tensions in OWI grew as various groups in the
organization went their own ways in trying to stimulate support
for the war. Finally the growing reliance on promotional methods
led the tensions to surface in the most vulnerable and challenged
area—the writers' division of the Domestic Branch. The writers
had worked well with MacLeish in the days of OFF, but after the
emergence of OWI, they had come under the control of Gardner
Cowles, Jr., who was much less interested in what they had to
offer. As head of the Domestic Branch Cowles worked closely
with the radio and advertising industries on the campaigns he
considered important. Such service for other branches of government, he believed, was the main function of OWI. As he saw it,
the independently originated pamphlets were peripheral, and
given their controversial nature, even expendable.[55]

Trouble broke out when Cowles reorganized the Domestic
Branch in February 1943. Heavy responsibilities fell to new assistants William Lewis, a former vice-president of the Columbia
Broadcasting System, and James Allen, a film executive and one-
time press agent for the Securities and Exchange Commission.
They in turn brought in other advertising and business executives, including Price Gilbert, former vice-president of Coca-
Cola. The writers came under Lewis's direction and the graphics
staff, which often worked with the writers, now reported to Gilbert.[56]

Shifts in direction reflected the influence of the new personnel.
A new publications policy aimed to conserve paper and to direct
activity more regularly through established channels. New guide-
lines from the leaders of the Domestic Branch governed the
writers and artists. Now the writers were to work only in response
to outside requests. The posters were to reflect only the more

benign side of the war. The writers and graphics staff resented
the new restrictions, and Henry Pringle, arguing that he was a
writer, not a copywriter, warned that the new policies would drive
creative individuals from the organization. His colleagues grew
increasingly upset at what they regarded as a turn away from the
fundamental, complex issues of the war in favor of manipulation
and stylized exhortation.[57]

The crisis peaked over a pamphlet dealing with the food question. Prepared in January, the pamphlet drew on Department of
Agriculture statistics and concluded with a grim assessment of
the food supply. Secretary of Agriculture Claude Wickard and
James F. Byrnes, then head of the Office of Economic Stabiliza-
tion, both objected to the OWI report, for they feared it would
aid the farm bloc in its campaign to gain higher priorities for
production of farm equipment. When the writers involved
refused to alter the pamphlet, their superiors refused to permit
its publication. Their sense of responsibility to other agencies
conflicted with the writers' sense of their own responsibility to
present the unadorned facts of the situation to the American
public. After an unsatisfactory conference with Cowles, the writers resigned.[58]

At about the same time, Francis Brennan, former head of the
Graphics Bureau, resigned for similar reasons. He wrote to Davis
that he resented the efforts within the agency "to make necessary
civilian actions appear palatable, comfortable, and not quite as
inconvenient as Guadalcanal." Sending a copy of the letter to
Harry Hopkins, Archibald MacLeish commented that he thought
it was "clear enough that OWI is no longer very much interested
in the innards of the war." A poster produced by the graphics
staff reflected that sentiment. The Statue of Liberty stood erect,
arm raised, holding four bottles of Coca-Cola. The caption read:
"The War That Refreshes: The Four Delicious Freedoms."[59]

A more public reflection of the tension came in an angry statement to the press issued on April 14 by Pringle, Brennan, young
historian Arthur M. Schlesinger, Jr., and a number of other members of the agency to justify their resignations. "There is only one
issue—the deep and fundamental one of the honest presentation

of war information," the statement said. "We are leaving because of our conviction that it is impossible for us, under those who now control our output, to tell the full truth. No one denies that promotional techniques have a proper and powerful function in telling the story of the war. But as we see it, the activities of OWI on the home front are now dominated by high-pressure promoters who prefer slick salesmanship to honest information. . . . They are turning this Office of War Information into an Office of War Bally-hoo." That statement, and the writers' quarrel in general, raised again the basic question of the role the Domestic Branch could play. Earlier the Office of War Information had chosen to serve not as an advocate of ideological issues but rather as disseminator of more general information. But even then the more serious and reflective presentation of the war had finally succumbed to the demands of public relations and what could have been an honest message had now become suspect.[60]

Davis reacted vigorously to the controversy. While he himself might well have signed the writers' statement had he been working in that division, Malcolm Cowley observed, as director his first reaction was to try to persuade those resigning not to leave. Now he rose to defend the agency. The writers may have been sincere, he told a press conference, but they were mistaken. "We deal in one plain commodity—the facts the people of this country need to win the war. . . . Emotional appeals of the type usually associated with promotional activities are not applicable to war problems." His disclaimer seemed to reflect his hope for the agency rather than the situation that had developed. But his denial was too late. The writers were gone, for their approach had been discredited, and now a curious public and an unfriendly Congress wondered just what the Office of War Information was trying to do.[61]

Congress, for some time, had been increasingly hostile, not only to OWI but to the Roosevelt administration in general. The New Deal was over, and while conservative Republicans and Southern Democrats who banded together in Congress came out in full support of military victory, they became more and more intolerant of other administration programs. During 1942 and

1943 Congress eliminated, as much for political as for practical reasons, the Civilian Conservation Corps, the Works Progress Administration, and the National Youth Administration. So too it scuttled the National Resources Planning Board and attacked Fiorello La Guardia's Office of Civilian Defense as a rearguard publicity organization for the president. The mid-term elections of 1942 only buttressed the conservatives and made their alliance all the more secure. Roosevelt's acknowledgment that Dr. New Deal had given way to Dr. Win-the-War did little good, for the Congress was a force to be reckoned with as it sought to enforce its own priorities.[62]

The Office of War Information became involved in the conservative effort to dismantle the liberal framework Roosevelt had created. Congress had been suspicious of OWI ever since its organization, and the random sniping that began then grew in intensity as the war continued. Representative John Taber, a conservative Republican from New York, was one of the earliest critics. In November 1942 he told Davis that the propaganda activities of his organization were hampering, not helping, the war effort. Other legislators claimed that the agency was making premature postwar commitments that could not be fulfilled. But most of the real hostility was directed at home front activities. Republicans in particular attacked the Domestic Branch as a New Deal publicity center which aimed mainly at obtaining a fourth term for President Roosevelt.[63]

Attacks began to increase in February 1943 when Senator Rufus C. Holman of Oregon came upon the first issue of *Victory,* an OWI publication designed for overseas use. He was particularly incensed by an article on "Roosevelt of America—President, Champion of Liberty, United States Leader in the War to Win Lasting and Worldwide Peace." Irritated by the large color photo of Roosevelt against the background of the American flag, Holman was even more irate at the characterization of the president as a kindly man whose own philosophy ran counter to "the toryism of the conservative reactionary." The whole magazine, Holman asserted, was but "window dressing" for another Roosevelt campaign. Agreeing with Holman, John Taber charged that *Vic-*

tory was an "outlandish, ridiculous, expensive type of getup," which wasted paper already in short supply and took up precious shipping space that could better hold bombs and bullets. Hostile Democrats added their fire. Senator Harry F. Byrd of Virginia indicated that his Joint Committee for the Reduction of Nonessential Federal Expenditures would investigate "all government propaganda ventures."[64]

Davis, conceding that the story on Roosevelt might have been better done, denied any partisan slant. *Victory* was directed solely at foreign audiences, he said. While the magazine might occasionally fall into the hands of American soldiers abroad, its purpose was to inform other peoples of America's contribution to the struggle. In describing the war effort, he explained in a press conference, "you have to say something about the President of the United States." Whatever Roosevelt's fourth term intentions, Davis continued, he would benefit little from the votes of South Africa, Egypt, or Australia. A Philadelphia newspaper, wondering at the fears of Roosevelt's opponents, asked: "What are they afraid of—that the Democrats in 1944 will sweep the fifth ward in Casablanca?" But Congress remained suspicious. Even Robert Sherwood's guarantees of "absolute impartiality" in political affairs failed to quiet their doubts.[65]

Other OWI materials heightened congressional hostility. *How to Raise $16 Billion,* the pamphlet on taxation, came under bitter attack. OWI considered the pamphlet fair, but various legislators resented its support for withholding taxes and argued that it misrepresented the Ruml plan, which enjoyed some important support. *Battle Stations for All,* the booklet dealing with inflation, attracted criticism for its support of policies that were still under congressional consideration. In the face of criticism from Capitol Hill Gardner Cowles, Jr., conceded that the publication was a mistake. But *Negroes and the War* drew the heaviest fire. Northern Republicans like Senator Henry Cabot Lodge, Jr., of Massachusetts felt it gave undue attention to the achievements of the New Deal. Mississippi Representative John Rankin took early aim and others followed. Representative A. Leonard Allen complained that the pamphlet favored racial equality. A statement that the pace toward that goal had quickened, he said, "smacks of an attempt to use the war to force upon the South a philosophy that is alien to us." Such congressmen, their ire aroused, were increasingly unsympathetic to anything OWI wanted to do.[66]

The Office of War Information was in trouble. The writers' walkout in April had drawn undesirable attention to an agency that had already lost much of the support it needed. Attacks came from all quarters as Congress began hearings in June on OWI's request for funds. Davis made the situation worse by choosing at that moment to criticize the press for what he considered inadequate treatment of the war effort. Some reporters "still seem to feel that a battle between a couple of administrators is bigger news than a battle between the American and Japanese navies," he said in a speech before the American Newspaper Guild in Boston. His words provoked the opposition of newsmen at just the time OWI needed support. Under those conditions, when another administrator under fire might well have turned to his chief for support, Davis had no place to go. For the president, who had created the organization in the first place, refused to get involved.[67]

Roosevelt's detachment was characteristic of his whole approach to his office, especially in time of war. As commander-in-chief in a cataclysmic struggle, he had his own priorities and they took precedence over all else. He assumed personal responsibility for important negotiations more than other presidents had, and given his fascination with the strategy and tactics of war, he carried innumerable details around in his head. Although he accepted the need for an American role in the postwar world, his view was subject to change, and even as he allowed the development of the notion of international organization, he seemed to favor big-power domination. Yet for all the planning behind the scenes, during the war he appeared to want victory first and foremost, as much an end in itself as a means of enforcing a measure of cooperation among allies with conflicting demands of their own. Despite the repeated requests from propagandists for specific declarations of war aims, he himself preferred to talk of the Four Freedoms and Atlantic Charter in general terms, with the assertion that anything else could wait until after the war. Uneasy about formal propaganda, unwilling to allow the power of publicity to drift from his own hands, he accepted the propaganda organization as a necessary if cumbersome addition to the war effort, but not one that demanded any more than his minimal support.[68]

Yet his treatment of OWI was no different from his treatment of scores of other organizations in the years since 1933. The president was a master at using men. His penchant for conflicting appointments, so evident before the organization of OWI, allowed him to play off his assistants against one another. Having set men on their own he could reserve the right to intrude if something really mattered to him, or simply allow his subordinates to work out their conflicting claims themselves. As Tom Corcoran later observed, "It reduced his responsibility for their mistakes. Since he wasn't directly involved, he could wash his hands of bad policies more easily." Even when officials came to him for support, he could put them off. He could charm people and send them away under his spell, firmly (but wrongly) convinced that he had taken their side. Or he would agree to see men on matters upon which he had not yet made up his mind, and then in his seemingly oblivious way, he would ramble on genially and refuse to allow them time to raise the point of their concern. Marriner Eccles, governor of the Federal Reserve Board, later recalled how one important meeting never got started, for the president insisted on listening to a Wagner opera on the radio and then discoursing on his love of the music for the rest of the time allowed. On another occasion, Eccles's time with the president was taken up watching him play with his little dog Fala and then scold the animal for "purging himself on the rug." Eccles was furious, but eventually recognized that he had simply fallen prey to FDR's way of avoiding controversial situations.[69]

So too the president could let his subordinates take the heat for him if that proved politically necessary. When the tax bill of 1943–44 emerged from congressional conference committee, it was full of inequities and failed to generate the revenue needed. Secretary of the Treasury Henry Morgenthau, Jr., recommended signing the bill nonetheless, but the president decided on his own to send it back to Congress with his provocative but valid assertion that the bill provided relief "not for the needy but for the greedy." Congress counterattacked and overrode the veto, and while Morgenthau observed that he had earlier opposed the president's course, he was now prepared to stand by his boss and take the brunt of the criticism. As he put it soon after, "I told my wife —I made the rather trite remark that somebody would have to be the ham in the sandwich, as between the President and Congress, and I was expecting to be it."[70]

Elmer Davis was also to take the barbs of critics of the administration when the president did not want to be further involved. Early in 1943 Roosevelt told both the OWI director and Domestic Branch head Gardner Cowles, Jr., that he would not intervene in what promised to be a difficult struggle in Congress over the 1944 appropriation for the agency. He was simply not willing to put his own credibility or credit on the line for something he was not particularly concerned about.[71]

And so the fight in Congress unfolded with OWI on its own pitted against the hostile senators and representatives who were determined to undermine the organization. After lengthy hearings, the House Appropriations Committee reduced the request for the Domestic Branch by nearly 40 percent to $5,500,000. It advised drastic cuts in films, publications, and graphics and then reported the budget favorably. On the floor of the House OWI's opponents pressed their attack. John Taber called the organization "a haven of refuge for the derelicts," and Representative Joe Starnes of Alabama termed the domestic propaganda "a stench to the nostrils of a democratic people." Davis's earlier membership in the American Labor Party came under attack, as did his organization's ostensible efforts on behalf of a fourth term for the president. Congressman Emmanuel Celler of New York tried valiantly to refute charges and defend the agency, but he was not strong enough. In the end, a majority composed of most Republicans and Southern Democrats voted 218 to 114 to abolish the Domestic Branch entirely. The Senate, a little less destructive, granted $3,561,499 for home front activities. The conference committee left the Domestic Branch with $2,750,000, just enough money, Davis noted, to avoid "the odium of having put us out of business, and carefully not enough to let us accomplish much." OWI had to abandon the Office of Publications and Motion Pictures Bureau and close its regional offices. It had to agree to work only through other agencies and not to generate materials for home use itself. None of the propaganda it produced for overseas consumption could be distributed within the United States. The Domestic Branch was now basically a coordinating agency which shuttled between other government agencies and the communications industry but did little more on its own.[72]

The one-time efforts of Archibald MacLeish in behalf of an independent information policy to communicate to the American people the real issues of the war had ended in naught. His hopes had been first circumscribed by the less aggressive members of his own organization, then sabotaged by the conservative Congress. Elmer Davis, caught in the middle of the squabbles within the organization and the larger struggles between his agency and the outside world, fought for survival, and on the domestic front that was about all he achieved. He had indeed become a scapegoat, and with his capacity for compromise had accepted the role, for he saw little choice if he was to continue to contribute in some way to the American war effort. Davis might have fought harder, but given the more necessitarian concerns of the president and the more political concerns of the Congress, such a fight would scarcely have made much difference.

The Domestic Branch therefore became the media-oriented coordinating mechanism, reflecting American tastes and American values, that certain of its members had advocated from the start. The liberals who had followed MacLeish were disappointed, for OWI's fate was but one more example of the war's devastating impact on the whole liberal cause. Davis, too, was disturbed, both at the attacks he had faced and the results they had brought. After the congressional action he wrote to Representative Louis Ludlow, who had labored on his behalf: "I do indeed feel pretty much like Job at the moment and sit here scraping myself with pot-sherds, not too greatly solaced by the mournful condolences of friends who point out wherein I have sinned. However, I do not think the time has yet come to curse God and die." He was determined to continue and even though, as Secretary of the Interior Harold Ickes noted in the summer of 1943, he was "literally making bricks without straw," he hoped that he would have smoother going with the propaganda aimed overseas. But there too struggles between liberal aims and necessitarian means threatened to cause still further trouble for the beleaguered OWI.[73]

3 Propaganda Abroad: A Vision Denied

The battle over the interpretation of the war, joined first in the home front information effort, became even more bitter in the foreign propaganda campaign. The liberal propagandists again sought to convey their vision of the meaning of the war and again faced ever-increasing resistance from others in the administration. The leaders of the OWI overseas program continued to see the war as a struggle in which freedom and democracy could triumph everywhere, a struggle that could bring a positive upheaval in the world at large. Because most of them shared the same convictions, they initially faced little of the internal dissension the Domestic Branch had known, especially since Elmer Davis left them largely to their own devices as he dealt almost exclusively with the domestic front. The troubles stemmed from the relationships with the more prominent leaders of the war effort outside of OWI. As the propagandists complained at length about the compromising positions taken by the Roosevelt administration, which proved willing to shelve commendable rhetorical aims in the interest of short-term military gain, the top-ranking officials they attacked were equally furious with the liberties the propagandists seemed to demand. In a series of ideological confrontations, those with broader authority blunted the aggressive thrust of the propaganda effort and demonstrated to all concerned that only with a belated reassessment of priorities could the battered agency hope to survive.

The propagandists engaged in the overseas program were a talented and forceful lot. Recruited both for their ability to express themselves and for their ideological commitment, they were used to speaking out and intended to continue to do so for the cause at hand. Coming from newspaper, theater, and radio circles, they often had similar backgrounds that contributed not merely to a shared sense of purpose but to a sense of companionship as well. And as the Overseas Branch grew from its modest beginnings into a large and spirited organization, a number of individuals took on a special importance in helping Robert Sherwood make it run.

James P. Warburg, who became the Overseas Branch's deputy director for propaganda policy, was one of the dominant figures of the group. Capable, creative, incisive, Warburg was a man of strong convictions who helped whip the organization into shape, although sometimes at the expense of appearing arrogant and intolerant of opposition. Born in Germany but raised in the United States and educated at Harvard, he followed family tradition and moved into the banking business. As he began a successful career, he also drifted into artistic and cultural circles, wrote lyrics and scores for musical comedies under the pseudonym Paul James, and came to know a variety of people who were prominent in the arts, among them Sherwood. Warburg had worked for the Roosevelt administration on banking and currency questions in the early days of the New Deal, but in short order broke with the president on financial matters and resigned. At first a friendly critic of the New Deal, he became disturbed at what he regarded as Roosevelt's hunger for power, but he began to reconsider his position as he saw that the United States could not avoid involvement in European troubles. An ardent interventionist who was horrified by Munich and wanted to do all he could to prepare the United States for a necessary war, he apologized to the president in 1940 and threw himself wholeheartedly into the task he now believed in. As war drew near he participated actively in the informal but acerbic debate over intervention, and even before Pearl Harbor he went to work as a special assistant to the Coordinator of Information, with responsibility for assembling a foreign language staff for Sherwood's new Foreign Information Service. In that capacity and in the more responsible positions he soon assumed, he left his imprint on the new organization.[1]

Working with Warburg, first in FIS and later in OWI, was newspaperman Joseph Barnes. Equally creative and equally committed, though somewhat more sweet-tempered and less outspoken than Warburg, Barnes brought a different perspective to propaganda. After a Harvard education that included service as managing editor, then president, of the *Crimson,* he spent some time studying in Russia, did some work there for the *New York Herald Tribune,* and at the end of 1934 decided to begin a career with the newspaper. He ran the Moscow Bureau for a couple of years, then in 1939 moved to Berlin, and a year later came back to New York where he became foreign editor of the paper. He too was an interventionist whose experience in Germany had led him to feel that since the war was going to involve the United States, the nation might just as well have a hand in determining the timing of its entrance. In the summer of 1941 he drifted into propaganda when Sherwood, whom he knew, asked him to help set up an office to monitor and analyze Axis propaganda. With Warburg, Barnes worked on the early staffing and was therefore responsible for the able but independent figures who joined the group. As Warburg came to assume responsibility for directives, Barnes became a deputy director in charge of operations and in time played a more and more political role in explaining to congressional committees just what the organization was trying to do. A solid member of the agency from its start, he too left his mark.[2]

Similarly important were two other figures who rounded out the top group. Percy Winner, like Barnes a newspaperman and foreign correspondent, was a playful gadfly whose convictions and sense of humor endeared him to Sherwood. His shortness complemented Sherwood's height, and the office staff remarked that they often looked like Mutt and Jeff as they walked off to lunch. Winner brought impressive credentials to the agency. After early service on a variety of papers he worked from the mid-1930s on as chief correspondent in North Africa for the Havas News Agency, as manager of the Rome Bureau of the International News Service, as foreign commentator for the Columbia Broadcasting System, and as director of the international division for the National Broadcasting Corporation. Joining the office of the Coordinator of Information in 1941, he brought to the organization an extensive background of observing European politics and a sense of the possibilities of the war, and in time became OWI's regional chief for Latin Europe.[3]

Finally there was Edd Johnson, another strong personality, who had worked as assistant managing editor of *Collier's* magazine, then as foreign news editor and director of the shortwave listening station for CBS, before moving into propaganda. He had a lively, if sometimes biting, sense of humor, although he could occasionally come across as opinionated, even abrasive, to outside observers. But he was firmly committed to his work, he could be relied on, and he played an increasingly important role in running the New York Control Office, which monitored all that OWI released.[4]

Those men had a firm sense of the war and of the part they wanted to play. Like Sherwood and MacLeish, they saw the struggle as a people's war, a necessary war that could reaffirm the values they held most dear. Less outspoken than either playwright or poet, they still clung to the same views. They shared the conviction, as Barnes later recalled, that wars could be won in the minds of men, and were confident that if their story was only told in full their audience—the rest of the world—would eventually believe it and support American ends. The overseas propagandists, like their domestic counterparts, therefore adhered faithfully to a "strategy of truth," for Sherwood, like MacLeish, insisted that a democratic society had to base any persuasive message on honest grounds. While enemy propaganda followed a "strategy of terror" that frequently included outright lies, the United States, even in the context of total war, could not afford such deception, which would only lend credence to the Axis charge that American ideals were hypocritical and hollow at best. American propagandists acknowledged that they made selective use of the truth and shaped it to their own ends. But they insisted vigorously that they were honest and forthright in what they did. Sherwood spoke for them all when he declared before the House Appropriations Committee in September 1942 that "the truth, coming from America, with unmistakable American sincerity, is by far the most effective form of propaganda," and he and his assistants were sure of their ultimate success.[5]

Sharing those convictions, the top staffers of the Overseas Branch worked extraordinarily well together. Many spent either all or much of their time in New York, where the Foreign Information Service had initially been established, partly because that was a key center for broadcasting purposes, but primarily because the early leaders wanted to avoid contact with any unsympathetic groups like the Congress and State Department in Washington. Even though the difficulties of rapid communication and coordination between Washington and New York were obvious with the formation of OWI, Sherwood and his subordinates preferred to leave the situation unchanged. Their group, which had grown from a single organization and not from several as the Domestic Branch had, enjoyed a sense of morale and companionship that the members were unwilling to see jeopardized by outside influences. Many indeed felt a tremendous loyalty and affection for Sherwood which led them to act as though they were working for him and not for the agency.[6]

The sense of independence in the Overseas Branch of OWI was heightened by Sherwood's shortcomings as an administrator. With Davis at first generally uninvolved with overseas affairs, Sherwood occasionally let his organization take a tack of its own. He was an imaginative propagandist who had a way with words, but he was totally inexperienced in running an office. Warburg observed in retrospect that Sherwood was "slow, unpunctual, and moody" in working with other people. He hated the paperwork necessary in his position and was bored by the daily routine. Lucille Gibbons, his private secretary, later recalled that piles of correspondence went into his office in the morning and came back at the end of the day untouched. If something demanded his attention, she finally resorted to the expedient of putting a darning needle through a document to force him to pay attention to it. Even that did not always work. Once Sherwood received a weekly directive and instead of duplicating or circulating it, he placed it in his pocket for future reference. Later, when asked why certain operations had not been carried out, he sadly remembered that the directive was still in the suit that had since gone to the cleaners. Sherwood gave an overall direction to the agency but then more often than not let his subordinates go off on their own.[7]

Working as a group, the propaganda leaders launched what became an enormous campaign. More and more people joined the organization and contributed to the activity in OWI. In New York, by the middle of 1943, the staff worked twenty-four hours a day on hundreds of productions in scores of different languages.[8]

The propaganda effort took a variety of forms. Many of the methods and media used on the domestic scene were employed in different ways abroad. News formed the backbone of the campaign, for Sherwood, early in the war, had decided to avoid emotional appeals on the assumption that the people abroad, deafened by the years of enemy propaganda, would respond best to a sober presentation of the facts of war. Spot news, therefore, transmitted over the air as soon after the fact as possible, made up much of the output, but it was supplemented by feature stories and interpretive pieces that helped place events in the framework of the war.[9]

The decision to use news as the basis for propaganda gave radio an important part in OWI's overseas activities. Only through radio could developments be reported immediately and could a sense of intimacy and personal contact be conveyed. Although at the beginning the United States had only about a dozen shortwave transmitters compared to Germany's sixty-eight, the radio effort got underway. The propagandists soon gained control of privately owned facilities, and they received some help rebroadcasting programs in mediumwave from the British Broadcasting Company. In time they took over facilities in Tunis, Palermo, and Bari, seized intact Radio Luxembourg, the second most powerful station in Europe, and just before D-Day set up ABSIE, the American Broadcasting Station in Europe, which operated out of London. So, too, in the Pacific the propagandists made rapid strides once the war was underway. To the single transmitter available when OWI was created, the agency added others on the West coast and then in Hawaii. Near the end of the war a mediumwave transmitter built on Saipan reached ordinary radios in Japanese homes. Once adequate resources were available, the "Yankee Doodle" signature of the "Voice of America" was heard in all corners of the globe.[10]

The propagandists of the Overseas Branch used printed materials to supplement the radio shows. While FIS had begun to produce leaflets on a limited basis, OWI developed that part of the program into a major operation. In addition to combat pamphlets, there were numerous other materials that carried America's message abroad. *L'Amérique en Guerre*, a four-page, weekly newsletter directed at Unoccupied France, sought to sustain the French with news of the Allied effort. It provided news and maps and regular quotations of American policy. Vice-President Henry A. Wallace's speech on "The Price of Free World Victory," with its vision of "the century of the common man," was distributed in booklet form in a wide variety of languages. It was meant to persuade readers of America's commitment to a better world. Other leaflets and posters showed American factories rapidly producing ships and planes in the quantities necessary to defeat the Axis. *The Life of Franklin D. Roosevelt* in cartoon form sought to affirm American determination to press on until the end, but it encountered a bitter reaction from Representative John Taber and his conservative colleagues and forced OWI to be more circumspect in its presentation of the president. A book program, headed by Chester Kerr, sent other published items overseas. *Victory* magazine, after surviving the trouble caused by the story on Roosevelt in its first issue, was the publication OWI favored most. An eighty-page, lavishly illustrated magazine printed on slick paper, it was sold, or sometimes given away, in friendly and neutral countries. It tried to inform people there about America and its part in the Allied war effort. *Victory* and the other publications continued to circulate until the end of the war and helped tell an American story that had never before been as fully or as directly told.[11]

The Office of War Information also produced documentary movies and newsreels for foreign consumption. It worked with the Board of Economic Warfare to arrange for the labeling of all goods sent overseas to Allied and neutral nations. It also established a line of specialty items. Packets of seeds had an American flag and a friendly message printed on the outside to identify the donor. Matchbooks, with the Four Freedoms inscribed on the inside of the covers, went abroad. "Soap paper," impregnated to lather quickly, carried a natural message: "From your friends the United Nations. Dip in water—use like soap. WASH OFF THE NAZI DIRT." A sewing kit included a special pincushion. One edge was shaped into a rounded rear end, and Hitler and Japanese General Hideki Tojo were caricatured on either side. The same rear end, serving both, provided the only place to stick the pins. Whatever the effect of such items, they probably provided those who received them with a few light moments in the midst of war.[12]

Finally, in the effort to reach around the world with America's message, the propaganda leaders oversaw the establishment of outposts overseas. The Foreign Information Service had already set up ten missions, and OWI continued to open new ones until there were forty at the war's end. In Britain, Australia, India, Iceland, and all the other locations, the outposts gathered information about local attitudes and distributed material about America, to help encourage support for America's ends.[13]

For all the resources at their disposal and for all the techniques at hand, the propagandists found their task more difficult than they had imagined it might be. They had a picture of America that they wanted to present, one that incorporated their own heartfelt aims and aspirations, and they had the means to present it, yet necessity dictated that they follow the lead of the top-ranking officials of the war and therein the difficulty lay. The policy laid down by military and diplomatic officers, and ultimately by the president himself, seemed all too often to have an unsettling ambiguity. Those officers may have had good reasons for refusing to commit themselves to given policies or courses of action until an appropriate time. Even so, the propagandists sometimes complained bitterly that the fuzzy lead they received made their own task difficult or even impossible to perform. They saw compromises made and values ignored, actions that seemed to undermine what they considered the basic aims of the war. Yet with no voice in the formulation of policy and little chance to express their complaints in ways that would be heard, they felt a constant strain between what they wanted to do and what the administration might continue to permit.

As much as possible they struggled to work within the bounds prescribed by the more powerful government institutions. As one staffer wrote, "If it is vitally necessary for one to chop down a tree and he has only a pocketknife, he begins to use that pocketknife in the most efficient way." OWI therefore quoted from speeches of the president and the secretary of state and from the statements of anyone else in the administration willing to give some direction to indicate current American sentiments and objectives. When those were vague, OWI either brushed over or ignored points of contention and indicated that solutions were on the way. Writers and broadcasters were told that "to overcome our lack of a clear political attitude toward the problems of Europe and Asia" they should "continue to use all available statements by United Nations' leaders which indicate that such an attitude is in the making."[14]

That was often easier said than done. When dealing with certain nations the ambiguities of American policy created problems that were particularly acute. In the case of France, for example, propagandists were never sure just where they stood. After France fell to the Nazis in 1940, the United States maintained relations with the pro-Nazi Vichy regime led by Marshal Henri Philippe Pétain, largely as a way of obtaining valuable political and military information about the situation in Europe. Whatever its justification, the American position aroused considerable resentment among American liberals and concerned parties abroad. Reflecting the delicate national position, an early FIS directive noted: "Until we receive new instructions from the State Department, we should ignore both Vichy and the Free French in our broadcasts as much as possible. We should neither praise Vichy for resistance nor blame Vichy for weakness; in fact we should not even let the French listener realize that we are aware of any special problem in the relations of Vichy with the Germans on the one hand and ourselves on the other." In time OWI criticized Nazi sympathizer Pierre Laval and expressed a guarded cordiality toward General Charles de Gaulle and the Free French movement, but followed the diplomatic lead in refusing to acknowledge the Free French National Committee as a government. As the war continued and French freedom became a foreseeable reality, propaganda continued to suffer from Roosevelt's reluctance to commit himself to future plans. Though Hull declared in an Easter speech in 1944 that the United States was willing to see the French Committee of National Liberation "exercise leadership" to help establish law and order in liberated areas, no mention of the committee as a "provisional Government" was permissible. Roosevelt's determination not to support de Gaulle at the expense of other Frenchmen left American policy deliberately vague. OWI propaganda could only reflect that somewhat nebulous position.[15]

Problems arose, too, in dealing with other nations where there were fierce internal struggles going on, especially if the propagandists found that their sympathies did not mirror those of the American administration. China was a case in point. That nation, a wartime ally of the United States, faced not only the ravages of the world war, but of civil war as well. Once the United States entered the war, Franklin Roosevelt treated Chinese President Chiang Kai-shek as an important colleague, for he hoped to use China to ensure ultimate stability in the Far East. But even Roosevelt recognized that Chiang Kai-shek's administration was inefficient, riddled with corruption, and up against serious challenges from the Chinese Communists. Steering a middle course in the larger interests of the war, the United States sought to placate Chiang with some financial and military assistance but never as much as he demanded to achieve his own internal aims.[16]

Under those circumstances, OWI had to proceed with caution. When the military effort in China seemed to falter, OWI tried against long odds to maintain Chinese morale and participated in psychological warfare activity directed against the Japanese armies of occupation. Leaflets included appeals to rescue downed airmen and encouraged Chinese laborers working on Japanese airstrips to slow down or cease their work. All the while, though, the struggle between the Kuomintang and the Communists hampered the propaganda work. Representatives of OWI, like some of the prescient observers in the diplomatic corps, occasionally reported the latest developments with notes on the favorable impressions made by the Communists. But OWI could do nothing that might weaken Chiang Kai-shek's position, for the generalissimo had Roosevelt's support and the State Department insisted that any upheaval would disrupt the war against Japan. OWI steered clear of the controversy, encouraged China to make "more active efforts to measure up to the full responsibilities of a major power," and continued under those circumstances to do the limited best it could.[17]

Similar problems stood in the way as the propagandists sought to deal with India. Committed in principle to an end to colonialism, Roosevelt faced Winston Churchill, who had once remarked that he had not become prime minister "in order to preside over the liquidation of the British Empire." While Americans looked with favor on the Indians' attempts to gain independence, Roosevelt could make little headway with Churchill, and indeed soon ceased to try. To relieve tension and to preserve Allied harmony, OWI agreed in August 1942 to a common front with Britain toward India. Reflecting American policy, the agency accepted the necessity of winning the war first and dealing with colonialism later.[18]

That decision notwithstanding, the attitude was sometimes hard to maintain. The identification of some American blacks with the Indian cause complicated the OWI stand. More vexing to representatives in the field, who were sympathetic to the mounting protest of Mohandas Gandhi and his followers, were the actions of Englishmen in India. The British sought to underscore Allied unity and to create the impression that the United States supported Britain in its dealings with subject peoples. Members of the outpost staff recognized the need for cooperation but were willing to go only so far. "OWI is not in India to fortify the cause of British imperialism," insisted representative Ralph Block.[19]

Block was right, but OWI's actions sometimes belied his words, for the agency, at home and abroad, had to follow the State Department's lead. Some of the proposed OWI literature therefore proved unacceptable. A pamphlet entitled *The United Nations Fight for the Four Freedoms* was found by the State Department to be "unsuitable for India as it might incite the Indians against the British." For the same reason OWI's Bombay office feared to issue speeches by Roosevelt and Vice-President Wallace that stressed their desire for equal opportunity regardless of race, color, or creed. Indian nationalists were understandably disillusioned by those actions and some members of the propaganda organization, upset at the difficulties of steering a middle course between the Indians and the British, wondered with good reason if the whole effort was worthwhile. But once again OWI persisted and tried to do what little it could until the end of the war.[20]

The more dramatic troubles arose in the major theaters of the war. There the propaganda leaders' problems in trying to portray what they hoped was a struggle for democracy became more urgent and certainly more difficult to resolve. The first crisis unfolded in North Africa, where the Western Allies launched, on November 8, 1942, their first major counterattack against the fascist forces.

The basic problems of communication and coordination with the policy making branches of government were characteristically present. Although top officials of the propaganda agency knew about the forthcoming invasion of North Africa, they still had to struggle to discover how they should describe it. Two days after the attack Archibald MacLeish asked Davis to secure from the military "their view on the question whether or not Africa is to be treated as a second front," while in the meantime MacLeish himself was trying to ascertain the State Department's view. With speed of paramount importance, OWI had to go to great lengths to find out how it should slant news of an invasion that had already occurred.[21]

But the major difficulties arose from the ideological convictions of the propagandists who had to watch what was going on. The problems were rooted in the political situation in North Africa. France, as a colonial power, had long controlled parts of the African continent, and when France fell in 1940 its possessions suffered the fate of the dominant land. Marshal Pétain, head of the Vichy regime, was therefore also in control of Morocco, Algeria, and Tunisia, and German influence predominated throughout. Liberals in the United States, including leaders of the foreign propaganda program, liked collaboration in North Africa no more than they liked it in France itself, and saw any potential invasion, whenever it took place, as a real movement for liberation that could destroy Nazi control.[22]

Once the North African invasion was underway, however, matters took a turn that infuriated liberals the world over. The Allies had hoped for a bloodless takeover. Robert D. Murphy, formerly counselor of the American Embassy at Paris and now Roosevelt's personal representative in North Africa, and General Dwight D. Eisenhower, who was leading the invasion, had both anticipated that Henri Giraud, a celebrated French general of World War I who had recently escaped from a German prison, could persuade the North African French to cease resistance. But when Giraud, at first reluctant to accept American leadership, proved unhelpful with the invasion already begun, Murphy and American General Mark Clark, eager to minimize bloodshed on both the Allied and French sides, turned instead to Admiral Jean François Darlan, commander-in-chief of the French Armed Forces, who was in Algiers to visit his critically ill son. Darlan had collaborated with the Germans and carried out Nazi policies in France and North Africa. Nonetheless, he was aware of the advantages of dealing with the Allies. He would call on the French to cease fire and then assist in the military operation in return for a promise that the Allies would not interfere with French control in North Africa, repressive as it might be. Citing both expediency and the need to place military needs before political considerations, Eisenhower and his superiors at home proved willing to accept the arrangement. They went along with the terms, Darlan fulfilled his part of the bargain, and the military effort unfolded more easily.[23]

The responses to the bargain were explosive. Liberals throughout the United States and Britain denounced it as a compact with the devil. Idealists who viewed the war as a crusade for a better world felt that principle had been sacrificed in the interest of military expediency. To people everywhere, Robert Sherwood later noted, "It seemed to confirm the impression that, while the Americans talked big about the principles of the Four Freedoms and the Atlantic Charter, they actually knew nothing about Europe and could be hoodwinked by any treacherous gangster who offered them collaboration."[24]

American propagandists who for the most part shared liberal sympathies were shocked by the Darlan deal, and their opposition persisted for the next several months. Unhappy with the American stance toward Vichy in the first place, they viewed the latest turn of events as intolerable. James Warburg contended in November that American policy was "most certainly going to destroy the belief of the peoples in Europe, in Russia, and in China in the good faith of the United States and in the sincerity of our war and peace aims." At the start of 1943 he still feared that American actions would "indicate to the world that when we 'liberate' a country, we shall make a practice of putting our friends in jail and of turning the 'liberated' country over to the enemies of democracy. If this impression is allowed to get abroad, the result of the North African campaign will be a political defeat irrespective of any military success." Wallace Carroll, formerly head of the London Bureau of the United Press, now in charge of the London OWI office, held the same view. Equally committed to upholding American principles although usually more temperate, he reported in December 1942 the anti-American reactions at all points along the political spectrum in Britain and voiced his own impression that the "moral authority of [the] President is being impaired." In spite of his own ultimate acceptance of the arrangement, he regretted the impression given to the rest of the world that America had "cast principle aside and struck a bargain with one of the most despicable of Hitler's foreign lackeys."[25]

In the first tense days after the Darlan agreement, OWI officials, despite their opposition, labored to make the best of the
situation. They sought a way to describe the matter that would
still stay within the boundaries of the truth. The Board of War
Information agreed on November 16 that the United States government, in an effort to divert public opposition, should issue an
authoritative statement emphasizing that the North African affair
was above all a military operation which did not give Darlan an
entirely free hand. Davis and MacLeish prepared a draft statement that advisers Harry Hopkins, Samuel I. Rosenman, and
Sherwood urged the president to issue to the press, and after
toughening it, he did so. He repeated several times that the
Darlan arrangement was a temporary one without permanent
consequences. The French people themselves, after liberation,
would determine their own fate. Roosevelt also followed OWI
suggestions in asking for the release of political prisoners in
North Africa and the abrogation of the Nazi decrees against the
Jews which were then still in effect. OWI, accepting Roosevelt's
statement as a directive for propaganda policy, advised its operators that "further discussion of Darlan should be dropped."26

But the hostile sentiments could not be so easily eliminated.
And while the complaints of the propagandists at home had but
a limited impact on the policy makers in the administration, they
did find a sympathetic response among OWI officials in North
Africa itself. Those representatives, making a first effort to assist
military operations, were working for the just formed Psychological Warfare Branch under General Eisenhower's broader command. While they were supposed to follow the commands of
their uniformed superiors, many had not yet absorbed military
values and remained loyal to OWI. They hated what they had to
do under the terms of the military agreement and fought back
whenever they could. They did destroy materials attacking Darlan and other Vichy representatives that they had brought with
them during the invasion. They also reluctantly allowed pro-
Vichy elements to take back control of newspaper and radio
facilities that had passed briefly into Allied hands as the landings
were underway. Percy Winner and others argued with Robert

Murphy and military leaders like General George S. Patton, Jr., to no avail, but the propagandists who were out in the field with transportation facilities either poor or unavailable found that they were freer to pursue their own bent. When Army officials prevented propagandists from using military communications to transmit sensitive information back to OWI, some of the field personnel responded by taking whatever liberties they could. Determined to describe conditions as they saw them, and to report the suffering that Jews and other political prisoners still faced, they simply bypassed military censorship and transmitted material to war correspondents who could then smuggle it out. In the words of C. D. Jackson, a former vice-president of Time, Inc., who later went to North Africa for OWI, many who were ostensibly under military control made the most of "a golden opportunity to indulge in their private 'kampf' against the enemy."[27]

The Army was infuriated by what was going on. Brigadier General Walter Bedell Smith, Eisenhower's chief of staff, finally declared, in Wallace Carroll's words, that "Europe and Africa together were too small to hold [Percy] Winner and the United States Army." Back at home, Secretary of War Stimson was disturbed by the unauthorized material that Elmer Davis was receiving from abroad and complained in December 1942 that Eisenhower was harassed at the very time when he should be devoting all his strength to the war in Tunisia.[28]

With the situation at home still tense, Elmer Davis determined to see what he could do. Eager to have open channels of communication, and fearful that serious underground criticism was filling the vacuum that resulted from the Army's restrictions on information, he sent Milton Eisenhower abroad in December to consult with his brother. The OWI representative chastened some of the more independent operators but, after listening to Winner and others, took them to present their case to the general, where they explained with but a small measure of success the difficulties of trying to work with former fascists and the need to solve the propaganda problems. Wallace Carroll later recalled that Milton Eisenhower had gone to North Africa to explain

OWI's position to his brother but ended up trying to explain his brother to OWI. That was true, but he was able to do more. Although he felt, as Vice-President Henry A. Wallace wrote in his diary, that "his brother should not be called on to do both military and political work," he did convey to Ike the need to explain the decisions that had been made. Milton Eisenhower left recommendations in North Africa for ensuring a smoother flow of news back to the United States, and General Eisenhower, in turn, asked to be informed about adverse political comment. A month later he lifted the veil of censorship and allowed editors and columnists to visit North Africa to see what was happening. He also procured for Davis summaries of local affairs that served to meet criticism within the United States.[29]

Milton Eisenhower's efforts might have ended the troubles had it not been for other events. In December 1942, Darlan had requested and Murphy had favored the appointment of Marcel Peyrouton to assist in the government of North Africa. Peyrouton, in the view of Assistant Secretary of War John J. McCloy, was a "sound, colonial, administrator." General Eisenhower viewed him in the same way. But Peyrouton had also been Vichy minister of the interior when the first anti-Jewish decrees went into effect. To liberals he was in the same class as Darlan. Unaware of his reputation, Eisenhower checked the appointment with the State Department, and while Under Secretary of State Sumner Welles advised against the move, Hull, believing the request originated with Eisenhower, allowed the appointment to be made. Peyrouton arrived in Algiers in mid-January, at about the time that President Roosevelt reached Casablanca to confer with Prime Minister Churchill, and then the storm broke. Archibald MacLeish found the appointment and Hull's justification for it "unfortunate and irritating," while Wallace Carroll again reported the bitter outcry he observed and later wrote that the appointment "stirred up all the sediment of the North African cesspool."[30]

Although the Casablanca conference drew attention away from the Peyrouton appointment, the incident only brought home to propagandists once again the almost insurmountable problems they faced in trying to advance their own idealistic interpretations of the war. They could talk all they wanted among themselves, and with others of similar persuasion, about the democratic values the war could bring in its wake, but they could do little to ensure that the war was conducted along the lines they approved. Reserving the right to complain, they had done so with the bitterness they felt, but that had hardly changed policy and had only left them in a more vulnerable position. Discouraged though they were, they still intended to press on.

With the North African adventure on its way to a successful military conclusion, the propagandists became increasingly concerned with other targets. Italy, just across the Mediterranean, seemed the next point of attack and propaganda concerns mounted accordingly. In the struggle with Italy, OWI leaders understood, the same issues were at stake as those faced, and compromised, in North Africa. The same basic questions of fascism versus democracy were involved, and some members of OWI were uneasy that those might again be subordinated to demands of expediency.

Percy Winner was particularly perturbed about what he feared was going on. "During the last few months," he wrote on July 19, 1943, in a memorandum to Sherwood, "we have deliberately and carefully emphasized the specifically military aspect of our propaganda warfare to Europe in general and to Italy in particular. We have subordinated, indeed in a certain sense taken a negative attitude toward the ideological aspect of our propaganda warfare." Winner wanted to make sure that the democratic values that the Allies embraced were not overlooked in the heat of military attack. Aware of "the latent civil war in Italy" that internal opposition to the fascists could spark, he wanted his colleagues to be certain that they were prepared for what upheaval might bring.[31]

Winner was uneasy about a message from Roosevelt and Churchill that had gone out to the Italian people during the Sicilian campaign. In that declaration of July 17 the Allied leaders, warning of the consequences of further resistance, emphasized their determination "to destroy the false leaders and their doctrines which have brought Italy to her present position." Winner wanted to know how far the Allies planned to go in rooting out fascist officials and their philosophies. It was simple enough to eliminate the leaders in the process of military attack. He feared, however, that "cautery of a symptom does not cure a disease of the blood stream." The extended exposure of Italians to fascist ideology indicated that something more was necessary.[32]

American policy and propaganda, Winner hoped, would concentrate on eliminating all traces of fascism. He had reason to question the American commitment to that aim, for public statements about the projected functions of Allied Military Government seemed to indicate that the Allies would try to prevent anarchy and to foster nonviolent solutions to internal problems. That policy, Winner argued, would be counterproductive. "Another palace revolution, a counter-revolution against a counter-revolution, any form of static, frozen 'order' imposed upon the Italians by alien soldiers will merely submerge the false doctrines we are pledged to destroy, and postpone a more dreadful day of reckoning." Aware of the "contradiction between immediate military aims and long-term political aims," he still contended that despite the temporary anarchy and confusion that might result, the Italians "should be stimulated to destroy the Fascist state."[33]

Percy Winner's concerns were well-founded. With Italian morale poor, with most of the country's army in the Balkans where Hitler insisted it stay, Roosevelt and Churchill hoped to take advantage of Italy's desperate condition to force the nation out of the war as quickly as they could. And that intention might well entail the kinds of compromises that many of the propagandists were unwilling to accept. The Allied leaders did seem less firm in their public pronouncements than they had earlier been. At the Casablanca conference in January 1942, they had declared that the Allied forces would fight until the unconditional surrender of the enemy had been achieved. Roosevelt had underscored that intention just two months before, in mid-May, when he had refused to hear any talk of offering the Italians a "peace with

honor" and had declared, "We cannot get away from unconditional surrender. All we can tell them [the Italians] is that they
will be treated by us and the British with humanity and with the
intention that the Italian people be reconstituted into a nation in
accordance with the principles of self-determination. This latter
would, of course, not include any form of Fascism or dictatorship." But now political conditions led him to change his mind.
He and Churchill, in their joint declaration of July 17, emphasized Italy's vulnerability and criticized Benito Mussolini's
"shameful leadership," but quietly tempered the phrasing of the
unconditional surrender doctrine. "The sole hope for Italy's survival," they said, "lies in honourable capitulation to the overwhelming power of the military forces of the United Nations. If
you continue to tolerate the Fascist régime, which serves the evil
power of the Nazis, you must suffer the consequences of your
own choice."[34]

Italy's position was serious. The campaign in Sicily, begun
earlier in July, was taking its toll in Axis lives and an invasion of
Italy itself was clearly next. The attacks on the fascists were
mounting and something had to give. Mussolini, faced with military defeat as well as corruption and inflation at home, on July
25 finally yielded to the pressure. Reluctantly he convened the
Fascist Grand Council, which expressed its lack of confidence in
him and left him no alternative but to resign. In his place King
Victor Emmanuel III appointed Marshal Pietro Badoglio, former
chief of the General Staff, notorious for his earlier role in Ethi-
opia, to serve as prime minister of a new Cabinet.[35]

On the Sunday evening when the world learned of the
upheaval in Italy, the full meaning of the events was not yet clear.
The abrupt shift seemed to be a sign that Italy was ready to yield,
yet a confirmed fascist and a king who had actively supported the
fascist regime were still in power. The Allied leaders, who had
perhaps hoped for the shift, but had not anticipated its form,
waited to see what would happen next. Members of OWI, like
other observers, had no sure sense of what was going on. But
they did have their own convictions buttressed by the reassur-
ances of the administration that the North African compromises

would not be repeated. They also had policy directives, composed earlier and neither amended nor withdrawn, which seemed applicable to the situation. The Italian Regional Directive of February 21, 1943, approved by OWI's Planning Board, which included representatives from the State Department, the Army, and the Navy, observed that " 'Fascism' includes not only Mussolini and his political and military accomplices, but the House of Savoy, which betrayed Italy to Fascism, and the industrialists who support Fascism." A secret contingency plan for propaganda to Italy in the event of invasion, a plan that C. D. Jackson took with him overseas in May 1943, sought to establish in advance ways of dealing with the Italian political situation. In response to questions the plan raised about how to handle the question of royal family, General Eisenhower told Jackson, who informed OWI, that although the Allied attitude was still not certain and a liberal monarchy might remain, propaganda should "not, however, spare criticism of House of Savoy for supporting Fascism." The July 17 message from Roosevelt and Churchill, with its warning that fascist doctrines and leaders would be exterminated, seemed to reinforce the other directives.[36]

OWI's more aggressive leaders, anxious to transmit the news of events in Italy to the rest of the world, were also probably eager to forestall new compromises like those in North Africa. With Davis in Algiers and Sherwood with the president, James Warburg, as deputy director for propaganda policy, took matters into his own hands. Warburg, like Winner, feared that as Italy began to wobble, the Allies might back off from their stated commitment to destroy all vestiges of fascism in the interests of short-term military aims. His fear was well-founded. American monitors revealed that the BBC, reflecting British policy, was claiming that the political change meant the end of fascism and that Italy had turned against the one remaining enemy—Hitler. Yet Marshal Badoglio's first proclamation held that "the war continues. Italy . . . maintains her faith in her given word" to Hitler to fight with Germany. Accordingly Warburg and his colleagues at OWI found the British position hard to accept. From New York Warburg cabled word of his discontent to Wallace

Carroll in London, but no action was possible until the next morning. Working only from the earlier policy instructions, Warburg then exercised his own authority and told the New York operators to treat the event "coldly and without any jubilation." It made no difference, he wrote in his guidance, "whether Mussolini or Badoglio or the King hold the leadership."[37]

OWI leaders in charge, once they had decided on the position they would take, made but limited attempts to obtain full clearance. The guidance, Warburg said later, was telephoned to Sherwood who approved it. The assertion that it made no difference who ruled was approved by a liaison officer from the Joint Chiefs of Staff. The State Department duty officer, who lacked authority to grant approval, was kept informed throughout the evening. But OWI, going through the motions of coordinating broadcasts with official policy, never did reach the leaders of the appropriate government departments. Sherwood, somewhat transparently, claimed after a few days that "it was a nice summer evening and it was Sunday. We couldn't get anybody on the phone." His comment reflected the feebleness of the efforts OWI made to consult those people who might have advised tempering or changing the broadcast plans already made.[38]

OWI broadcast word of the shift in Italy, but in news stories indicated that the basic nature of the fascist regime seemed unchanged. It also used commentary and samples of American opinion to express caution at the upheaval, and there it got into trouble. Commentator John Durfee said that the American people did not view Mussolini's resignation as an event of real importance. They would continue to fight fascism "irrespective of whether it is Mussolini, or Badoglio, or the Fascist King himself " who led the struggle for Hitler. Even stronger was the assessment of Samuel Grafton, a columnist who wrote for the *New York Post*, whose judgment OWI quoted over the air:

> Fascism is still in power in Italy. It has put on a new face, that's all. Italian Fascism has rouged its cheeks and its lips and is trying to see whether a smile will not do more for it, than the famous frown by which it lived so long.

The moronic little king who has stood behind Mussolini's
shoulder for 21 years has moved forward one pace. This is
a political minuet and not the revolution we have been wait-
ing for.[39]

Grafton's comment summed up the liberal position and by
using it, and others like it, OWI leaders were indicating their
interpretation of the events that had transpired. Warburg later
asserted that he wanted American broadcasts to communicate to
the BBC, which monitored them, OWI's displeasure with the
softer British line. He hoped that by presenting samples of
American opinion he could get British radio to shift its emphasis
to something he regarded as more acceptable. Because Grafton's
language was strong he authorized that commentary for use only
once and only in English, although due to a misunderstanding it
went out five times. It should not have caused significant trouble,
but unknown to OWI, other Americans, unsympathetic to the
propagandists' aims, were listening to the programs.[40]

The *New York Times* had just begun monitoring OWI's output
on a twenty-four-hour basis. If it was suspicious of the propaganda going overseas, the *Times* found what it was looking for in
the broadcasts concerning Italy. On Tuesday, July 27, the newspaper carried a front-page story and a column by Washington
correspondent Arthur Krock, notorious as a defender of State
Department policies. "OWI Broadcast to Italy Calls Ruler 'Fascist' and 'Moronic Little King' " blared the headline. Krock found
the OWI commentary disturbing, for he felt it could make it more
difficult to use the king and marshal "to provide the bridge to a
democratic government" in Italy if that was what the Allies chose
to do. The *Times* also called attention to OWI's use of John
Durfee, an "imaginary" political commentator, and there it hit
the jackpot. OWI did indeed use several *nom de plume* commenta-
tors in overseas broadcasts. John Durfee, born but a week or two
before, was in reality James Warburg. OWI outposts had been
alerted that his commentary would paraphrase the political thrust
of OWI directives as a quick way of communicating a message,
particularly in case of emergency. John Durfee had acted as ex-

pected on that fateful Sunday evening. It was simply unfortunate for the organization that his mythical existence should have been discovered in the midst of an already controversial incident.[41]

The Office of War Information was in trouble. That very afternoon, at a press conference, when asked whether the OWI broadcasts were authorized, Roosevelt indicated that neither he nor Sherwood nor the State Department had given approval. Deeply involved himself in assessing the implications of the Italian shift, the president was not happy about the public controversy or about what the propagandists had said. "I think Bob Sherwood is raising Hell about it now," the president said. "It ought never to have been done." As the newspapers quickly picked up the story of the presidential rebuke, over the next few days Krock broadened his initial attacks. Roosevelt's response, he asserted, showed that "once again a group of administration employees had made and carried out a 'foreign policy' of its own" and one that was shaped "according to the personal and ideological preferences of Communists and their fellow-travelers in this country." OWI's actions, he continued, imperiled both international negotiations and the lives of American soldiers abroad. Other papers continued in the same vein. "Just as long as OWI follows the policies of its nitwits, its half-baked international politicians, and its Communist lunatic fringe, just so long will innumerable opportunities be presented for mischief quite as bad as this," argued George Rothwell Brown of the *New York Journal-American.* Drew Pearson in his column "The Washington Merry-Go-Round" was more clever. In view of Warburg's role in the recent activities, he suggested renaming the propaganda agency the "Office of Warburg Information."[42]

The use of John Durfee drew the greatest fire. Where Krock had lambasted OWI for using "its own private Charlie McCarthy," other papers went further. The *New York World-Telegram* carried a three-column photograph of the mysterious John Durfee on its front page on July 29. It showed a hat, coat, and gloves—with no flesh visible to support them—working at a typewriter. Along with the picture was an obituary of the thirty-three or seventy-two-year-old American political commentator.

Thomas L. Stokes in the same paper concluded that John Durfee must be related to John Doe and Joe Doakes, but found it puzzling that "in this nation of 130,000,000 people, many of whom are literate, more of whom can talk," OWI found it necessary to invent a character to speak to audiences abroad. *Life* magazine picked up the photo and the stories and gave them national circulation. Generalizing about the incident, an editorial in the *World-Telegram* said "the whole thing smells of dishonesty." Both that editorial and columnist Brown in the *New York Journal-American* proposed that the State Department take over the Overseas Branch entirely.[43]

OWI leaders, though somewhat disconcerted, stood by their position. Their ideological convictions no less intense, they still shuddered at the thought of another compromise with the forces of reaction. They may have hoped naively that by establishing their own stance over the air they could exert an influence on policy still to be determined, but those hopes had proved unfounded. Now what they had all along feared was indeed happening, and that only fueled the charges of critics who asserted the propagandists were far off base.

The Allies were coming to terms with the new regime. Badoglio, on assuming power, was eager for peace with the forces opposing him. He was unwilling to risk an open rupture with Germany, however, until he could conclude a settlement under which the Allies would protect Italy from the German troops still in his land. Churchill and Roosevelt, meanwhile, had to decide how they would deal with the situation.[44]

The British and American leaders were in close communication in those first crucial days. The prime minister informed the president on July 26 that he "would deal with any non-Fascist Italian Government which can deliver the goods." He enclosed his "Thoughts on the Fall of Mussolini" that had been given full approval by the British War Cabinet. There he pointed to the probability that the king and Badoglio would seek to negotiate an armistice with the Allies. It was necessary, Churchill said, to decide just what the Allies wanted. The "supreme aim," he went on, was "the destruction of Hitler, Hitlerism, and Nazi Germany."

Before the House of Commons on July 27, Churchill was more reserved. Expressing satisfaction at the fall of Mussolini, he refused to commit himself about Badoglio. But he did say that with Italian affairs in a state of flux, "It would be a grave mistake . . . so to act as to break down the whole structure and expression of the Italian state."[45]

Roosevelt, more indecisive, initially stood back and waited to see what would happen. Then on July 28, the day after he had rebuked OWI for its controversial broadcasts, he spoke firmly about Allied intentions toward Italy. "Our terms to Italy are still the same as our terms to Germany and Japan—'unconditional surrender,' " he said. "We will have no truck with Fascism in any way, shape, or manner. We will permit no vestige of Fascism to remain." Yet Roosevelt saw no alternative to Badoglio, and as Percy Winner had earlier feared, was unwilling to risk political chaos in Italy. Accepting Churchill's proposal, the president told the press on July 30 that he would deal with any non-fascist, whether he "be a King, or a present Prime Minister, or a Mayor of a town, or a village." It was now clear that he was willing to overlook the king's long acceptance of the Mussolini regime and Badoglio's exploits on behalf of the Duce. Military expediency was again the president's prime consideration.[46]

OWI, vulnerable even before the president had made up his mind, was now in an even more untenable position. The liberal leaders of the Overseas Branch had expressed their own convictions over the air, and they now had to defend themselves before powerful critics. Efforts to argue that their public position was consistent with Allied policy at the time hardly spoke to the fact that the propaganda agency had not sought to determine new directions the administration might have been considering. Nor were attempts to explain that OWI was not alone in its assessment of "the moronic little king" particularly helpful. Although James Warburg pointed out that the *New York Sun* had soon afterward called Victor Emmanuel "a timorous little king," that the *New York World-Telegram* had referred to him as "the craven king," and that an editorial in the *New York Times* on the very day that Krock's first attack appeared had spoken of Italy's "conniving puppet king," it made little difference, for the damage was already done. Roosevelt, once again able to turn things to his own advantage, in Joseph Barnes's words, let OWI "take the rap as whipping boy in a maneuver which was, or was thought to be, in the national interest." The president had exonerated Sherwood even though Sherwood was involved, and that left Warburg and Barnes to take the public blame. A few days after the explosive broadcasts Sherwood called the incident a "regrettable slip" and pledged that in the future OWI would refer anything at all controversial to the State Department and Joint Chiefs of Staff. OWI leaders, chastised, had to accept the criticisms their action drew with the reluctant resolve to be more faithful to policy in the future.[47]

Despite the uproar, those pledges proved constraining, for most of the top propagandists continued to disagree bitterly with Allied policy as it unfolded. In the aftermath of the "moronic little king" episode, it was clear that Roosevelt and Churchill were prepared to deal with Victor Emmanuel and his new prime minister if that would help in the struggle against Hitler. The Italians, in turn, were ready to seek an armistice, for their nation had become a battleground after the fall of Mussolini as Hitler had poured troops into Italy in an effort to protect Germans there and to hold the country. When in response to Italian overtures, the United States and Britain insisted that any agreement be based on unconditional surrender, Italy objected, in the hope that it could be treated as a prospective ally and not as a defeated enemy. Through the end of August 1943, therefore, a stalemate ensued.[48]

American propagandists at home and abroad criticized the Allied actions, but now more quietly and only among themselves. Though Badoglio had dissolved the Fascist party two days after he succeeded Mussolini, the prospect of dealing with former fascists remained as disturbing as ever. Wallace Carroll in London decried the latest "resort to expedience," while Warburg at home complained that by attempting to avoid disorder at all costs, the present policy would simply preserve "in Europe that very political and economic status quo which gave birth to the

Communist revolution and to the Fascist and Nazi counter-revolutions." Allied actions, he feared, would lead the people of Europe to "regard us not as liberators but as the agents of reactionary suppression."[49]

Still, the Allied leaders were not to be restrained. Secret negotiations with the Italians finally culminated in compromise with an armistice signed on September 3—the same day the invasion of Italy began. That "short" agreement pertained to military matters alone and made no mention of unconditional surrender, but the "long" armistice, signed on September 29, included the term and took care of other concerns. With that settled the American propagandists sought to assist the war effort however they could. Without discussing the character or future of the Italian king or government, they concentrated on encouraging the Italian people to assist in the liberation of their country. As the campaign unfolded OWI played it up as the first landing on the mainland of Europe. The propaganda material appealed to the Italians to increase their resistance to the Germans. It sought to stress unification around the Badoglio government as a way of effecting the speediest liberation of the country. When a broader Cabinet was finally formed in the spring of 1944, OWI hailed it as "the first expression of a democratic government in liberated Europe."[50]

Despite the subsequent efforts at cooperation, the "moronic little king" episode had left its mark. OWI, long battered by others in and out of the administration, was now more vulnerable than before.

OWI's liberal views had already caused trouble with Secretary of War Stimson and the rest of his department. Stimson, suspicious of OWI for much of the war, often assumed that security leaks came as a result of OWI's activities. When during the North African invasion he became irritated with hostile newsmen who sat "with their feet on the desks in Algiers and their tentacles in the cesspool of gossip," he was prepared to see to it that no further correspondents arrived. On one occasion, when well-known correspondent Edgar Ansel Mowrer was scheduled to go to North Africa for OWI, Stimson stepped in. While the Casa-

blanca conference was meeting he "did not think it was wise for
a man who had formed such decided, not to say passionate views,
on the Darlan situation" to enter that area. Later, when Elmer
Davis demanded a meeting with the president to discuss the
matter, Stimson saw to it that the appointment with Roosevelt
was cancelled. Finally, at another meeting with Davis and Secretaries Hull and Knox, Stimson reaffirmed "the ticklishness of
Eisenhower's position" and his own opposition to "sending another nuisance down there." Mowrer stayed in the United
States.[51]

On another occasion, when Davis gave Stimson a request for
some 134 agents to go to North Africa and, as the secretary
observed, to "bombard the Germans with leaflets fired from our
cannon and mortars and to generally frame up a great psychological warfare against them," Stimson noted in his diary that he
"thought it was half-baked and by the time I got through it here
it seemed thoroughly half-baked, if that is possible." The War
Department also made it difficult to send stenographic and cleri-
cal help to assist OWI personnel already in North Africa. One
general refused to allow nonmilitary women stenographers to go,
while another refused to allow Army personnel in the United
States to go to Africa to perform those tasks. OWI seemed sty-
mied at every corner.[52]

So too the State Department had long caused problems for the
propaganda organization. It often proved slow in dispatching
OWI people to the outposts, and also denied to some passports
or transportation priorities to prevent them from going overseas.
Ruth Shipley, head of the Passport Division in the State Department, refused passports on orders from her superiors and occasionally on the basis of her own independent judgments. One
person assigned to London as an administrative officer was
delayed for seventy days because of an allegation that he had
once worked as a labor union organizer. Robert Parker, overseas
outpost representative in Ankara, Turkey, assumed his post only
after having his passport at first refused by one of the assistant
secretaries of state. John Houseman had similar trouble, for
though his citizenship papers were coming through, Shipley de-

cided that his current alien status disqualified him for government travel at the time.[53]

The State Department proved troublesome in other ways as
well. It demanded copies of OWI codes, messages, and letters
that traveled between the Overseas Branch and its representatives abroad. Occasionally it held up transmission of OWI messages to the outposts. It also exerted its influence through the
various American embassies, which were supposed to oversee the
OWI outposts. Joseph Barnes, preparing to accompany Wendell
Willkie around the world, learned that Paul West, OWI representative in Cairo, was "not receiving the fullest cooperation"
from American Ambassador Alexander C. Kirk. In Turkey, an
open confrontation occurred. When Ambassador Laurence A.
Steinhardt refused to pass on mail to OWI representative Robert
Parker, Parker kicked down an embassy door to get the mail. That
caused repercussions in Washington and necessitated elaborate
explanations and apologies in order to repair the strained relationship.[54]

With the Office of War Information already under quiet but
effective attack from the two most important departments in the
government, the "moronic little king" incident jolted the agency
still further. Elmer Davis recognized the damage done by the
president's remarks about OWI on July 27, soon after the episode had taken place, and understood that his organization was
in trouble.

Something clearly had to be done if propaganda was to play
any part in the rest of the war. The beating the Domestic Branch
had taken from Congress and the battering the Overseas Branch
had received for its controversial broadcasts led Milton Eisenhower to write in early August, "The fundamental necessity now
is for the President to do something appropriate to restore the
prestige and strength of OWI." And so Davis drafted a letter for
Roosevelt to sign that stressed OWI's "fine record and . . . valuable service to the war effort" and alluded to the broadcasts the
night Mussolini resigned but evidenced little concern about
them. The letter had evidently been prepared at the suggestion
of the president himself, but the OWI director may well have

been a victim of Roosevelt's practice of letting those to whom he was talking believe that he took their side. In any event, despite Sherwood's prodding, the letter was never sent. In fact, the president undermined Davis's and OWI's position still further by leaving him at home when he went to the Quebec conference in August, even though Brendan Bracken, British minister of information and Davis's opposite number, was there. Now OWI's vulnerability was out in the open for everyone to see. "The President, if he chooses, can disperse the cloud that has fallen over the OWI in this particular, and send the professional courtiers on other scents of favor's decay," wrote Arthur Krock in the *New York Times*. "With a few words of reasonable explanation, should he wish to take notice of the episode, he can remove Mr. Davis from the shadow of the doghouse. If he wishes to lift OWI from the slump of morale which the Quebec incident and certain plainer misadventures have produced—notably Mr. Roosevelt's reprimand of its overseas branch's broadcasts after the fall of Mussolini—the President should say those few words, or authorize them to be said for him."[55]

With the president hardly likely to act by himself, Davis decided to make one more effort in his own behalf. His organization therefore took its stand on the whole question of the release of military and diplomatic information which had been a sore point for the past year. In the middle of July 1943 Davis had sent the president a sample letter that could go to the War and Navy Departments to discourage them from using the excuse of security to withhold military news that could be made public. By the end of August the need for support was even greater. "The Office of War Information is at present under heavy attack—mostly partisan, malicious, and unjustified; but partly due to our failure to attain the standing contemplated by, and to perform all the duties assigned to us in, Executive Order 9182," he wrote to the president. Then Davis underscored the necessity of changes in OWI's relationship to the State, War, and Navy Departments. OWI should have authority to determine what news to release and should be supplied with the information it needed to formulate appropriate propaganda policies. If such measures were im-

possible, he respectfully recommended "that the President dras-
tically reorganize the Office of War Information, changing its
name, its Director, and its assigned functions; otherwise its enemies and his are likely to cripple it or even destroy it."[56]

Roosevelt, realizing that he could procrastinate no longer,
agreed to back Davis. In letters to the secretaries of state, war,
and navy on September 1, the president directed that OWI exercise authority over the release of news and be provided with the
material it needed. It was a limited gesture, as OWI leaders knew,
but at least it gave them some mandate to continue their work.[57]

Davis also moved to impose his own control over the Overseas
Branch of his organization, which had long pursued a course of
its own. The problem was hardly a new one, but earlier Milton
Eisenhower alone had recognized the need for greater guidance
of overseas operations. Since Eisenhower was not prepared to
take a strong stand against Sherwood's assistants, his proposals
for better integration went unheeded.[58]

There was a good deal that Davis had to do, for the New York
office had assumed more and more power with little direction
from above. There was an Overseas Planning Board in Washington, but Sherwood and his top associates seemed to feel that
policies should originate at the operating level. The playwright
acknowledged that the New York staff members had sometimes
concealed what they did from Washington to prevent anything
from being done about it. The New York group had also moved
to formalize existing arrangements. An administrative memorandum in December 1942, issued with Davis's approval, had
seemed to strengthen the New York group. While the OWI director several months later had taken the first steps to regain some
of the authority in Washington, he had not been wholly successful. A staff order in February 1943 had set up seven regional
divisions within the Overseas Branch, strengthened the Overseas
Planning Board, and made Davis chairman of it. Though closer
supervision had resulted, the men in charge of operations still
retained a good deal of flexibility.[59]

Davis was ready to take further action when, toward the end of
1943, the Overseas Branch attempted again to assert its independ-

ence. A reorganization in September merged the seven regional divisions into three. Yet the Overseas Editorial Board established in New York at about the same time seemed to assume a greater measure of responsibility for the procedures the agency followed. Then in November the Overseas Branch staff advanced proposals that would have left New York with almost total authority for overseas propaganda. At that Davis balked. To Sherwood he wrote: "Whatever alterations may be made will have to proceed from the major premise that the seat of the government is in Washington, and so are the headquarters of OWI."[60]

Davis recognized that the organization had almost drifted out of his hands. The Domestic Branch had been nearly eliminated. The Overseas Branch, which he had neglected, had received, in the latest budget, $34 million, or more than 90 percent of OWI's total appropriation. Increasingly, Davis felt the New York office "was running away with the OWI." It functioned as a "closed corporation" that he could not penetrate. Davis neither controlled operations nor saw communications that the New York office failed to forward promptly to Washington.[61]

Davis set out to assert his authority. Since Milton Eisenhower had left OWI during the summer of 1943 to become president of Kansas State College, on December 1 Davis appointed as associate director Edward Klauber, an old friend who had served as best man at his wedding. Klauber came to OWI with a tough reputation from his days as executive vice-president of the Columbia Broadcasting System. Known there as William Paley's "hatchet man," he was to serve the same function for the director of OWI.[62]

Soon after taking office, Klauber spent two days in New York to find out what was going on. There he asked what were described as "vague or philosophical questions." More specifically, on one occasion he asked what tasks a particular individual performed. He was informed that the person involved was an "expediter on the policy level." With that and other answers leaving him cold, and adding little to his information about the New York office, he was more determined than ever to see things cleaned up.[63]

At about the same time Davis received further evidence to support his growing belief that the independent activities of the New York group were having a harmful effect on the overseas information program. In early December Wallace Carroll and three of his top assistants suddenly resigned from the London office. Carroll was angry at the lack of support from the Overseas Branch at home. Preparations for the invasion could not go on with the feeble cooperation he felt he was receiving from the American-based offices. Communications, he asserted, went unanswered, and people in the United States neglected to push through things that they did not approve. Carroll complained that the Overseas Branch even ignored recommendations that Davis himself had approved on a trip to London. Davis was distressed by the resignations, especially since in his isolation he had been unaware of the difficulties that Carroll had found intolerable. Now, with Klauber's help, he prepared to take action of his own.[64]

By mid-September Sherwood was aware of the case against his part of the organization. To Warburg he wrote that he knew the line was "that I am a notably worthy and noble fellow—and an effective pleader on both ends of Pennsylvania Avenue—and (of course) a cracking good playwright—but that I'm so hopelessly inept as an administrator or executive that under me are our old friends, Anarchy and Chaos, each in a neat box on the Civil Service Chart." He understood too the charge "that I have inadequate control over the Overseas Branch and therefore sterner and more vigilant authority must be set up in Washington." Frankly upset by the situation, he counseled Warburg that they all had to be careful.[65]

Davis, nonetheless, moved forward on the course he had determined. In early 1944, following Klauber's survey of operations, he undertook to reorganize the Overseas Branch. Under the proposed arrangement Sherwood would be director of propaganda and information with responsibility for developing propaganda policy. A new executive director, responsible to Davis, would have full control over all operations. New deputy directors to assist the executive director were named. The Overseas Editorial Board in New York was dissolved. There was no place in the new plan for Warburg or Barnes or Johnson, the three officials who seemed to Davis responsible for the situation that existed.[66]

Sherwood balked at the proposal. Supported by Warburg who told him that Davis's plan was "irrational" and "irresponsible" and "would seriously damage the war effort of the United States," he denied Davis's right to insist on the personnel changes. His resistance would ordinarily have been cause for dismissal, but Sherwood could exploit his own ties to the White House. When he indicated that he was appealing to the president and would recommend splitting OWI into separate foreign and domestic agencies if no other solution was possible, Davis, too, carried the dispute to Roosevelt. The changes he proposed were necessary, he informed the president, if OWI was to accomplish its assigned tasks. "It is pretty hard to sail any craft when the first mate permits himself to be at the head of a mutiny against the skipper," Davis wrote, but since Sherwood had said that he would accept Roosevelt's decision, Davis was willing to keep his overseas director with OWI "provided, and so long as, he recognizes the full authority of the head of this office and behaves accordingly."[67]

The drama was played out through the White House. Roosevelt asked for further information, which Davis provided. According to most observers "it is evident that our Overseas Branch is so confusingly organized, and so shot through with intrigue and office politics, that it can never operate as effectively as it should so long as Mr. Sherwood is its operating head," he wrote to the president. He cited efforts of the New York group "to prevent me from exercising the authority over the Overseas Branch" that had been officially granted. On the whole, he argued, the inner clique did not even perform its work particularly well. He pointed to the resistance that led Carroll to resign. In conclusion, he said that he could not continue without the authority to meet all of his responsibilities.[68]

Sherwood in turn defended his own record and the record of his group. Although Warburg assisted him with an answer to Davis's charges and emphasized "that any compromise . . . would

be tantamount to total defeat," Sherwood's response to the president was straightforward and dispassionate. He cited congressional support for the Overseas Branch and quoted the accolades
of a number of top military leaders. He defended his subordinates from the attacks against them. He answered Davis's charges
one by one, acknowledging some, disclaiming others. Both he
and Davis knew that some of the charges were "trivial." Both also
knew that the charges themselves were less important than the
real question of who was going to control what was left of OWI.
That was what the president had to decide.[69]

In characteristic fashion Roosevelt delayed. As was often the
case in the controversies among his subordinates, he hoped they
could settle the matter themselves. The Davis-Sherwood dispute,
however, had gone too far. Both men called for some resolution
by the president so the agency could begin to function properly
again, and at the end of January 1944 the press picked up word
of the fight and spread it throughout the country. Newspapers
speculated that Byron Price, director of censorship, would soon
undertake responsibility for propaganda as well. As the issue
grew more and more heated some action became imperative at
last.[70]

On February 2 Davis and Sherwood appeared at the White
House together. Roosevelt, for all of his tolerance and even en-
couragement of disagreement within his administration, had little patience when the arguments became public. "The President," Davis noted, "told us that he wished he had a good long
ruler, the kind that school boys' hands used to be slapped with
when he was in school; that he was good and God damned mad
at both of us for letting a thing like this arise and get into the
papers at a time when he had a war to think about." Roosevelt,
according to Davis, also "said that it must be clear that I was the
head of the Agency and responsible for its operations but that he
did not want Sherwood sent to Guam, as they used to say in the
Navy." Then Roosevelt, in a familiar move, ordered them into
the cabinet room to work out a compromise. They had trouble
reaching agreement that day but on February 5, "in order to
promote harmony of operation and to avoid misunderstanding,"

they signed a statement which recorded the nature of their relationship. "The Director of OWI," it said, "being responsible for
both the policies and the operations of the Overseas Branch, has
complete authority over both." He could initiate any steps he
considered desirable. He would be informed of all actions under-
taken by the branch and would pass on all appointments that
might be made.[71]

It was a clear-cut victory for Davis. Still, in the reorganization
that followed, Roosevelt's wish to save Sherwood's pride was
honored. On February 7 Davis told the press that "Mr. Sherwood
will soon make a brief trip to London to make final arrangements
there for expanded psychological warfare operations in consulta-
tion with military authorities and representatives of other Allied
governments, after which he will continue active direction of the
Overseas Branch from headquarters in Washington." At the
same time he announced that Edward W. Barrett, formerly a
writer and then associate editor of *Newsweek* before going to work
for the Office of the Coordinator of Information, now on duty for
OWI in North Africa, would serve as executive director of the
Overseas Branch under Sherwood. In reality Barrett assumed all
of Sherwood's authority at home, and in September 1944 assumed his title as well, when Sherwood resigned from OWI and
returned to the United States to work on Roosevelt's campaign
for reelection. The rest of the reorganization followed Davis's
earlier plan. He announced that the resignations of Warburg,
Barnes, and Johnson had been requested and received. Soon
thereafter he appointed new deputy directors for the main re-
gions of the world.[72]

The responses to the upheaval were mixed. Arthur Krock
hailed the results. Davis, he wrote, had "finally asserted his directive." William L. Shirer in the *New York Herald Tribune,* Joseph
Barnes's old paper, felt otherwise. Davis, Shirer asserted, should
have acted earlier instead of disrupting a functioning propaganda
organization with military responsibilities. Editorials in the *Herald Tribune* were similarly critical. One on February 8 claimed that
Davis "has been tough at the wrong moment, with the wrong
people and over the wrong issue." Another three days later noted

that "a reorganization carried out for obscure and unexplained reasons of office politics simply exposes it to all the slings, arrows and dead cats of blind criticism and embittered prejudice." Davis steadfastly defended his decision. He had never doubted the loyalty of the men involved, he said, but he had decided that they were not contributing to the kind of teamwork he considered necessary in the latter stages of the war.[73]

Davis was convinced that his actions were necessary even though for a time they caused a certain awkwardness. Sherwood left for London, he told Warburg, "with a very heavy heart." Davis, an equally decent and sensitive man, was also subdued. Publicly he declared that "there's no question of anyone winning or anything of the sort." When asked how he liked his job now he simply answered, "It is a lot less uncomfortable than wading in the mangrove swamps of New Guinea, or climbing up and down the slippery mountains of Italy, as my son is doing." Yet he and his close colleagues in the Office of War Information still felt that the results were for the best.[74]

Thus ended the hopeful, idealistic, and often independent efforts of the liberal propagandists in the Overseas Branch to affirm what they insisted were the real purposes of the war. In quiet discourse few in Washington would have disagreed with their ultimate ends, but that was hardly the question. The president had a different conception of how the war would unfold— one which depended upon as quick and uncomplicated a military victory as he could arrange. Always willing to delay on sticky issues that could cause trouble with the other members of the Grand Alliance, he was ready to make the compromises that others found more difficult to accept. The propagandists, eager to keep their values alive, were moderately successful at doing so until their purpose conflicted with more expedient efforts to prosecute the war. Then something had to give, and the propagandists were most vulnerable of all.

Elmer Davis, under attack from without and within, battered by the Congress and ignored by the aggressive staffers of his own organization, knew he had to act if he was to salvage anything for the rest of the war. He probably shared the convictions of those in the Overseas Branch he had to struggle to control. But once again, he was willing to make the compromises that he regarded as necessary if he and his agency were going to survive.

And so the aggressively liberal leaders of the Overseas Branch had to go and others more moderate and willing to work along with those in charge had to take their place. Barrett was, in the words of one journalist, no "human firecracker" but he was "quiet and serious and efficient"—just what Davis believed the organization needed. Sober and sensible too was Wallace Carroll, who came back to OWI as deputy director with responsibility for propaganda to Europe. Barrett and Carroll were men with whom Davis could work to do whatever the agency might still be able to do. OWI's own initial message had been denied, but with the cross-channel invasion impending, there might still be a role on the military front.[75]

4 Propaganda Abroad: The Military Message

It was ironic that the propaganda effort, launched with such liberal and idealistic ends, made its greatest contributions in the military theaters of the war. With the ideological bent of the early leaders blunted by the "moronic little king" episode in Italy, those who then took charge saw no alternative but a more circumscribed campaign. More and more they accepted the policy decisions that governed the conduct of the war and devoted themselves to doing what the administration asked. The military side of propaganda, at the start of the struggle but a small, halting, and only occasionally successful venture, grew by the latter stages of the war into an integrated part of the attack. And with a prominent role in both the last campaigns in Europe and the final thrust at Japan, the much criticized OWI could quietly argue that propaganda had really come of age.

The propaganda work to assist the military that became known as psychological warfare had started early in the war as simply one part of the broader OWI program. The liberal leaders of the organization, always interested in projects they could undertake to assist the war effort, soon discovered, in spite of some rough beginnings on the military front, that their service to the Army proved more successful than their larger attempt to interpret the issues of the war. The military propaganda campaign, carried out both by agents in the field under military command and by staffers who provided support from home, came into its own at just about the time that ideological confrontations, particularly in Italy, threatened the very existence of OWI. And so Elmer Davis and the aides he trusted most determined to emphasize OWI's military role at the expense of all others. Earlier they had fought off challenges from others in Washington who wanted to take over psychological warfare, and that bureaucratic victory, one of the few they enjoyed, allowed them to carry on. Even though the direction of what they did shifted more and more from the Washington offices to the military command, in the new arrangements that slowly evolved propaganda was finally given a part to play in bringing the war to an end.

At the start of World War II the possibility of a role for military propaganda seemed remote indeed. American military officials, understandably skeptical of any unproven techniques, had to be persuaded of the ultimate utility before they would make any moves. Unfortunately for OWI, the Army's first involvement had not fared particularly well. In June 1941 the Army had established a "Special Study Group" in its Military Intelligence Service to coordinate intelligence and to integrate early psychological warfare planning with War Department programs. After Pearl Harbor the group became known as the Psychological Warfare Branch, and while it did develop some propaganda plans for the Army, it never received a totally sympathetic response. When OWI was established, Colonel Oscar Solbert, head of the Army group, asked to be detailed to the new organization in the hope that proximity to the planning of foreign propaganda would give him greater authority. Robert Sherwood for his part believed that Solbert would have inside information that would help OWI, but both were disappointed, for Solbert had neither special knowledge nor access to anything OWI might want. Major General George V. Strong, head of Military Intelligence, viewed him as "a messenger boy" and even in that role Solbert did not function well. Lacking precise information about impending military events, he was in New York attending a horse show at the time of the North African invasion. Soon afterward the Army abolished his unit.[1]

A more helpful beginning grew out of an OWI initiative of July 1942 when Archibald MacLeish and James Warburg went to London to organize the agency's main overseas operational base. While MacLeish concentrated on establishing an American information program and on making provisions for broadcasts to American troops in Britain, Warburg sought to interest military leaders in OWI's potential contributions to projected attacks. To

General Dwight D. Eisenhower, who had recently arrived in London to plan those operations, and to the combined British-American staff Warburg explained what OWI could do. Eisenhower indicated that he was receptive to Wallace Carroll, then with the United Press but soon to take control of OWI's London office. "I don't know much about psychological warfare," Eisenhower said, "but I want to give it every chance." He felt that there was a role for propaganda in the TORCH operation—the invasion of North Africa—then being organized. He agreed that OWI personnel in London could begin formulating plans, but insisted that representatives involved be attached to his staff and subject to his command.[2]

Under those conditions, OWI sent Percy Winner to London to start making the necessary arrangements. With the occasional help of Carroll, Winner worked with Ritchie Calder of the Political Warfare Executive—the British propaganda arm—to develop directives for the propaganda that would accompany the attack. Winner's main theme was that liberation had now begun, and in support of it he developed appeals to the French patriotic spirit and drafted messages for use in the landings of the very first day. In propaganda programs designed to keep the Axis nations ill at ease, he suggested that other invasions could occur any place else at any time.[3]

Because the propagandists in London had learned the secrets of the coming attack, Eisenhower insisted they now follow military command. To that end he incorporated OWI and PWE personnel as well as those from the American Office of Strategic Services and the British Ministry of Information into a new Psychological Warfare Section, soon known as the Psychological Warfare Branch, of Allied Force Headquarters. Heading the new unit was Colonel Charles B. Hazeltine, whose appointment reflected the primitive regard for propaganda activities in the early days of the war, for Hazeltine was a cavalry officer who knew nothing at all about his intended tasks.[4]

Hazeltine was nonetheless determined to make the best of the situation. To the members of his section he declared: "I don't know anything about propaganda, but I believe in its power. I know the army and I understand organization. We're on trial until we produce the goods. So you write the words and I'll sell the army on their value." He did. He was a scrounger, well-aware of official and unofficial Army methods for procuring supplies and getting things done. On Gibraltar, a few days before the invasion, he organized his crew, a motley but eager group of several dozen American and British soldiers and civilians.[5]

The organization of the new Psychological Warfare Branch was a significant development in the conduct of Allied propaganda during the war. It established the principle, continually reaffirmed, that operations in theaters of action would be subject to military control. In those early days the main offices of OWI at home were not always pleased with what was going on but understood they had no real choice in the matter. Military contributions they might make, no matter how small, would take place under the military terms of attack.

Thus began the organized psychological warfare campaign. If arrangements were not always certain and tactics not always clear, there was still going to be some role for propaganda in the first counterattack of the war. As the North African battle began on the morning of November 8, 1942, members of the new PWB landed with Allied troops along the Mediterranean coast in Morocco and Algeria. Some attempted to assist the landing with radio and megaphone requests for surrender. Near Casablanca the U.S.S. *Texas* broadcast over mediumwave warnings to local military leaders against armed resistance which were effective until a ship's salvo disrupted the delicate radio equipment. At all points PWB agents sought the surrender of enemy forces and the cooperation of the French.[6]

As the campaign got underway PWB "psychological warriors" moved to seize North African media facilities that could be used for Allied publicity. They took over newspaper plants, radio studios, and movie theaters that they could use for their own messages to Europe and Africa. In time they set up propaganda shops which contained publications and pictorial displays lauding the Allied cause and they even operated mobile units to carry the message to the hinterlands. They knew they had important work to do, for as Ernie Pyle, the noted war correspondent, wrote, "the German propaganda here had been expert," and left what Milton Eisenhower called an "intellectual blackout" in the area. Knowing only what the Germans wanted them to know, North Africans were persuaded that the Axis would win, and PWB therefore moved to counter those impressions.[7]

After the devastating deal the Allies made with Darlan, the propagandists found themselves at a loss. They shared the anti-Vichy sentiments of their colleagues in the United States and favored General Charles de Gaulle and the Free French movement. They had carried to North Africa several hundred thousand leaflets attacking Darlan and other Vichy representatives. Those they destroyed after the agreement with the admiral, but the propagandists remained disturbed by the American action. They also found their own hands tied. The Darlan agreement provided for the return to the French of control over communications media, and so PWB had to give up the radio stations and newspaper plants it had seized, and try instead to work with the pro-Vichy elements who had opposed the Allies for the past several years.[8]

Disconcerted, PWB members grumbled about the restrictions and even took liberties with them whenever they could. Those independent efforts compromised PWB's already tenuous standing with the Army. Fortunately for the propagandists, Milton Eisenhower's visit to North Africa to consult with Ike helped smooth things over and led the Army to restructure the psychological warfare organization. In early 1943 Allied Force Headquarters established an Information and Censorship Section which was part of Eisenhower's staff. It had responsibility for public relations, propaganda, and news to and from home. Brigadier General Robert A. McClure, who had participated in the original London conferences on psychological warfare, was head of the new unit, while psychological warfare remained under the direction of Colonel Hazeltine, who was now directly responsible to McClure. The reorganization established PWB more firmly as a military body and secured a place for it in the military hierarchy. The changes portended smoother operations. Even though some members of PWB still insisted, in C. D. Jackson's words, on applying their own "individual enthusiastic interpretation of the Four Freedoms," even though Colonel Hazeltine occasionally seemed eccentric, subject to alcoholic binges and sometimes unable to understand the work of his organization, and even though General McClure was more occupied with his broader Information and Censorship Section than with PWB itself, conditions did improve. Propagandists in the field began to understand just what they could do and began for the first time to enjoy some limited success.[9]

In the Tunisian campaign PWB dropped twenty million leaflets that had some effect in contributing to the demoralization of the enemy. Leaflets with such themes as "You Are Surrounded" and "Drowning Is a Nasty Death" rained on Axis territory from Royal Air Force planes. Americans who had grumbled that "you can't kill a Heinie with a spitball" watched as the number of Axis soldiers surrendering began to rise. As deserters carrying leaflets arrived at Allied lines in March and April, the American Army became more enthusiastic about the PWB program and General James H. Doolittle for the first time sent planes under his command to drop leaflets over enemy lines. Although military force was the main cause of the capitulation by early May of more than a quarter of a million German soldiers stationed in North Africa, OWI could claim that propaganda had played a part.[10]

True, leaflet warfare still had a low priority in the broader scheme of things and military men still resented civilians in combat areas. Nonetheless, the success of PWB in the TORCH campaign provided a base in North Africa from which to carry the propaganda war to the rest of Europe. And in the operations that followed psychological warfare was to play an even larger part.[11]

The experience at Pantelleria further helped the cause of psychological warfare. Allied forces attacked that island fortress located midway between Tunisia and Sicily in June 1943. With both bombs and leaflets they sought to gain control of the garrison of 10,000 men. Despite the air attacks, the Italians ignored the demands for surrender. Finally new leaflets told the enemy soldiers to demand that their commander end the hopeless struggle. After one more round of bombs the Italians, obeying instructions in the leaflets, demonstrated their readiness to yield by laying out a large white cross on the airfield. When asked about the effect of the leaflets, the garrison commander removed one from his own pocket and related how his men, kneeling in prayer, had implored him to surrender.[12]

Propagandists acknowledged that leaflets alone could not bring about surrender. But Elmer Davis and others argued on the basis of experience that when enemy soldiers were "militarily in a tough spot, propaganda gives them the shove." Leaflets helped make it safe for antagonists who were already vulnerable to give up. They did not need to use surrender passes or other such materials when they found them, but could hide them away for future use. Several times PWB refined the safe-conduct items after questioning prisoners who had yielded. Commanders watching surrenders increase might still have reservations about the leaflets' ultimate efficacy but were willing to use the materials nonetheless.[13]

As the Allies moved toward Sicily, propaganda played an even larger role than it had in earlier campaigns. Before the landings on July 10 airplanes dropped millions of PWB leaflets over the island. More leaflets fell as the invasion began. They asserted that the Allies were coming as friends to release Italians from fascist domination and to help reestablish a free nation. PWB radio broadcasts carried a proclamation by General Eisenhower and up-to-date reports on the operations. Later radio programs and leaflets aimed at Sicily and Italy carried a message from Prime Minister Churchill and President Roosevelt which told the audience: "The time has come for you to decide whether Italians shall die for Mussolini and Hitler—or live for Italy and civilization." PWB combat teams, with a more clearly defined mission than in North Africa, accompanied the troops and aimed their efforts at both enemy soldiers and the local population. They prepared propaganda materials and took over presses and radio stations in captured cities. In Palermo, using the partially destroyed equipment from two fascist newspapers, PWB brought out a new paper, *Sicilia Liberata*. In less than a fortnight its circulation jumped from 2,000 to 50,000. With a greater sense of confidence, unhampered by political conditions that had proved restrictive in North Africa, PWB teams moved forward to win over the Sicilians.[14]

Allied efforts were successful. Psychological warfare units, on interrogating the first Italian prisoners of war in Sicily, found that they had read and believed Allied leaflets. One Italian general, Robert Sherwood told a Senate committee, confessed, "I could do nothing to maintain the morale of my men when they were plastered with hundreds of your leaflets every day." Colonel Hazeltine told of a PWB officer who flew over Trapani and dropped leaflets telling the townspeople to put out white flags if they wanted to save their city. "By the time he flew back after his leaflets had been dropped," Hazeltine said, "the town looked as though all the washing in the world were hung out there. Every habitable quarter showed white." Such experiences helped persuade other Army officers of propaganda's value. General George S. Patton was one of those converted by the results in Sicily. When he came around others followed. At the end of the thirty-eight-day campaign psychological warfare enjoyed greater stature than before.[15]

In the campaign against Italy itself, PWB played an active part and made a number of contributions that won it acclaim. In early September 1943 the organization helped call attention to the Italian surrender. Marshal Badoglio had accepted an armistice and had agreed to announce the surrender over Radio Rome, but American military forces, which had operations keyed to the announcement, remained anxious, for rumors were circulating that Badoglio might back off from his promise. When PWB monitors revealed that no announcement was forthcoming, it was clear that the marshal had reversed himself. Eisenhower then decided that rather than call off all plans, the announcement should go out anyway to force the Italian's hand. Algiers radio sent it out, and soon after Badoglio appeared on the air to confirm the surrender.[16]

PWB also claimed a role in bringing about the surrender of the Italian fleet after Italy's capitulation. The Allies feared that the fleet would fall into German hands, but because of the long-standing fascist ban on listening to Allied programs, there seemed to be no way to reach it. Maurice Pierce, an OWI radio engineer with PWB, therefore shifted a transmitter in Algiers from its normal signal to the international distress frequency that all naval ships listen to at all times. A message then went out every fifteen minutes that urged the fleet to proceed to Malta. Some ships reached Allied ports. Others, lacking air cover as they attempted to surrender, were destroyed by the German Luftwaffe. Whether the Italian commanding officers had followed instructions from their superiors or from Allied propagandists, OWI relished the comment of British Admiral Sir Andrew Cunningham, who said to an aide: "Tell General McClure that they've accomplished in one day with propaganda what I've been trying to do for three years with the Navy." That light remark was played up heavily by OWI when it next tangled with Congress.[17]

PWB leaflet operations grew heavier, too. The Germans, now tenaciously resisting the Allies in Italy, were the main targets. By December 1943, fifteen million PWB leaflets fell upon northern Italy weekly, and there were requests for even more. Distributed by plane and by shell, they were having some effect in encouraging Germans to surrender. Lieutenant General Mark W. Clark of the Fifth Army reported that soldiers often picked up *Passierscheine*—safe-conduct passes—and waited for the right moment to give up. He sensed the value of propaganda and indicated his intention to keep using it. Leaflet warfare survived occasional complications. Bill Mauldin, war reporter and cartoonist, described how a group of sadistic soldiers in Anzio made life difficult for PWB. Ordinarily the Americans shot leaflets over enemy lines and then ceased fire until the Germans gathered them up. Once, however, they fired the leaflets, waited for the Germans to surface, and then unleashed explosive fire. "Psychological warfare probably got as sore about that as the surviving Germans," recorded Mauldin. "Our leaflet barrages were distrusted for a long, long time after that." Elsewhere, though, distribution went more smoothly. Soldiers gradually recognized the value of propaganda and accepted its use.[18]

As the Allies pushed on, PWB units moved into liberated areas and assisted in the occupation. The psychological warfare groups issued the necessary military instructions. They brought in OWI-compiled recorded music, features, and other broadcast material for use over Italian radio, and produced their own newspapers for the Italians. And they learned lessons as they went along. In tiny Lampedusa, an island with several hundred poor fishermen which lies between Sicily and Africa, PWB members established the first free newspaper in enemy lands. One side of the first single-page issue contained necessary military announcements. The other, noted James M. Minifie, deputy psychological warfare officer of the Anglo-American Fifteenth Army group in the Mediterranean, "urged the Lampedusans to embrace the four freedoms and to cease defecating in the public highway." When the local citizens protested that it was inconsistent to deny an old freedom while demanding that they accept new ones, the sergeant/editor in charge refused to take them seriously. And so, Minifie went on, they assembled in the piazza and "with one accord they struck a blow for freedom." While Italians everywhere seemed independent and individualistic, PWB efforts to deal with them during the next year proved more successful for all concerned.[19]

In those first campaigns of the war, PWB was playing a more and more active part. Slowly but surely the organization was gaining a reputation for being something more than a group of crackpots who were not willing to fight. As that happened, OWI members at home began to make a more sustained effort to help their colleagues in uniform overseas. For all the complaints voiced about the military's direction of policy at the front, OWI staffers at home were active from the start in providing the support for PWB that they could best give.

In the North African campaign, OWI, like the BBC, sent out spot announcements telling of the attack. The recorded voice of President Roosevelt, in French, told listeners of the landings, while other messages, some from General Eisenhower, continued for the next few days. All transmitters were constantly alive with news of the invasion. In the moments available the strains of "La Marseillaise" and "The Star Spangled Banner" filled the air. OWI radio broadcasts also interpreted the invasion for overseas audiences. Following official policy, OWI pointed out that other fronts "from Norway to Finland to the islands of the Eastern Mediterranean" might open up at any moment. North Africa would serve as a stepping-stone to the rest of Europe, for the invasion was but the start of a thrust that could not now be denied.[20]

In Italy too OWI supported PWB propaganda attacks launched from overseas. The agency had long been trying to encourage the spirit of rebellion in Italy, as when it tried to arouse the ire of Italians by repeating stories that were circulating about olive oil —necessary for cooking in Italy—being used to lubricate German tanks. As the results in North Africa became clear, OWI blamed the inordinately ambitious Mussolini for involving Italy with the treacherous Hitler. It continued to assert that the Italian people could bring the day of liberation closer by their own efforts. Now was not yet the time for open revolt, but broadcasts made it clear that resistance could come through sabotage and in other less obvious ways. After the political upheaval in Italy, one OWI directive recognized the responsibility "to make the wagon of victory roll faster and faster down hill," and to that end the organization encouraged the Italian people to assist in the liberation of their country. As the invasion occurred OWI played it up as the first landing on the mainland of Europe. The propaganda material appealed to the Italians to increase their resistance, and sought to stress signs of unification around the Badoglio government as the speediest way of effecting the liberation of the country. The earlier ideological concerns clearly had been subordinated to military ends.[21]

As OWI worked in ever more deliberate ways to assist the military effort overseas, the agency also had to defend its right to engage in that kind of propaganda at all. With their very mandate under attack from all directions, the leaders of the organization recognized that they had to retain control of the activity that was probably least controversial and most successful of all that they might try. Yet they faced a vigorous challenge from Colonel

William Donovan, now head of the Office of Strategic Services, which Roosevelt had set up on June 13, 1942, at the same time that he created OWI.[22]

Donovan recognized that he could use his new organization to retain some influence over propaganda. The executive order establishing OWI was vague about who would control information activities pointed toward the enemy. It gave OWI authority to formulate and execute programs to promote intelligent understanding at home and abroad, but said nothing about propaganda that could weaken the enemy. Although OWI assumed that its mandate covered military propaganda, Donovan disagreed. He insisted on the division between open, general, informational activities, and those tied to front-line operations. OWI could control the former, which Donovan considered propaganda chores. The latter, which he regarded as psychological warfare tasks, he claimed for his own organization.[23]

Donovan claimed authority "to initiate, formulate, and develop plans for psychological warfare, . . . to coordinate psychological warfare activities of other U.S. Government agencies, . . . [and] to designate the executive agencies for implementing approved psychological warfare plans," as he pressed his attack. Although OWI was able to hold him off at first, once the North African invasion had revealed the possibilities of military propaganda, he was more determined than ever to have his way. To that end, he won the Joint Chiefs of Staff to his side, for as a military man at heart, Donovan was more acceptable to the JCS than the civilians of OWI. When the JCS issued a draft directive in early December 1942 which gave OSS authority for "the planning, development, coordination, and execution of the military program for psychological warfare . . . in furtherance of actual or planned military operations," OWI fought back. "A more flagrant and obvious disregard for the expressed will of the President," Archibald MacLeish declared, "has rarely been displayed in any draft document prepared in this government," and Elmer Davis circulated his comments "on the proposal to cut off one leg of my pants and give it to Bill Donovan, who already has pants of his own."[24]

Once the directive in its final form was issued, some members of OWI—Joseph Barnes, James Warburg, and Robert Sherwood, among others—said they would resign if it went into effect. Although both in late December and in early January Davis received assurances from Roosevelt that OWI was to continue to do what it had been doing, the president refrained from intervening publicly in the quarrel. With more important matters on his mind, he again preferred to stand apart from the bureaucratic struggles that he tended to encourage for as long as he could.[25]

The War Department, however, was becoming concerned about the interagency conflict. Secretary of War Stimson wrote to Roosevelt in February that both Davis and Donovan "have differed vigorously and at length as to scope and jurisdiction of their respective duties. As the head of the War Department and thereby the civilian head of the administration of the Army, I am rather in the position of the innocent bystander in the case of an attempt by a procession of the Ancient and Honorable Order of Hibernians and a procession of Orangemen to pass each other on the same street. I only know that every Army commander hereafter conducting operations in a foreign theater, if the present differences persist, will be subjected to great embarrassment and danger to his operations."[26]

Milton Eisenhower's negotiations with Lieutenant General Joseph T. McNarney, deputy chief of staff of the War Department, finally ended the impasse, and on March 9, 1943, Roosevelt issued an executive order which stated: "The Office of War Information will plan, develop, and execute all phases of the federal program of radio, press, publication, and related foreign propaganda activities involving the dissemination of information." It modified the OSS military order of June 13, 1942, "to the extent necessary" but OSS remained intact and under JCS control. The executive order also demanded coordination of propaganda programs with military plans and required JCS approval of OWI's materials. Perhaps because the North African experience was still in the president's thoughts, the order also stated that "parts of the foreign propaganda program which are to be executed in a theater of military operations will be subject to the control of the theater commander."[27]

With that the matter ended, and although there was occasional carping as the war in Italy dragged on, Donovan did retreat and OWI emerged with its authority affirmed. Regardless of whatever else happened, the organization could still work on its military propaganda program during the coming campaigns.[28]

With OWI's proprietary interest in propaganda intact and with the experience derived from its first military efforts in mind, Davis, in the wake of the "moronic little king" incident, had a clear sense of his agency's future direction. Although Percy Winner voiced his discontent with "the degree of subordination of political-strategic propaganda to military-tactical propaganda," a directive in January 1944 guaranteed that such subordination would continue. "From now on," the directive stated, "political warfare will be even more directly serving military operations in the European theater." Whatever the earlier debates and the earlier hopes for the organization, the new way was evident for all to see. The ideological crusade had ended, but there was still work to be done.[29]

In the last phases of the war in Europe, OWI worked increasingly through military organizations. As planning began for the invasion of France, Brigadier General McClure, who had come to oversee psychological warfare activities in North Africa, arrived in London to assume similar propaganda duties, and he became chief of the new Psychological Warfare Division, Supreme Headquarters, Allied Expedition Force (PWD/SHAEF), when it was organized in early 1944. Like the preceding military groups, PWD consisted of both American and British military and civilian personnel. Realizing that its greatest contributions could come by working through McClure's PWD, OWI expanded its London operations. OWI had organized its London office in July 1942. At first a comparatively small operation, it became a major center of activity, which by D-Day in June 1944 had some sixteen hundred people at work. They supported PWD tasks and supplied men and materials that enabled the military organization to function smoothly. Once again, as it had done in the earlier campaigns, OWI headquarters in Washington provided policy guidance to the London office and in coordination with its British counterpart worked out broad policy lines for PWD to follow. But as before the principle of military control prevailed. PWD recognized OWI directives when it could but pursued its own lines when it perceived any military advantage in doing so. OWI leaders at home were not entirely happy with the arrangement, but within the context of the wartime chain of command they could do little else but comply.[30]

PWD, better integrated than its predecessors into the military chain of command, was able to be more aggressive in its propaganda attack. Political warfare plans were included in the extensive Bodyguard campaign to deceive the Germans before the Normandy landings of June 6, 1944. PWD members spent a good deal of time planning for the invasion and coordinating their role in the struggle that would follow. Some, even before D-Day, began to broadcast a series of instructions entitled "The Voice of SHAEF," while others worked on the leaflets they would use either to warn civilians to evacuate particular areas or to carry messages from the military command. On the morning of the attack itself a three-man psychological warfare team led several other teams ashore. Carrying some leaflets in shells ready for firing, they were also prepared to request London to drop others over designated language areas when they saw what was going on. In time they brought over printing presses and did some of the production themselves in what became a huge propaganda effort. In the Normandy invasion alone the Allies dropped nine million leaflets, and in the three months that followed they dispatched 800 million more.[31]

The propagandists pressed home their attack. PWD sound trucks moved as close as possible to enemy forces and then broadcast what the GIs called *Schweinheils*—pig calls—that revealed to the Nazis their desperate plight. Leaflets and miniature newspapers assured the Germans of good treatment and detailed the care that prisoners received. There were different items for different groups. Propagandists directed *Nachrichten für die Truppe*

toward German troops. They aimed *SHAEF,* another daily newspaper which had pages in an assortment of languages, at foreign
prisoners and workers in Germany. Most important in the leaflet
campaign were the increasingly refined safe-conduct passes that
the Allies dropped behind enemy lines. In German, French, and
English each pass stated: "The German soldier who carries this
safe conduct is using it as a sign of his genuine wish to give
himself up. He is to be disarmed, to be well looked after, to
receive food and medical attention as required, and to be
removed from the danger zone as soon as possible." Each pass
bore the facsimile signature of Dwight D. Eisenhower, which was
intended to make it look more like an official contract and less like
an appeal.[32]

As the military struggle continued, so too did the propaganda
campaign. By the final surrender of Germany the number of
leaflets dropped since D-Day reached over three billion, while
radio operations expanded in the same way. Maurice Pierce, the
OWI engineer who had assisted in bringing the Italian fleet to
port, entered Luxembourg with the first troops. The Germans
had been destroying radio stations as they retreated, but on a
wild chance Pierce borrowed tanks and moved toward the large
transmitter that belonged to the powerful Radio Luxembourg.
He was able to capture it in September 1944. William S. Paley,
chief of Allied radio propaganda at SHAEF, then moved to protect the station from the Germans, from the company that owned
it, and from other groups that showed interest. With Radio Luxembourg the Allies could blanket Europe and even reach Germans on sets that received only German wavelengths.[33]

Like the American Broadcasting Station in Europe (ABSIE),
Radio Luxembourg relayed news and feature broadcasts that
originated elsewhere and also performed military tasks and
released programs of its own. During the attack on Aachen, in
western Germany, as the Allies moved weapons into position, the
radio station issued an ultimatum to the town. Although that
particular appeal went unheard when Aachen's power failed, the
town fell nonetheless. The Allies, recognizing that propaganda
appeals might speed military success, were willing to use them

whenever possible. More widespread were the general programs that aimed to undermine German morale and eventually to induce surrender. Sometimes staffers read excerpts from captured German letters, not yet posted or delivered. They responded to the news of a potato shortage in Germany by claiming that Hitler's V-weapons were propelled by fuel distilled from potatoes and each time a missile went off, 15,000 Germans lost their potato ration for a week. They also used jokes, either those they made up or others related by prisoners, to make their points. One served to remind listeners of German shortages and manpower problems. In German one voice asked, "Why did Grandpa join the Volkssturm?" Replied the other: "Because he had no one to take care of him now that Grandma's in the Luftwaffe."[34]

Another radio scheme took shape through "Operation Annie" —what *Time* magazine termed "the most dramatic underground radio station in wartime Europe." The American Twelfth Army Group ran the station from an isolated house in Luxembourg each morning from 2:00 to 6:30 A.M. Taking certain liberties, it pretended to be a German station, run from within the Reich by a small group of loyal Rhinelanders who felt the Nazis were not being truthful about their desperate position. Programs consisted of authentic war news, reports from the front, miscellaneous gossip, and music. Once an audience had been established, "Annie" could begin to play sly tricks with immediate ends in view. One program reported that the Allies had dropped fake food ration stamps. By naming communities where that had not been done, staffers sent people scurrying to stores to try to get rid of what they thought were false cards as soon as they could. The high point of the campaign came when German troops in the Eifel Mountains were surrounded by Allied forces but still had safe areas for retreat. "Annie," with a reputation for truthfulness firmly established, labeled other areas as safe and led the Germans into an Allied ambush. As Germany's defeat grew near, the propagandists decided that the station had served its purpose. A staged scuffle, broadcast over the air, left "Annie" in ruins—with the job done.[35]

Such campaigns, organized by propagandists in the field, were largely beyond the control of OWI at home. The organization's leaders in Washington and New York continued to subscribe to their "strategy of truth" as they laid out general lines of policy, yet they understood that there was little they could do about the actions taken by psychological warfare personnel under military command thousands of miles away. OWI could feign innocence when the propaganda in the field occasionally strayed from the truth, and at the same time could legitimately claim that such occurrences came only infrequently and never approximated the large-scale fabrications for which the Axis powers were known.

In general the military propaganda efforts met with a favorable response from the Army. There were still moments of friction, however. General Patton, for example, usually cooperative with psychological warfare programs, at one point reacted vigorously to a suggestion that he use more leaflet warfare against enemy soldiers. "I'm not here to write 'em letters," he announced, "I'm here to kill the S.O.B.'s!" Another officer complained that an issue of the tiny newspaper *Internenbanner* which showed the treatment that prisoners of war received "looks like a damned travel folder to me," and American soldiers under fire often resented the conspicuous sound equipment which they feared would only draw further attacks. Still, on a number of occasions propaganda did contribute to enemy desertions and that ensured that the efforts would go on.[36]

All the while OWI continued to provide support from home. The organization had long been seeking to undermine Germany's will to resist, and from mid-1942 on it carried on the optimistic Foreign Information Service line that the United Nations had gained the offensive. It stressed that the defeat of the Nazi regime would not mean the destruction of the German people, while at the same time it warned that the longer the war lasted, the more damage it would do to everything inside the Reich. In the months that followed, OWI continued to emphasize that German defeat was inevitable, that only through surrender could Germany minimize the misery that would follow. With its message, the agency hoped to increase unrest in the Nazi state and to reduce the efficiency of the German war machine.[37]

Occasionally OWI became involved in specific campaigns. In early 1943 it had begun to work with the Navy's Special Warfare Branch (Op–16–W) on a series of broadcasts aimed at challenging inflated claims of German submarine success. By that time the worst days of the battle of the Atlantic were over, but victory was not yet in sight. Propaganda might help bring the end nearer. The Navy and the Office of War Information cooperated closely on the project, which unfolded smoothly, perhaps because it began at the Navy's initiative. The Special Warfare Branch, working from intelligence materials, provided OWI with radio scripts and platters for the broadcasts of Commander Robert Lee Norden, USN (in reality Lieutenant Commander Ralph G. Albrecht). Over the next twenty-seven months 309 Norden broadcasts went out over the air. They cited the actual locations of vessels that the Germans claimed they had sunk. Norden questioned why no noncommissioned officers were ever rewarded for sinkings. Soon the German estimates of submarine sinkings began to drop to more realistic levels and two petty officers were suddenly awarded for their work. German prisoners spoke of the propaganda broadcasts after they were captured and one U-boat captive even requested a personal interview with Commander Norden.[38]

OWI waged other campaigns on its own. As the invasion of France approached, the Allied Air Forces sought to overcome the German air arm. Despite the bombings of factories and other installations, German planes refused to come out and fight. Wallace Carroll proposed that OWI bait the German Air Force. At the end of March 1944 the propaganda effort began. The first directive advised an indirect approach. OWI wanted to undermine the Luftwaffe's prestige and to arouse the German people sufficiently so that they in turn would place pressure on the policy makers. Operators were told to ask, "Where is the Luftwaffe?" That question—"Strictly deadpan" according to one directive—was repeated over and over. Soon after the campaign began, German planes started to respond more actively to air attacks. Whether they were stirred by propaganda or by the desperate need to defend the German homeland, their appearance gave the

Allied Air Forces new chances to meet them in combat. The results were favorable to the Allies. Whenever the German planes did fight, OWI wondered why they had not fought harder. In time, as German air strength seemed to decline, OWI spoke more bluntly about the Luftwaffe's impotence. Broadcasts emphasized the German dilemma. The air force could participate in battle and risk destruction or stay on the ground and watch German reserves destroyed. German Propaganda Minister Joseph Goebbels finally claimed the weather kept the German planes grounded. The moment of truth came on D-Day when the Luftwaffe was again mostly quiet. The Allies, using propaganda to assist military force, had succeeded in drawing the air force out and leading it to destruction.[39]

With the approach of D-Day OWI launched still another campaign. The Germans had been glorifying their coastal defenses for several years. Sherwood in London proposed that the Allies proclaim that the Germans had to hold the Atlantic Wall if their defenses were to remain secure. OWI began to draw parallels between the Maginot Line that had failed France in 1940 and the Atlantic Wall now. The propagandists hinted that by putting their faith in static defenses the Germans were victims of a "Maginot mentality." The attack aimed to "build up to the conclusion that any breach in Germany's coastal defenses will be a major military disaster." As soon as the Allies then established a beachhead, their penetration would constitute success.[40]

For D-Day itself OWI had copies of statements and communiqués from the Supreme Allied Commander and his Headquarters which the organization was to begin using upon receiving a signal from the field. At the same time the propagandists at home, like their colleagues abroad, intensified the campaign to induce enemy surrenders. Soon after the landings the Office of War Information began to stress the overwhelming Allied strength that the Germans now faced. When Sherwood reported that some prisoners in Normandy gave overwhelming force as the reason for their capitulation, Carroll seized on that rationalization as the key to a new approach. OWI directives stated that propaganda should "indicate to the Germans that submission to overwhelming force constitutes an honorable way out." Broadcasts and other messages should say that the Germans were overpowered, not that they deserted.[41]

As the campaign unfolded after the Normandy landings and the Allies raced toward Germany, OWI became more enthusiastic than ever before. A new propaganda campaign to assist the military effort became more pointed than other campaigns had been. "From now on," noted a central directive in July, "our propaganda offensive will run boldly in advance of our military offensive. We shall proceed on the implicit assumption that the German will to resist can be broken and will be broken by next December." To that end OWI took propaganda risks previously discouraged. With news stories it worked to create the impression that Germany was crumbling and could fall at any time. A month later OWI, reflecting the optimism of Supreme Headquarters, moved up the date for the anticipated collapse of Germany to November 15. Soon after the agency went further and, without mentioning a date, began to proclaim that "the end of the war is in sight."[42]

Complementing that effort, OWI engaged in several other projects. Seizing on the July 1944 attempt to assassinate Hitler, it interpreted the episode as an indication of the existence of a much larger peace movement in Germany. Meanwhile the organization had inaugurated a campaign to force Hitler to show himself before the German people. The fuehrer had not appeared at any mass meetings for over a year. OWI began to try to commit him to a date for a public appearance. It sought to generate rumors that his health was failing and to stimulate anxiety about his withdrawal from public view. German propaganda denied that anything was wrong, and Hitler did speak over the radio. But OWI hoped that his failure to appear personally would create doubts about Germany's capacity to survive.[43]

At the same time OWI attacked Germany's flanks. Following the State Department line, it began to take a tougher attitude toward the neutral nations in Europe. Any aid given to the enemy would now be held against the neutrals. Hinting that "the military situation is such that the neutrals must play their part in

supporting the cause of the Allies," OWI told Sweden, Switzer-
land, Spain, Portugal, and Turkey to cooperate before it was too
late. The propaganda organization also warned the satellites that
now was the time to get out of the war. Holding out longer would
only be to their disadvantage. To countries like Hungary where
Jews were in serious trouble OWI warned that further atrocities
would bitterly prejudice Allied public opinion. The Hungarians
were already accountable for their associations with the Nazis in
the slaughter of the Jews. Such warnings, Davis notified Cordell
Hull, would continue until news came that Jews were safe.[44]

And all the while the struggle with Germany continued, OWI
persisted in trying to find a way, through channels, of getting
around the unconditional surrender formula to which the Allies
still adhered. Roosevelt, with Churchill's approval, had announced the policy in January 1943, in large part to assure members of the Allied coalition that despite the Darlan deal the
United States would fight to the finish, and also to placate the
Soviet Union as the Allies postponed opening a second front in
Europe. In his statement to the press as the Casablanca conference ended, Roosevelt said that unconditional surrender did
"not mean the destruction of the population of Germany, Italy,
or Japan," but only the destruction of the enemy philosophies.
Indeed, although he neglected to mention the incident to the
press, the president seemed to be thinking of Ulysses S. Grant's
magnanimous gesture in allowing the Southerners to keep their
horses after Robert E. Lee's surrender at Appomattox had ended
the Civil War.[45]

Whatever his intentions, the response from the propagandists
came almost at once and persisted throughout most of the war.
They argued that the phrase unconditional surrender obscured
the need for arrangements and plans that could take effect as
soon as fighting ceased. Use of the term might well lengthen the
war, they believed, by allowing enemy populations to believe that
an unimaginably severe fate lay in store upon total defeat.
Months before he left office, James Warburg complained that the
rigid declaration left the ultimate fate of the enemy unclear. That
ambiguity, he claimed, caused unnecessary complications, for

without some indication—however tough—of what might happen to them after unconditional surrender, the Germans would continue to fight. In the spring of 1944, Wallace Carroll was able to argue the same thing when he observed that the lack of definition allowed Goebbels to persuade the Germans that "unconditional surrender means slavery, castration, the end of Germany as a nation."[46]

Yet through all the criticism the president stood firm. In the Italian war he had turned aside all requests for public modification of his policy, even though the surrender was not, in fact, unconditional, and he continued on the same course in the German campaign. In April 1944 recommendations came from General Eisenhower and from General Walter Bedell Smith, his chief of staff, asking for a clarification of unconditional surrender that would delineate the bases of Allied treatment of a defeated Germany. The military officers wanted an Anglo-Russian-American statement to define surrender policy, guarantee the maintenance of law and order, and detail the arrangements for dealing with Nazis, war criminals, and other Germans. But the president refused to accept the proposal and ordered, as Cordell Hull later wrote, "that the subject be given no further consideration without his approval."[47]

In the face of all that resistance from above, the propagandists were finally able to extract a modest clarification of the policy they had to observe. In mid-1944 the State Department approved the German translation of "unconditional surrender" as "bedingungslose Waffenniederlegung." Clumsy as the phrase was, OWI felt it was helpful for it indicated clearly that the Allies sought the surrender of the armed forces and not the people.[48]

Then, as attention began to focus on what postwar Germany might indeed be like, the propagandists finally had a chance to make the clarifications they had long desired. The Morgenthau plan, advanced by the secretary of the treasury, accepted by Roosevelt and Churchill at the second Quebec conference in September 1944, and aimed at "converting Germany into a country primarily agricultural and pastoral in its character," was a propaganda disaster, and allowed Goebbels to say that the Allies would change Germany into "one vast potato patch." But in the face of bitter attacks from the press and the political opposition, Roosevelt backed off and authorized the drafting of an alternative plan to cover the various stages of the occupation. Incorporated in a series of versions of JCS 1067, that plan, completed only after the national election, was substantially less severe.[49]

With JCS 1067 the propagandists at last had material they could use. And when the psychological warfare officers at Supreme Headquarters drafted a series of thirteen statements that described what Allied Military Government would be like for the Germans, OWI was able to use those points to launch a campaign of its own. By broadcasting the statements—which noted, for example, that National Socialism would be dissolved and Nazi courts closed, but that other German courts after a purge would remain open, and that the property of all Germans would be respected—OWI was able to assure the Germans of just what lay in store without making any outlandish promises. Though the Civil Affairs Division of the War Department cut the effort short in a few months with the argument that the statements would only complicate the task of military government when it was finally established, OWI had been able to meet the Goebbels challenge and assure most Germans that they would indeed be able to survive.[50]

Despite concerted military and propaganda attacks Germany continued to fight. Even before OWI's anticipated dates for victory arrived it became clear that the war would last longer. The success of the German V-2 rockets helped raise morale, and Hitler's counteroffensive in the Ardennes in December made it certain that the struggle would drag on into 1945. As OWI recognized that the war would continue, it took the line that a longer war would be most destructive to the German people. The propagandists also continued to play upon the theme of Allied solidarity that they had developed throughout the war. The Allies were working together, not only in war, but towards a better peace. Churchill, Roosevelt, and Stalin were cooperating in the pursuit of common ends. There were occasional disagreements, to be sure, but the basic unity remained and would contribute to Germany's defeat.[51]

Then in early 1945 the Allied offensive accelerated on all fronts. OWI repeated to the Germans that they could take actions that would help bring the war to a close. The propaganda agency counseled them to engage in passive resistance wherever possible, to avoid conscription, and to try to prevent a scorched earth policy. "Our overall aim," one directive noted, "is to cause the maximum of confusion and panic in Nazi Germany, in order to hinder the German High Command and the Nazi Party from taking effective measures to meet new advances we make in the West." OWI sought to encourage evacuation, to clog the roads, and to add whatever strain it could to the Nazi military effort.[52]

The propagandists at home and abroad knew they were on the right track. German radio stations engaged in widespread jamming to keep enemy broadcasts from being heard. Because Allied programs still got through, Nazi leaders ruled that Germans could not listen to foreign radio. They similarly forbade reading leaflets. Earlier in the war the penalty had been hard labor. By April 1944 the Nazi state had decreed the death penalty for reading or keeping Allied materials. Yet after D-Day Anthony Eden, the British foreign secretary, told the House of Commons that 77 percent of the German prisoners questioned in Normandy admitted that they had heard or seen Allied inducements to give up the struggle. Forty percent had leaflets with them when they surrendered.[53]

By April 1945 the end was near. Rejecting an offer from Heinrich Himmler, head of the German police, to make a separate peace on the Western front, the Allies held out for total capitulation, although they did accept individual surrenders from German soldiers who wanted to give up. The numbers mounted until between 75,000 and 100,000 Germans had yielded that way. At the end of the month, as Hitler committed suicide, Germany collapsed. On May 7, 1945, the long-awaited day finally arrived and Germany ceased to fight.[54]

With one phase of the devastating war over, attention now

focused on the Pacific campaign. OWI had long been involved in activities in that part of the war, yet the propaganda effort reflected the military priorities of the leaders of the struggle. At the Arcadia conference in Washington in December 1941 and January 1942, Roosevelt and Churchill had agreed to concentrate first on the defeat of Germany. While the American Navy battled the Japanese fleet in the Pacific, more men and supplies went to Europe, and so it was with propaganda. The Pacific program, limited at the start, grew gradually during the next few years but only became sizable and coordinated with the military effort in the last year of the war. Then, as in Europe, the propaganda leaders worked with the Army and Navy officials to bring the fighting to a long sought end.[55]

Differences in the way the propaganda program unfolded and became integrated with the military in the European and Asian theaters reflected the significant differences in overall command. In Europe there had been a unity under a single commander. In the Pacific OWI found itself responsible to a number of different leaders in the various theaters of war. It worked under General Joseph W. Stilwell when he was in charge in Burma and China, under General Douglas MacArthur in the southwest Pacific, and under Admiral Chester Nimitz in the campaign against Japan directed from the Hawaiian Islands.[56]

More significant than the number of commands were the attitudes of the military officials involved. Eisenhower was open and usually cooperative, though he always insisted on final control. The leaders in the Pacific were less receptive. The Navy, generally suspicious of propaganda efforts, insisted on rigid security. At a March 1943 meeting with Admiral Nimitz's Command Staff, Lieutenant Colonel Benjamin Stern, on duty for OWI, noted "that (a) inasmuch as the Navy is in complete control of Oceania and Pacific operations, it is jealous of its prerogatives; (b) is afraid of any operation which might jeopardize its own plans and (c) possesses the usual Naval service distrust of civilian organizations." His reception had been cool. "I felt like a lone Nazi in Moscow," he reported. Even worse, there was "a general lack of belief in the worthwhileness of OWI efforts along propaganda lines and covert doubt as to its general usefulness."[57]

With General MacArthur there had been some hope of cooperation. Several weeks after the attack on Pearl Harbor he had requested broadcasts, and then leaflets, to counter Japanese propaganda in the Philippines. Promptly the Foreign Information Service complied. Pleased, MacArthur asked the FIS to provide a regular, daily news service. In late February 1942, however, all that changed. In the midst of the Japanese attack on the Philippines, Roosevelt ordered MacArthur to leave the islands to assume a new command in Australia, and a few months later the Philippines fell to Japan. MacArthur, an OWI officer reported in August 1943, was furious, for he felt that Roosevelt had "betrayed" him. Help that he expected never arrived. MacArthur, "a bitter man surrounded by bitter men who owed all their loyalty —indeed their very lives—to the General," had little use for OWI "for the OWI is linked to the Administration." When the Office of War Information tried to establish contact with MacArthur's headquarters in Australia, the representatives "received the impression that we were not welcome and that we were just a civilian New Deal agency interfering in things of which we knew nothing." The military granted no requests, and one colonel declared categorically: "No OWI man will ever be allowed into the forward areas."[58]

Leaders of the Office of War Information, regretting their inability to participate more fully in Pacific campaigns, made efforts to achieve integration. Those were unsuccessful until July 1944, when Roosevelt took Davis with him to Honolulu where he met with both Nimitz and MacArthur. Davis explained what OWI could do and assured the military officers that a coordinated propaganda campaign was possible without dangerous information leaks. Both commanders agreed to accept OWI's assistance. Though Nimitz, somewhat tentative, was unsure of how well psychological warfare would work in his theater, his staff began working with OWI. MacArthur was more enthusiastic. As he prepared to return to the Philippines, he was ready to accept any assistance he could get.[59]

Before MacArthur landed in October 1944, OWI provided

leaflets and trinkets with the message "I Shall Return" that were smuggled to guerrillas on the islands. As the invasion commenced, an OWI team accompanied the first forces in Leyte and conducted front-line propaganda against the Japanese. Almost immediately it began to put out the first issue of the Leyte-Samar edition of the *Free Philippines*. Broadcasts carried MacArthur's voice. Further leaflets, telling Japanese troops of the progress of the war, encouraged their surrender. When the Army moved toward Manila and took the city in March 1945, OWI worked from there.[60]

Even as OWI provided men and resources to do what was specifically asked, propagandists at home assisted the struggle by issuing broadcasts and statements that followed the official line of those in charge of the war. OWI had long been trying to create distrust and doubt within the Japanese home population. Broadcasts, designed to cause a schism between the Japanese government and people, claimed that the government had failed to serve the interests of the common folk. Its defeat would not mean their defeat or the end of Japanese culture. Radio stories also played upon cleavages between various groups in Japan. They pointed to friction between the Army and Navy that increased as the war dragged on. They emphasized economic difficulties that also worsened as the fighting continued.[61]

As victories in the various theaters in the Pacific mounted OWI reported those successes via shortwave and standard medium-wave broadcast band to the Japanese home population. The capture of Saipan in mid-1944, it declared, was a real milestone. It marked a break in Japan's inner defenses and gave the Allies a position from which to bomb the sacred homeland. When Saipan-based B-29s began to attack Japan in November 1944, the propagandists hailed the raids as a new phase in the war. Meanwhile they played up Germany's disastrous failure in Europe. With Germany's final collapse in 1945, a weekly directive noted, there was "an unprecedented opportunity to dramatize to the . . . Japanese people and troops the hopelessness of continuing the war and their isolation from the rest of the world and each other." Further resistance meant only further destruction.[62]

All along OWI had been urging the Japanese to get out of the war, but the Japanese proved reluctant to surrender. Their tenacity seemed to stem from the notion of Japanese superiority prevalent during the war. Although the Japanese had long manifested both a self-consciousness and a fear of inferiority in their contacts with Westerners, by the 1930s they had developed an aggressive nationalism expressed in terms of national traits of superiority. Stressing reverence for the emperor and emphasizing Japan's unique national polity, the sentiment had a mystical quality. Many Japanese professed to believe that the Yamato spirit, which according to traditional theory dated from the founding of Japan, would help overcome the strongest enemy, and keep the Army and Navy from defeat. Tied to that attitude was the equally strong feeling that the Japanese in battle had but two alternatives: victory or death. Dying for his emperor and nation was the supreme duty for the Japanese soldier. Capitulation, on the other hand, was considered to be the ultimate disgrace. Surrender, reported anthropologist Ruth Benedict, left the Japanese soldier in a void. It cut him off from all ties with his former self. It left him rootless in his own culture.[63]

OWI sought to break down those traditional attitudes. Effective propaganda, under the circumstances, awaited military success. As the American offensive gained momentum, the propaganda attack mounted as well. One leaflet entitled "Do Not Rest Your Ladder Against a Cloud" pointed out that the Japanese exaggerated their own fighting capabilities. American power and American spirit were routing the forces of Japan. At the same time OWI tried to undermine the idea that no Japanese surrendered. It sought to remove the stigma from surrender by arguing that it was no disgrace to yield to overwhelming force when the military situation was hopeless. The German surrender afforded a telling lesson. Another martial nation, confronted with power it could not overcome, had given up.[64]

As they worked to make the prospect of surrender more palatable, propagandists considered the criticisms of early prisoners. Americans learned that the demand for surrender should not be stated directly. Rather the Japanese should be asked to "come over to our side." Even there it was necessary to be careful. Offers of food and drink could be used but had to avoid seeming like bribes or charity. One leaflet, while depicting a tempting plate of Japanese food in a variety of colors, told the soldiers that it was their duty not to die but to live and help rebuild their country. That same appeal took other forms as well. To demonstrate that becoming a prisoner was not the ultimate end, OWI began a campaign to show the high positions some Japanese now held even though they had been captured in the Russo-Japanese War of 1904–05. In the same vein a leaflet compared a German admiral who surrendered in World War I and then served faithfully in World War II with a Japanese naval officer who committed "seppuku" (slit belly) on Saipan. The text asked: "What good is seppuku when it leaves a man without sons to bear his name and carry on his family line? Do you want to be the last of your line, or do you want a family too?"[65]

The surrender campaign, developing slowly, finally bore results in the battle for Okinawa which began on April 1, 1945. By then propagandists both at home and abroad were working closely with the military authorities in a well-coordinated attack. The Okinawa campaign was the largest amphibious operation in the Pacific war to date. It was also the first time American troops in the East had to deal with a sizable local population. Psychological warfare promised to be particularly helpful there. A week before the landings began, some leaflets warned civilians to take cover and to remove themselves from battle areas, while other printed materials addressed the Japanese troops. Although the civilians did not cause much trouble, the Japanese forces fought tenaciously. At the end of two months, even as the Americans drew nearer to victory, the resistance continued, but after severe casualties, most of the remaining enemy troops were rearguard Japanese and Okinawan soldiers. And once American force had cleared the way, propaganda moved into play. In the middle of June 1945, one American front-line division ceased firing for an hour as loudspeakers from tanks and landing craft broadcast a message that told enemy soldiers how hopeless their position was and emphasized to them that surrender would not reflect adversely on their fighting spirit. Only a few Japanese surrendered at that moment, but a week later several thousand gave up, many with leaflets in their hands. Not all soldiers surrendered. Some committed suicide; others fought to the finish. Nonetheless, by June 30, 1945, there were 10,755 prisoners—both soldiers and civilians—more than in any previous Pacific campaign. That news provided OWI with a powerful propaganda message as American forces turned their attention to Japan.[66]

As they sought to demoralize and discourage the Japanese people, OWI had to handle two questions with extreme care. The first was that of unconditional surrender—still controversial as it had been throughout the European campaign. Some members of OWI, even while staying within the bounds imposed, argued, as they had in Europe, that the formula seemed to do more harm than good. The Japanese government had taken the unconditional surrender line, cabled one representative from abroad, and used it to argue that an Allied triumph would mean "prostitution and castration" for the Japanese people, as well as destruction of the government. Despite the constant repetition, the terms of the formula remained shrouded in an ambiguity the propagandists would have been happy to avoid.[67]

The other, and related, question involved the disposition of the Imperial House. The emperor of Japan played a profoundly important role in Japanese life. He reigned "By the Grace of Heaven." He sat upon "the Throne occupied by the same Dynasty changeless through ages eternal." As he watched over the Japanese people, he bore no responsibility for whatever setbacks occurred. Others always took the blame for mistakes. Propagandists, recognizing that unique position, had long avoided direct attacks on the emperor for they knew that such barbs would only draw the Japanese closer together. But now some decision had to be made about what might happen to the institution after the war. The emperor could prove helpful, Joseph Grew, former ambassador to Japan, observed in April 1944, in helping to maintain civil order after the defeat of Japan. Nonetheless, the counterargument that a promise to preserve the emperor would dilute the unconditional surrender doctrine carried weight with many other American officials. Since through mid-1945 the issue remained unresolved, the propagandists found they had to hedge and say, without elaboration, that the question was under discussion. Without significant clarification of either question, OWI could only follow the lead from above and continue to do all it could, both by pursuing the programs already underway and by assisting the military in efforts of its own.[68]

One important military program that took place with OWI support involved Captain (later Admiral) Ellis M. Zacharias of the American Navy. Zacharias had long believed that a positive approach to the Japanese might well bring an end to the war, and his optimism had some basis in experience, for he had been a student of the Japanese language and culture for the preceding twenty-five years. A career naval officer after his graduation from the Naval Academy, he had been sent to Japan in 1920 by the Navy to learn all he could of the language and people. In the years that followed he became fluent in the language and developed some close friendships with highly placed Japanese officials. All of his experience persuaded him that if the Japanese were approached properly, they might well be willing to cease their fight.[69]

Earlier in the war he had suggested to Admiral Nimitz's staff a series of psychological warfare broadcasts, but the Navy officers had no interest in his idea. Then at the end of 1944 he proposed another propaganda scheme to Captain Waldo Drake, on loan to OWI as a liaison officer between the propaganda group and Pearl Harbor headquarters. Zacharias wrote of his expectation that a more liberal government would soon assume power in Japan. He argued that the propaganda agency, working through an "official spokesman," should focus on the Japanese High Command. It was vulnerable, and if dealt with carefully, he implied, it might prove less resistant to a movement for peace. Drake showed Zacharias's somewhat vague letter to Elmer Davis, who was impressed but wanted Zacharias to elaborate his ideas. Zacharias did, and in March 1945 found himself assigned to temporary duty in Washington to develop his plans further. There he decided to work through the Navy's Special Warfare Branch (Op–16–W). He met with Secretary of the Navy James Forrestal and then sketched out his thoughts about a potent psychological warfare campaign.[70]

Drawing on his own sense of Japanese psychology, Zacharias stated that the mission was: "To make unnecessary an opposed landing in the Japanese main islands, by weakening the will of the High Command, by effecting cessation of hostilities, and by bringing about unconditional surrender with the least possible loss of life to us consistent with early termination of the war." He hoped to plant seeds of doubt within the High Command, for weakening it could encourage disintegration all along the line. Zacharias felt the Japanese were basically realistic people who would not resist further once total collapse had begun. He therefore proposed that a United States government spokesman should address particular Japanese officials openly and directly. The spokesman would point out the hopelessness of the Japanese situation. He would exploit cliques within the High Command which disagreed with current strategy and he would play up Japanese admissions of weakness. He would explain the meaning of unconditional surrender by emphasizing that it meant only the cessation of hostilities as directed by President Roosevelt and not the onset of a campaign of violent punishment against the Japanese people.[71]

Secretary Forrestal and Admiral Ernest J. King approved the plan. Then Davis and the OWI staff, after arranging for Zacharias to serve as the "official spokesman," steered the plan through the War Department and the Joint Chiefs of Staff. Zacharias and his aides drew up a "Declaration by the President of the United States," which explained unconditional surrender and was to provide a starting point for the broadcasts. Davis presented the declaration to Roosevelt. Before any further action could be taken, on April 12, 1945, the president died. In the days that followed nothing was done. As Germany moved toward final collapse, Zacharias arranged for Harry S. Truman to see the statement. In his announcement of Nazi Germany's defeat in May, the new president issued the declaration and thereby started an elaborate propaganda campaign in the Pacific.[72]

Within two hours Zacharias was on the air to Japan. He identified himself as an official spokesman and mentioned prominent Japanese individuals with whom he was familiar. He noted Japan's hopeless position and then addressed himself to the question of what would happen after the war. "I am in a position to guarantee with authority that the desperate phrase 'victory or extermination' is a deliberate misrepresentation of fact," he said. He then read Truman's proclamation. It stated that unconditional surrender meant the end of the war, the end of military leadership in Japan, the return of soldiers and sailors to their homes. It meant an end to suffering in Japan. It concluded: "Unconditional surrender does not mean the extermination or enslavement of the Japanese people." Zacharias ended by telling the Japanese: "Your future lies in your own hands. You can choose between a wasteful, unclean death for many of your forces, or a peace with honor."[73]

Soon other broadcasts followed at weekly intervals. In them Zacharias repeated Truman's explanation and probed the failures of Japanese leadership. He continued to "reiterate authoritatively that unconditional surrender is a military term" that did not mean the destruction of the people. Zacharias encouraged Japanese leaders he knew to pursue a sensible course of action. He told of the fall of Okinawa and outlined the dismal implications of that defeat.[74]

After the fourth broadcast the head of the Domei News Agency, acting as a spokesman over the air, questioned further the meaning of unconditional surrender, and Zacharias made efforts to respond. In his twelfth broadcast on July 21, 1945, he explained that Japan had only two alternatives: "One is the virtual destruction of Japan followed by a dictated peace. The other is unconditional surrender with its attendant benefits as laid down by the Atlantic Charter." The reference to the Atlantic Charter, with its pledges of no aggrandizement and promises of self-determination, was a new departure, but Zacharias was on firm ground for he had cleared all items in his broadcasts at the highest levels.[75]

At the same time he approached the question of the emperor,

not in his broadcasts, but in an anonymous letter to the *Washington Post* on July 21, 1945. That letter said that if the Japanese wanted to know about "Japan's future national structure (Kokutai), including the emperor's status after surrender, the way to find out is to ask." There were diplomatic channels that could be used for any clarification necessary. The message hinted at a solution but did not suggest one.[76]

When the Allied leaders, after meeting together, issued the Potsdam Proclamation on July 26, Zacharias had something further to use. That document repeated the phrase "unconditional surrender" but still outlined a series of terms, which included the removal from authority of the Japanese responsible for the war, punishment of war criminals, occupation of Japanese territory, and the cession of certain Japanese possessions. Japanese soldiers could return to their homes, Japan could retain some industrial capacity, and the Allied occupation would end when "there had been established in accordance with the freely expressed will of the Japanese people a peacefully inclined and responsible government." The statement said nothing about the emperor because there was still controversy over the question, but it was nonetheless something Zacharias could use to clarify what might happen when the war came to an end.[77]

Meanwhile OWI maintained a growing complement of programs to Japan. Broadcasts continued unabated and were evidently viewed as threatening by those in power, for the Japanese, like the Germans, issued injunctions against listening to the messages and even tried jamming to deny a choice to the home population. At the same time OWI was working on an intensive leaflet campaign. From the start of the war until May 1, 1945, ninety million leaflets had been dropped in the Far East. In the subsequent three months alone ninety-eight million were released. B-29s now dropped leaflets as well as bombs over the home islands. Using the Potsdam declaration in leaflets entitled "Here are the Peace Terms," OWI repeated the demands for surrender and the assurances that the Japanese would neither be enslaved nor destroyed.[78]

More potent propaganda followed on July 27 in the leaflets and broadcasts which warned that at least four of eleven cities mentioned would be destroyed in the next few days. Inhabitants were advised to evacuate to escape harm. The bombs continued to wreak their destruction and soon the same warning was attached to another list of cities. Then on August 6, 1945, the United States dropped an atomic bomb over Hiroshima. That awful device stunned the Japanese. An American broadcast immediately announced the event and emphasized Truman's statement that if the Japanese failed to accept the terms of the ultimatum of July 26, "they may expect a rain of ruin from the air the like of which has never been seen on this earth." Leaflets quickly appeared that announced: "We are in possession of the most destructive explosive ever devised by man." They advised the Japanese to ascertain what had happened at Hiroshima and then to petition for surrender. Other leaflets emphasized Russia's entry into the war. When the Japanese government subsequently made a peace offer but did not inform its own people, OWI conveyed the message in broadcasts and in still another top-speed leaflet campaign. In the final days of the war the propagandists had all the help they wanted and acquitted themselves as they had always hoped they might. On August 14, five days after the explosion of another atomic bomb at Nagasaki, Japan agreed to surrender. The war was won.[79]

Crushing military force, as in Europe, had led to victory. The atomic bombs were only the last weapons in an arsenal that had been systematically used to strip Japan of its conquests and to close in on the homeland itself. But even before the bombs exploded and Russia entered the fight, OWI had helped the Japanese explore the issue of unconditional surrender as the Asian nation considered ending the war. Through the Zacharias broadcasts and the other methods it used, the agency had presented those clarifications that policy makers were willing to accept. Neither Zacharias nor the leaders of OWI went as far as they wanted to go. Given more time and greater flexibility, their approach might have produced results without the final bombs, but the president and his advisers decided otherwise, and OWI understood that it had to work within the confines of higher policy if it was to work at all.

And so once again OWI had assisted the military effort in bringing on the triumphant end. The agency which had started out in a sea of troubles had come into its own by the middle of the war and had then increasingly and successfully integrated its efforts with those of the military in the last campaigns of the war. Some of the early founders of the organization would have frowned on the emphasis placed on military coordination, but they were no longer around, and the agency, as reconstituted, accepted the only role left for it to play. The propagandists involved, both at home and in the field, both in the East and in the West, understood that their task was to assist the military, and once that commitment was made, they were able to do so in ever more creative ways. By working within the confines imposed, they abandoned some of their original expectations but were able to make contributions as important, perhaps, as those they had long had in mind.

Epilogue

American propaganda reached maturity after a long, hard fight in World War II. And with maturity the inflated expectations of the prewar period gave way to more realistic assessments of what propaganda might do. The public fear of the insidious lure of propaganda was now laid to rest, as was the early hope that propaganda could play the decisive role in winning the war. In the end the radio, leaflet, and film campaigns of OWI and other organizations played a useful part in the struggle, but always in conjunction with a host of other weapons that were equally if not more important. Although President Truman cited OWI for an "outstanding contribution to victory" as he abolished the wartime agency by executive order on August 31, 1945, he and others, both in and out of the agency, now had a clearer idea of the contributions propaganda could make. And they understood too that those contributions had come only when the propaganda veered away from its first independent interpretations and began to reflect the more practical American aims in the war.[1]

The exaggerated expectations of the early years were easy enough to understand, for they reflected the popular stereotypes of propaganda so prevalent in the decades before the war. Political scientist Harold D. Lasswell made the point that was echoed in both popular and academic circles in his 1927 study of *Propaganda Technique in the World War*. There he concluded that "when all allowances have been made, and all extravagant estimates pared to the bone, the fact remains that propaganda is one of the most powerful instrumentalities in the modern world." It is, he went on, "the new dynamic of society." Lasswell and others continued to develop that argument in the next decade and their work helped create the image of propaganda as an irresistible force. Even though further psychological research in the late 1930s reduced the sense of fearsome omnipotence, the leaders who carved out a place for propaganda in World War II still believed in the ultimate efficacy of their work.[2]

The men who organized OWI had no doubts about their powers of persuasion. They were not popularizers of propaganda trying to ratify the value of their product, but were rather men at once committed to a cause and convinced they could have an effect on the world at large. They had a message, the truth of which they never doubted, that affirmed the value of democracy over any totalitarian threat, and they were sure that if they could simply repeat it loudly enough and often enough, it would win the hearts and minds of all who heard. Their hopes and expectations rested on the claims of the two decades since the end of the last war, and if the claims in retrospect seemed somewhat naive, they were nonetheless fervently and honestly embraced.

To the propagandists' dismay, the second major war of the century demonstrated not only the limits of their expectations but also the infinitely more complex nature of the entire war effort. OWI found itself constantly jostling with other agencies and organizations that had both a voice in its affairs and responsibility for the larger struggle. The Departments of State, War, and Navy, jealous of their own prerogatives, were loathe to grant OWI the latitude it wanted. Furthermore, Secretaries Hull, Stimson, and Knox did not see much value in propaganda or psychological warfare at all. Congress often misunderstood what the agency was doing and regularly tried to cut back on operations it considered questionable. And the president refused to help, for despite his own impressive powers of persuasion, he was suspicious of propaganda not under his direct control and had his own concerns that took precedence over everything else.

At the same time the propagandists faced the troubling conflicts between the values of democracy and the requirements of war. Unwilling to sacrifice the tenets they considered most important in the struggle, they insisted on using truth as the basis for propaganda in order to affirm the values they were determined would prevail. But their dedication to the "strategy of truth" drew the sometimes justified criticisms of those who wanted to see a more pointed campaign. Sherman H. Dryer, on the basis of long experience with radio, was most explicit when he called the propaganda policy a handicap. The truth, he wrote in 1942, "will enhance the integrity of our officialdom, but it is a moot question whether it will enhance either the efficiency or effectiveness of our efforts to elicit concerted action from the public." Despite such criticism, the leaders of OWI held firm to their own beliefs. They were, to be sure, selective about the materials they used, and when possible they tried to use "the tactics of clarity and vividness" that Harold Lasswell demanded, yet they refused to compromise their convictions. They might well have defined their role in a democratic society more broadly, but their own commitments to what they considered the democratic way made them unwilling to try. Instead they continued to affirm their values, even when the very operation of democracy made their task more difficult to perform, even when partisan squabbling attested to the vitality of the political system but intruded on the activities at hand.[3]

As members of OWI wrestled with their problems and sought to work within self-imposed constraints, they knew that propagandists in other lands were reaching different solutions to many of the problems they all faced. Every major power undertaking some kind of propaganda effort had to decide how it would shape its message to the world at large. And as the American propagandists developed their own lines, they watched their counterparts in other systems respond in predictable ways.

In dictatorships, of course, it was easy for the government to speak with a single voice. In Germany propaganda had long been centralized, and under the direction of Joseph Goebbels the message that emerged was often inflated, exaggerated, and distorted in the interests of achieving the hoped-for victory. On the home front Goebbels was generally successful in maintaining the morale of the German people, although he had some trouble when the promised short war dragged on and on. To the outside world Nazi propaganda supported the blitz effectively, but as the German armies ran into trouble the contradictions and boasts were increasingly evident and undermined the credibility of the whole German line. Japan's propaganda message was also firmly controlled, even though that country had no one propaganda minister. Propaganda in the field, not necessarily confined to the truth, accompanied the great conquests and helped further the Japanese cause. Victories were hailed and defeats hidden from the public eye, for the Japanese war leaders had a message they wanted to convey both to the people who were falling under their rule and to the Japanese at home, and by skillful use of the press and other facilities they got that message across. In the Soviet Union propaganda had long supported the goals of Soviet policy. With Russia part of the Allied cause, propaganda still continued under centralized direction to reflect Russian aims in the war. If materials sometimes had a heavy Marxist-Leninist orientation, that was but a reflection of the control that was part of the Soviet way.[4]

Only when they looked toward Britain could American propagandists find support for their own line of attack. The British political system rested on the same bases as that of the United States, and British propaganda hence suffered from many of the same constraints. There was a minister of information in the War Cabinet, and in 1941 a new Political Warfare Executive took responsibility for foreign propaganda work. Yet Britain endured the same bureaucratic struggles, the same compromises entailed by a rigid dedication to a truthful line of attack, and the same troubles caused by the indifference of a chief executive, despite Prime Minister Winston Churchill's own sensitivity to the power of words.[5]

American propagandists, who could not help comparing their own task with that of propagandists overseas, had no illusions about the limitations they faced—limitations that they believed were inherent in the nature of the society in which they lived. In the light of their own values and commitments, they accepted the constraints and within what they perceived as the realm of the possible they did the best they could.

Yet it was not merely the constraints they saw in the democratic system that limited the thrust of American propaganda. Nor was it the interminable quarreling that characterized Washington for the duration of the war. Rather the greatest limitation came from the nature of the American commitment in the war itself. Propaganda for democracy in the hopeful, idealistic terms of the early founders of OWI was simply out of place in a war that policy makers claimed they were fighting for the purposes of military victory alone. The president and his advisers had a sense of the role the United States could play both during and after the war, and as the struggle continued they moved to define their vision. Yet the first step, they insisted, was winning the war, and they were therefore willing to compromise whenever they felt it might bring a speedy end to hostilities, even when the compromises seemed to call into question the very reasons for going to war. There were reasons, to be sure, for American support for Admiral Jean François Darlan in North Africa, or for Marshal Pietro Badoglio in Italy, and those justifications governed the course of the struggle. The reasons were ones the propagandists did not like, yet slowly they came to understand that they did not really have much choice in the matter. If they wanted to emerge from the bureaucratic mare's nest in which they constantly found themselves, they had to accommodate themselves to what others saw as the realistic aims of the fight. Grudgingly the leaders of OWI began to shift their point of view. As some people left and others arrived to help in an ever-expanding effort, the agency first accepted, then seized, its new line of attack.[6]

The military-oriented propaganda was one result of that transition. The material generated was serviceable, useful, though hardly as crucial as proponents twenty years before might have claimed. But by now most observers understood that and accepted the propaganda for what it was worth. As General Eisenhower noted after the war, "The exact contribution of psychological warfare toward the final victory cannot, of course, be measured in terms of towns destroyed or barriers passed." Yet he still felt that propaganda was "an important contributing factor" in the overall context of the war. Wallace Carroll reflected wisely somewhat later that propaganda was "a weapon of a definite but limited utility." If used extensively enough, under favorable conditions, propaganda could occasionally produce visible results. More concrete contributions were harder to claim.[7]

Still another result of the adjustment of OWI was a portrayal of America and the American way of life that was meant to persuade people around the world of the righteousness of the American cause. That portrait, which established the contours of most of the work done, emerged from an effort to reflect those qualities that might describe ordinary Americans in their ordinary tasks in the optimistic assumption that such a representation could give faith and sustenance around the world. The men who headed OWI knew they had to combat a distorted image of America as a decadent, gangster-ridden society that had emerged from American film and other arts and then been embellished by Axis propaganda. In their directives and in the material they produced the nation appeared as a mighty, dedicated, wholesome country which somehow had the better interests of all mankind at heart.[8]

All American virtues were visible in that general scheme. Americans were sympathetic, even sentimental, according to a directive in October 1942. They combined "an idealistic aspiration towards Utopia with shrewd, hard, horse sense. . . . They are slow to anger, but, once aroused, they finish what they start." Another directive characterized Americans as "an aggressive people, tough and virile—who can take the initiative, who hit hard and like to hit hard." Having conquered a continent, they were now prepared to apply their talents to the military venture at hand. The stories that emerged from those directives reflected the images the policy makers wanted to convey. A booklet entitled *Small Town, U.S.A.* told the story of Alexandria, Indiana. It was a quiet, pleasant town of 4,801, like thousands of other small towns across the country, where the people, always hard-working, dedicated, industrious, now supported the war in the factories and armed forces. Similar stories appeared in *Victory*, set against stories of Americans in action. Americans, quiet and peaceful by nature, could compete with anyone when driven to war.[9]

Most of the propaganda stressed in some way American power and productivity. Early messages sought to create the image of "a gigantic mechanical monster which, slowly put together in the

New World, is now on the move and is gathering momentum as it heads straight for Berlin and Tokyo." Despite Axis successes, the United States was creating the greatest fighting machine ever known. The first issue of *Victory* carried on the cover a color picture of an American bombardier at his controls. The caption underneath said that "Two Million Men Will Fight in 185,000 U.S. Planes." A story inside pointed out that as many as twenty-five bombers a day were already being flown to England. One factory produced a four-engine bomber every hour. The color photos of assembly lines in the center fold depicted the country's productive might. While some readers might remain skeptical, it was an imposing message that *Victory* presented. Other materials conveyed the same impressions. OWI's film *Autobiography of a Jeep* told in sixteen different languages the story of the vehicle that had come to symbolize the war effort wherever it went.[10]

Not only was America powerful; it was committed as well, and it would see the war through to the end. The United States would help lead world affairs, the propagandists said, because the nation clearly provided an example that others might well follow. That theme, which persisted throughout the war and into the period that followed, reflected a traditional American attitude of dominance. Elmer Davis stated the case early for OWI. The basic message was "that we are coming, that we are going to win, and that in the long run everybody will be better off because we won." He continued to make that point throughout his tenure. There was "no question . . . that the victory of our side will prove to be . . . a good thing for the whole world," he told an audience in mid-1943, and he repeated such statements again and again in public appearances that followed.[11]

Other OWI statements elaborated upon Davis's assertions. An Overseas Branch statement of principle in June 1942 said that "the things we stand for and believe in constitute the one ideology that men of freedom and good will can turn to," and it was America's responsibility to make that ideology known. A draft statement for OWI use entitled "America in the World" appeared at the end of the war but reflected perceptions that had been crystallizing all along. "In this interdependent world," the statement said, "there is no region in which the United States can renounce its moral and ideological interest. . . . We believe that 'power cannot be left idle like money in an old sock; it must be used constantly and wisely.' But we believe further that by serving our national interest, intelligently conceived, we serve the general interest as well." America would act as it saw best, OWI claimed, and the entire world would benefit.[12]

In part to prepare the world for an important American role, in part to engender sympathy for the Allied cause, OWI constantly sought to generate an appreciation for the American way of life. It issued stories on everything from ballet to baseball. It showed Americans fighting boll weevils, planting victory gardens, and going to church. And it showed them governing themselves. *Victory* was filled with pieces on the Iowa state legislature, Rochester's city manager form of government, and the electoral process on which all government was based. All in all, the treatment was overwhelmingly optimistic. There were faults, to be sure, in American society. But even while reporting problems to the rest of the world, OWI slanted them so that the overall picture remained hopeful. As a coal strike threatened in mid-1943, an OWI directive noted that bad news should be reported, but presented as an example of the democratic process in action. Blacks should be treated "in a casual, matter-of-fact way," another directive indicated. Stories should neither avoid them nor go to excessive lengths to play them up. The racial disturbances that erupted during the war years reflected difficulties that American democracy was prepared to confront. They too could be acknowledged with the note that progress was always taking place.[13]

OWI, in that composite picture, had finally hit on a vision of America that was not only noncontroversial but which reflected the ways that others represented the war as well. The same virtues came through in the *Why We Fight* films that producer Frank Capra made for the War Department. They were reflected too in American advertising for the duration of the struggle, as public relations men sketched the war as a struggle for the American way of life and stressed the components—both spiritual and material—that to them made America great. And perhaps most important of all, the general image seemed consonant with the way ordinary Americans viewed the war. Both Bill Mauldin and Ernie Pyle noted the lack of interest among soldiers in the large causes or politics of war. Soldiers were interested in other things—home above all—as John Hersey learned in writing about the marines on Guadalcanal. They hungered for the simple things they remembered and longed to see once more. Judged against the broad spectrum of home front life, OWI's picture of aims and aspirations, of power and purpose, was incomplete to be sure, but it captured the optimism and confidence usually felt, met with almost universal approval, and was in the end the part of OWI's work that came across best.[14]

The propaganda of war had finally come to represent the war being fought. The image of America was an encouraging one and probably buoyed up Americans at home even as it held out hope for people in occupied lands in the desolate days of the war. Afterwards that image, widely held throughout the United States, became a two-edged sword. Struggling to get along in the postwar world, Americans held on to their image of a powerful and righteous nation. Efforts to deal with other states in the years that followed were sometimes complicated by an unfortunate American sense of superiority.

Still, that result was an unintended if perhaps unavoidable consequence of the war. Engaged in the mightiest struggle of all time, the United States had to use all resources available. The picture of America that emerged was often all that the State, War, and Navy Departments, all that the White House, would allow. If it was inflated, it nevertheless reflected the way most ordinary Americans viewed themselves as they worked to defeat the Axis powers. In the end American propaganda reflected American policy, and indeed America itself.

Notes

PROLOGUE

1 Harold D. Lasswell, *Propaganda Technique in the World War,* pp. 10, 18–24, 42.

2 James R. Mock and Cedric Larson, *Words that Won the War: The Story of the Committee on Public Information, 1917–1919,* p. 4; LaMar Seal Mackay, "Domestic Operations of the Office of War Information in World War II" (Ph.D. diss., The University of Wisconsin, 1966), p. 178.

3 [Edward P. Lilly], "Government Information before June, 1942: 'Confusion Confused' " (Chapter 1 of official OWI history), p. 2, Box 64, Records of the Office of War Information, RG 208, The National Archives, Washington, D.C.; Mock and Larson, *Words that Won the War,* p. 235; George Creel, *How We Advertised America,* p. 4.

4 William E. Leuchtenburg, *The Perils of Prosperity, 1914–1932,* pp. 44–46; Walton E. Bean, "George Creel and His Critics: A Study of the Attacks on the Committee on Public Information, 1917–1919" (Ph.D. diss., Graduate Division of the University of California, 1941), pp. 6, 10, 13; Paul M. A. Linebarger, *Psychological Warfare,* p. 68; Daniel Lerner, *Sykewar: Psychological Warfare against Germany, D-Day to VE-Day,* p. 15.

5 Barry Alan Marks, "The Idea of Propaganda in America" (Ph.D. diss., University of Minnesota, 1957), pp. xi, 24, 65–66, 69–71, 160–61.

6 James Duane Squires, *British Propaganda at Home and in the United States, From 1914 to 1917;* H. C. Peterson, *Propaganda for War: The Campaign against American Neutrality, 1914–1917.*

7 Otis Pease, *The Responsibilities of American Advertising,* pp. 2, 11, 18, 87, 97, 109–11, 172, 203; Frank W. Fox, "Advertising

and the Second World War: A Study in Private Propaganda"
(Ph.D. diss., Stanford University, 1973), pp. 36–37, 58; John
Morton Blum, *The Promise of America: An Historical Inquiry*, pp.
115–18.

8 Marks, "Idea of Propaganda," pp. 96, 122; John Morton
Blum, *V Was for Victory: Politics and American Culture During
World War II*, p. 21.

9 Address of the President of the United States, *Congressional
Record*, 77th Cong., 1st sess., vol. 87, pt. 1, 44–47 (6 January
1941); Declaration of Principles, Known as the Atlantic Char-
ter, By the President of the United States of America and the
Prime Minister of the United Kingdom, 14 August 1941, U.S.
Department of State, *Executive Agreement Series*, no. 236.

CHAPTER 1

1 Peter Sage, "From Poetry to Prose: Archibald MacLeish and
the Defense of Democracy" (Yale Misc. Mss. 70, Manuscripts
and Archives, Yale University Library, New Haven, Connecticut), p. 3; "MacLeish, Archibald," *The National Cyclopaedia of
American Biography*, vol. F, pp. 39–40.

2 Sage, "From Poetry to Prose," pp. 15–16; Richard H. Pells,
*Radical Visions and American Dreams: Culture and Social Thought
in the Depression Years*, pp. 183, 314; Signi Lenea Falk, *Archibald MacLeish*, p. 79.

3 Sage, "From Poetry to Prose," pp. 17, 19; Interview with
Archibald MacLeish, 4 November 1974.

4 Archibald MacLeish, "The Irresponsibles," pp. 116–17.

5 Archibald MacLeish, "The Affirmation," p. 12; Archibald
MacLeish, "The Attack on the Scholar's World," p. 4; Mac-
Leish, "The Irresponsibles," pp. 110–11.

6 MacLeish, "The Affirmation," p. 14; Archibald MacLeish,
"Look to the Spirit Within You," p. 21; Archibald Mac-
Leish, "The American Cause," p. 116.

7 Archibald MacLeish, "We Cannot Escape History," p. 41;
Archibald MacLeish, Address at Inaugural Dinner, Freedom
House, 19 March 1942, Beinecke Rare Book and Manuscript

Library, Yale University, New Haven, Connecticut; Archibald MacLeish, *American Opinion and the War: The Rede Lecture Delivered before the University of Cambridge on 30 July 1942,* p. 28.

8 MacLeish, Address at Inaugural Dinner, Freedom House, 19 March 1942, Beinecke Library; Archibald MacLeish, Press Conference, 21 January 1942, Box 42, Records of OWI.

9 Profile of Robert Emmet Sherwood, November 1942, Box 18, Records of OWI; Walter J. Meserve, *Robert E. Sherwood: Reluctant Moralist,* pp. 20–22.

10 John Mason Brown, *The Worlds of Robert E. Sherwood: Mirror to His Times, 1896–1939,* p. 193; R. G., "The Author," p. 8; Meserve, *Robert E. Sherwood,* p. 142.

11 Brown, *Worlds,* pp. 13, 90, 96, 119, 195, 208, 210, 220; Robert Emmet Sherwood, *Idiot's Delight,* pp. 189–90.

12 Brown, *Worlds,* p. 347; Sherwood to Walter Winchell, 2 October 1938, PPF 7356, Franklin D. Roosevelt Papers, Franklin D. Roosevelt Library, Hyde Park, New York.

13 Robert Emmet Sherwood, *Abe Lincoln in Illinois,* p. 139; Alfred Haworth Jones, *Roosevelt's Image Brokers: Poets, Playwrights, and the Use of the Lincoln Symbol,* pp. 45–46; Meserve, *Robert E. Sherwood,* pp. 137, 141.

14 Meserve, *Robert E. Sherwood,* pp. 142, 144; Robert E. Sherwood, *There Shall Be No Night,* pp. 153–54, 162.

15 Robert E. Sherwood, "Rush All Possible Aid to Britain!" p. 15; Meserve, *Robert E. Sherwood,* p. 15; Robert E. Sherwood, "The Front Line Is in Our Hearts," pp. 21, 103.

16 John Mason Brown, *The Ordeal of a Playwright: Robert E. Sherwood and the Challenge of War,* pp. 82–89; Sherwood, "Rush All Possible Aid to Britain!"; Sherwood, "The Front Line Is in Our Hearts."

17 Brown, *Worlds,* pp. 208, 385–86; Brown, *Ordeal,* p. 101; Meserve, *Robert E. Sherwood,* pp. 168, 170.

18 Robert E. Sherwood, "The Power of Truth," p. 62.

19 Roger Manvell and Heinrich Fraenkel, *Dr. Goebbels: His Life and Death,* pp. 178, 192, 194; Adolf Hitler, *Mein Kampf,* p. 181; Willi A. Boelcke, "Editor's Introduction," *The Secret Con-*

ferences of Dr. Goebbels: The Nazi War Propaganda, 1939–43, pp. xvi–xvii; Anthony Rhodes, *Propaganda: The Art of Persuasion: World War II,* pp. 13, 16, 18–19; William L. Shirer, *The Rise and Fall of the Third Reich: A History of Nazi Germany,* pp. 247–48.

20 Arthur M. Schlesinger, Jr., *The Age of Roosevelt: The Coming of the New Deal,* pp. 534–35; William E. Leuchtenburg, *Franklin D. Roosevelt and the New Deal, 1932–1940,* pp. 328–29.

21 Allen Irving Safianow, "The Office of War Information" (Master's thesis, Cornell University, 1968), pp. 1, 4–6; David Lloyd Jones, "The U.S. Office of War Information and American Public Opinion during World War II, 1939–1945" (Ph.D. diss., State University of New York at Binghamton, 1976), pp. 14–16.

22 [Lilly], "Government Information," pp. 6–7; Richard W. Steele, "Preparing the Public for War: Efforts to Establish a National Propaganda Agency, 1940–41," p. 1645, n. 16; Michael Darrock and Joseph P. Dorn, "Davis and Goliath: The OWI and Its Gigantic Assignment," pp. 227, 229; Safianow, "The Office of War Information," pp. 6–10.

23 [Lilly], "Government Information," pp. 7–9; Darrock and Dorn, "Davis and Goliath," p. 229; United States Bureau of the Budget, *The United States at War: Development and Administration of the War Program by the Federal Government,* p. 211; Sydney Weinberg, "What to Tell America: The Writers' Quarrel in the Office of War Information," pp. 73–74.

24 Blum, *V Was for Victory,* p. 17; Steele, "Preparing the Public for War," pp. 1647–48; Safianow, "The Office of War Information," pp. 12–14; Weinberg, "What to Tell America," p. 75.

25 [Lilly], "Government Information," pp. 14–15; Steele, "Preparing the Public for War," p. 1652; Executive Order 8922, Establishing an Office of Facts and Figures in the Office for Emergency Management in the Executive Office of the President, 24 October 1941, *Federal Register* 6, no. 210 (28 October 1941), p. 5477.

26 MacLeish to Harry Hopkins, 27 October 1941, Harry Hop-

kins Papers, Franklin D. Roosevelt Library, Hyde Park, New York; Blum, *V Was for Victory*, p. 22.

27 *New York Herald Tribune*, 9 October 1941; [Lilly], "Government Information," pp. 14, 21; Darrock and Dorn, "Davis and Goliath," p. 229.

28 Weinberg, "What to Tell America," p. 76; Blum, *V Was for Victory*, pp. 22–23; [Lilly], "Government Information," p. 16; Darrock and Dorn, "Davis and Goliath," p. 229.

29 [Lilly], "Government Information," p. 16; Blum, *V Was for Victory*, p. 23.

30 MacLeish to Harold Smith, 20 February 1942, Archibald MacLeish Papers, Library of Congress, Washington, D.C.

31 Harold F. Gosnell, "Organization of Information Activities for Defense and War, 1940–1942," Series 41.3, Unit 169, pp. 16.2, 16.3, 16.4, Records of the Bureau of the Budget, RG 51, The National Archives, Washington, D.C.

32 "Rockefeller, Nelson Aldrich," *The National Cyclopaedia of American Biography*, vol. I, p. 196; Bureau of the Budget, *United States at War*, p. 218; Gosnell, "Organization of Information Activities," p. 16.4.

33 Corey Ford, *Donovan of OSS*, pp. 11–12, 69–75, 98–105, 107, 110; R. Harris Smith, *OSS: The Secret History of America's First Central Intelligence Agency*, p. 1; "Donovan Strategy," *Newsweek*, 17 November 1941, p. 21.

34 Gosnell, "Organization of Information Activities," pp. 288–91; Ford, *Donovan of OSS*, p. 108.

35 "Report of Elmer Davis to the President on the Office of War Information," printed in U.S., Congress, House, Foreign Operations and Government Information Subcommittee of the Committee on Government Operations, *Hearings, Government Information Plans and Policies, Part 2*, 88th Cong., 1st sess., 1963 (hereafter cited as "Report of Elmer Davis"), p. 244; R. Harris Smith, *OSS*, pp. 1, 21; Ford, *Donovan of OSS*, pp. 109, 110, 112, 174; William Phillips, *Ventures in Diplomacy*, p. 335.

36 Bureau of the Budget, *United States at War*, pp. 218–19; [Lilly], "Government Information," pp. 9–10; Personal notes of OWI historian from a luncheon conference with

Llewellyn White, 4 August 1944, Box 43, Records of OWI.
37 [Lilly], "Government Information," pp. 10–11; Sydney Stahl
   Weinberg, "Wartime Propaganda in a Democracy: America's
   Twentieth Century Information Agencies" (Ph.D. diss., Columbia University, 1966), p. 335; R. Harris Smith, *OSS*, p. 2.
38 "Report of Elmer Davis," p. 221; Weinberg, "Wartime Propaganda," pp. 338–40; Plan for Political and Psychological
   Warfare against Germany, 4 March 1942, Box 35, Records
   of OWI; Sherwood to Harry Hopkins, 17 December 1941,
   Hopkins Papers; Bureau of the Budget, *United States at War*,
   p. 219.
39 Weinberg, "Wartime Propaganda," p. 217; Ford, *Donovan of
   OSS*, p. 125; Gosnell, "Organization of Information Activities," p. 325.
40 Ford, *Donovan of OSS*, p. 126; [Edward P. Lilly], "Formulation of OWI Charter" (Chapter 2 of official OWI history), p.
   9, Box 64, Records of OWI.
41 Memorandum, Edgar A. Mowrer to Elmer Davis, 23 July
   1942, Box 7, Records of OWI; Charles A. H. Thomson,
   Overseas Information Service of the United States Government, p. 21;
   Weinberg, "Wartime Propaganda," p. 343; Breckinridge
   Long, *The War Diary of Breckinridge Long: Selections from the Years
   1939–1944*, pp. 234, 257.
42 Memorandum, Sherwood to Donovan, 20 October 1941, OF
   4485, Roosevelt Papers; Darrock and Dorn, "Davis and Goliath," p. 227; [Lilly], "Formulation of OWI Charter," p. 1;
   A. H. Feller, "OWI on the Home Front," p. 55.
43 Milton S. Eisenhower, *The President Is Calling*, pp. 22, 53, 69,
   81, 93; "Eisenhower, Milton Stover," *The National Cyclopaedia of American Biography*, vol. I, p. 332; [Lilly], "Formulation
   of OWI Charter," pp. 5–6; Gosnell, "Organization of Information Activities," p. 339; Harold F. Gosnell, "The Framing
   of the Office of War Information Executive Order," Series
   41.3, Unit 160, pp. 11–14, Records of the Bureau of the
   Budget; Harold F. Gosnell, "Overhead Organization of the
   Office of War Information," Series 41.3, Unit 170, p. 1, Records of the Bureau of the Budget.

44 [Lilly], "Formulation of OWI Charter," pp. 6–7; Gosnell, "Organization of Information Activities," pp. 339–41; Gosnell, "Framing of the Office of War Information Executive Order," p. 15; Bureau of the Budget, *United States at War,* pp. 220–21.

45 [Lilly], "Formulation of OWI Charter," pp. 7–8; Gosnell, "Organization of Information Activities," pp. 341–42; Gosnell, "Framing of the Office of War Information Executive Order," pp. 20–23; Bureau of the Budget, *United States at War,* p. 221.

46 [Lilly], "Formulation of OWI Charter," pp. 8–11; Gosnell, "Framing of the Office of War Information Executive Order," pp. 23–26; Gosnell, "Organization of Information Activities," pp. 342–43; Memorandum, Donovan to Roosevelt, 16 May 1942, PSF 102, Roosevelt Papers.

47 [Lilly], "Formulation of OWI Charter," p. 11; Gosnell, "Organization of Information Activities," p. 344.

48 Richard Lauterbach, "Elmer Davis and the News," pp. 13, 55; "Man of Sense," *Time,* 22 June 1942, p. 21; N. C. [Norman Cousins], "Elmer Davis, Director, Office of War Information," p. 8; "A Job for Elmer Davis," *The New Republic,* 22 June 1942, p. 848; MacLeish to Roosevelt, 16 June 1942, OF 4619, Roosevelt Papers; H. I. Brock, "Uncle Sam Hires a Reporter," p. 8.

49 Brock, "Uncle Sam Hires a Reporter," p. 8; [Lilly], "Formulation of OWI Charter," p. 12; Profile of Elmer Davis, August 1943, Box 42, Records of OWI.

50 Elmer Davis, "Broadcasting the Outbreak of War," p. 581; David Holbrook Culbert, *News for Everyman: Radio and Foreign Affairs in Thirties America,* p. 133; Roger Burlingame, *Don't Let Them Scare You: The Life and Times of Elmer Davis,* p. 155; Darrock and Dorn, "Davis and Goliath," pp. 229–30; Brock, "Uncle Sam Hires a Reporter," p. 8.

51 Davis to Louis Ludlow, 11 May 1944, Box 11, Records of OWI; Burlingame, *Don't Let Them Scare You,* pp. 121, 151; Elmer Davis, "Roosevelt: The Rich Man's Alibi," p. 468; Philip Chalfant Ensley, "The Political and Social Thought of

Elmer Davis" (Ph.D. diss., The Ohio State University, 1965), pp. 74, 81.

52 Elmer Davis, "The Road from Munich," p. 40; Elmer Davis, "The War and America," pp. 450–62; Elmer Davis, "We Lose the Next War," p. 347; Elmer Davis, "Is England Worth Fighting For?" p. 35; Elmer Davis, "America and the War," p. 12; Lauterbach, "Elmer Davis and the News," p. 58; Culbert, *News for Everyman,* pp. 146–47; Alfred Haworth Jones, "The Making of an Interventionist on the Air: Elmer Davis and CBS News," pp. 77–93.

53 Burlingame, *Don't Let Them Scare You,* p. 186.

54 "Notes and Comment," in "The Talk of the Town," *The New Yorker,* 14 March 1942, p. 13; Burlingame, *Don't Let Them Scare You,* pp. 186–87; Davis to Hopkins, 25 March 1942, Hopkins Papers; Lauterbach, "Elmer Davis and the News," p. 13.

55 [Lilly], "Formulation of OWI Charter," p. 13; Burlingame, *Don't Let Them Scare You,* p. 193.

56 Executive Order 9182, Consolidating Certain War Information Functions Into An Office of War Information, 13 June 1942, *Federal Register* 7, no. 117 (16 June 1942), pp. 4468–69.

57 [Norman Cousins] N. C., "Elmer Davis," p. 8; [Lilly], "Formulation of OWI Charter," pp. 14, 16.

58 [Lilly], "Formulation of OWI Charter," pp. 16–17; Elmer Davis, Lecture—Role of Information in World War II (delivered at the Naval War College), 16 November 1951, pp. 7–8, Elmer Davis Papers, Library of Congress, Washington, D.C.

59 Executive Order 9182, pp. 4468–69; [Lilly], "Formulation of OWI Charter," pp. 17–18; Creel to Davis, 4 August 1942, Davis Papers.

60 Eisenhower, *The President Is Calling,* p. 128; [Lilly], "Formulation of OWI Charter," pp. 20–21.

61 [Lilly], "Formulation of OWI Charter," pp. 18–19; Creel to Davis, 4 August 1942, Davis Papers.

62 Eisenhower, *The President Is Calling,* p. 128; Brock, "Uncle Sam Hires a Reporter," p. 8.

CHAPTER 2

1 Feller, "OWI on the Home Front," pp. 56–57.

2 Lester G. Hawkins, Jr., and George S. Pettee, "OWI—Organization and Problems," p. 21.

3 "Cowles, Gardner, Jr.," *Current Biography: Who's News and Why, 1943,* pp. 145–48; "Dynasty in Radio," *Business Week,* 4 November 1944, pp. 81–84.

4 MacLeish, *American Opinion and the War,* pp. 13–16, 27–28; Memorandum, Basic Policy Statement on OWI Objectives, MacLeish to Davis, Eisenhower, Sherwood, and Cowles, 19 August 1942, Box 5, Records of OWI.

5 Memorandum, MacLeish to Davis, Eisenhower, Cowles, Sherwood, 30 November 1942, Box 6, Records of OWI.

6 Memorandum, Sherwood to Davis, Eisenhower, MacLeish, and Cowles, 2 December 1942, Box 6, Records of OWI; Memorandum, MacLeish to Eisenhower, 2 December 1942, Box 6, Records of OWI; Davis, at bottom of Memorandum, MacLeish to Davis, Eisenhower, Cowles, Sherwood, 30 November 1942, Box 6, Records of OWI; Memorandum, Eisenhower to MacLeish, 1 December 1942, Box 6, Records of OWI; Memorandum, Eisenhower to MacLeish, 3 December 1942, Box 6, Records of OWI.

7 Memorandum, MacLeish to Eisenhower, 5 December 1942, Box 6, Records of OWI; Davis note at bottom of Memorandum, MacLeish to Davis, 7 December 1942, Box 6, Records of OWI.

8 MacLeish to Davis, 12 August 1942, MacLeish Papers; MacLeish to Davis, 17 October 1942, MacLeish Papers; Memorandum, MacLeish to Eisenhower, 5 December 1942, Box 6, Records of OWI; *New York Herald Tribune,* 31 January 1943.

9 Donald F. Drummond, "Cordell Hull, 1933–1944," pp. 184–85, 189, 199, 209; Schlesinger, *Coming of the New Deal,* p. 190; Dean Acheson, *Present at the Creation: My Years in the State Department,* pp. 30–31.

10 Elting E. Morison, *Turmoil and Tradition: A Study in the Life and Times of Henry L. Stimson,* pp. 378, 424; John Morton Blum,

From the Morgenthau Diaries: Years of War, 1941–1945, pp. 241–42; Cordell Hull, *The Memoirs of Cordell Hull*, 2:1109–10; [Henry A. Wallace], *The Price of Vision: The Diary of Henry A. Wallace, 1942–1946*, p. 67.

11 Drummond, "Cordell Hull," p. 195.

12 Weinberg, "Wartime Propaganda," pp. 219, 342, 344–45; Thomson, *Overseas Information Service*, p. 21; Gosnell, "Organization of Information Activities," pp. 310, 324; "Report of Elmer Davis," pp. 232–34, 237; [Edward P. Lilly], "Developing Overseas Operations" (Chapter 4 of official OWI history), pp. 56–57, Box 64, Records of OWI; Bureau of the Budget, *United States at War*, p. 231; Harold F. Gosnell, "Relationship between Planning and Intelligence in Overseas Propaganda," Series 41.3, Unit 171, p. 57, Records of the Bureau of the Budget; Memorandum on an interview with Robert Sherwood, Harold F. Gosnell to Pendleton Herring, 26 May 1943, Series 41.3, Unit 153d, Records of the Bureau of the Budget; U.S., Congress, Senate, Subcommittee of the Committee on Appropriations, *Hearings, National War Agencies Appropriation Bill for 1944*, 78th Cong., 1st sess., 1943, p. 236; Davis to W. Warren Barbour, 19 November 1943, Box 11, Records of OWI; Long, *War Diary*, p. 257.

13 Morison, *Turmoil and Tradition*, pp. 167–68, 388–90, 399, 402, 410, 414, 425, 427.

14 "Running the War," *Time*, 7 September 1942, pp. 24–25; "End of a Strenuous Life," *Time*, 8 May 1944, p. 14; "In Line of Duty," *Newsweek*, 8 May 1944, p. 31; "Knox, [William] Frank[lin]," *The National Cyclopaedia of American Biography*, vol. F, pp. 25–26.

15 Ernest K. Lindley, "Marshall and King," p. 37; "King, Ernest Joseph," *Current Biography: Who's News and Why, 1942*, pp. 458–60; "One Year of War," *Time*, 7 December 1942, p. 30; Robert McCormick, "King of the Navy," p. 20; U.S., Congress, House, Subcommittee of the Committee on Appropriations, *Hearings, Second Supplemental National Defense Appropriation Bill for 1943*, 77th Cong., 2nd sess., 1942, pp. 449–50.

16 U.S., Congress, House, Subcommittee of the Committee on Appropriations, *Hearings, National War Agencies Appropriation Bill for 1944,* 78th Cong., 1st sess., 1943, p. 700; "Report of Elmer Davis," p. 224; Elmer Davis, "War Information," p. 30.

17 Hull to Davis, 8 July 1942, Box 5, Records of OWI; Davis to Hull, 10 July 1942, Box 5, Records of OWI; "Report of Elmer Davis," p. 237.

18 Diary of Henry L. Stimson, vol. 39, 17 June 1942, p. 96, Henry L. Stimson Papers, Yale University Library, New Haven, Connecticut; Davis, Account of First Day in Office, 16 June 1942, Davis Papers; Richard N. Current, *Secretary Stimson: A Study in Statecraft,* p. 201; Bruce Catton, *The War Lords of Washington,* p. 190.

19 Catton, *The War Lords of Washington,* p. 192; Darrock and Dorn, "Davis and Goliath," p. 233; "Report of Elmer Davis," p. 225.

20 Diary of Henry L. Stimson, vol. 39, 9 July 1942, pp. 152–53; "First Time Up for Elmer," *The New Republic,* 20 July 1942, p. 83.

21 Diary of Henry L. Stimson, vol. 39, 10 July 1942, pp. 157–58; "Report of Elmer Davis," p. 225.

22 Davis, Lecture—Role of Information in World War II, 16 November 1951, p. 29, Davis Papers.

23 Burlingame, *Don't Let Them Scare You,* p. 200; Darrock and Dorn, "Davis and Goliath," p. 234.

24 Davis, Account of First Day in Office, 16 June 1942, Davis Papers; Davis, Lecture—Role of Information in World War II, 16 November 1951, pp. 25–26, Davis Papers; Burlingame, *Don't Let Them Scare You,* p. 201.

25 Davis, Lecture—Role of Information in World War II, 16 November 1951, pp. 26–28, Davis Papers; Burlingame, *Don't Let Them Scare You,* p. 202; Lauterbach, "Elmer Davis and the News," p. 55.

26 Burlingame, *Don't Let Them Scare You,* pp. 202, 204; Darrock and Dorn, "Davis and Goliath," p. 234.

27 Martha Byrd Hoyle, *A World in Flames: A History of World War*

II, pp. 125–35, 201; Davis, Lecture—Role of Information in World War II, 16 November 1951, p. 28, Davis Papers.

28 Minutes, Board of War Information, 16 December 1942, Box 41, Records of OWI; DeVoto to Davis, 28 March 1944, Davis Papers.

29 Mary Elizabeth Clark to Roosevelt, 9 June 1942, OF 5015, Roosevelt Papers.

30 Richard Polenberg, *War and Society: The United States, 1941–1945*, pp. 19–22; Darrock and Dorn, "Davis and Goliath," pp. 235–36.

31 Catton, *The War Lords of Washington*, pp. 155–75; Polenberg, *War and Society*, pp. 16–18; Richard R. Lingeman, *Don't You Know There's a War On? The American Home Front, 1941–1945*, p. 238; Jerome S. Bruner, "OWI and the American Public," p. 132; Blum, *V Was for Victory*, p. 35.

32 Catton, *The War Lords of Washington*, p. 187; William J. Small, *Political Power and the Press*, p. 18.

33 Edwin Emery and Henry Ladd Smith, *The Press and America*, pp. 588–89; Delbert Clark, *Washington Dateline*, pp. 310–11; Small, *Political Power and the Press*, pp. 83–86.

34 Bruner, "OWI and the American Public," pp. 129–33; Weinberg, "What to Tell America," p. 78.

35 Weinberg, "What to Tell America," pp. 75–76, 82; " 'We Could Lose this War'—A Communiqué From the OWI," *Newsweek*, 17 August 1942, p. 30; *New York Herald Tribune*, 8 September 1943.

36 *The Unconquered People*, Box 1697, Records of OWI; *Divide and Conquer*, Box 1697, Records of OWI; *The Thousand Million*, Box 1697, Records of OWI.

37 *How to Raise $16 Billion*, Box 1697, Records of OWI.

38 *Battle Stations for All*, pp. 1, 5, 8, 46, Box 1697, Records of OWI.

39 *Negroes and the War*, Records of OWI and Franklin D. Roosevelt Library; David Lloyd Jones, "The U.S. Office of War Information," pp. 357–60.

40 Richard Dyer MacCann, *The People's Films: A Political History*

of U.S. Government Motion Pictures, p. 118; Gregory D. Black and Clayton R. Koppes, "OWI Goes to the Movies: The Bureau of Intelligence's Criticism of Hollywood, 1942–1943," p. 48; Clayton R. Koppes and Gregory D. Black, "What to Show the World: The Office of War Information and Hollywood, 1942–1945," pp. 89–90.

41 MacCann, *The People's Films,* pp. 119, 129–30, 135–37.

42 Dorothy B. Jones, "The Hollywood War Film: 1942–1944," p. 13; Peter A. Soderbergh, "The Grand Illusion: Hollywood and World War II, 1930–1945," p. 17; Walter Wanger, "OWI and Motion Pictures," pp. 105–06, 108; Memorandum, Taylor M. Mills to Truman K. Gibson, Jr., 1 May 1944, Box 1484, Records of OWI.

43 Black and Koppes, "OWI Goes to the Movies," pp. 44, 46, 49; Wanger, "OWI and Motion Pictures," p. 100; Lingeman, *Don't You Know There's a War On?* pp. 182–84.

44 Black and Koppes, "OWI Goes to the Movies," pp. 44, 49–52; Koppes and Black, "What to Show the World," pp. 90–92.

45 Dorothy B. Jones, "The Hollywood War Film," p. 10; Black and Koppes, "OWI Goes to the Movies," p. 50.

46 Dorothy B. Jones, "The Hollywood War Film," pp. 4–6; Soderbergh, "The Grand Illusion," p. 18; Black and Koppes, "OWI Goes to the Movies," pp. 53–54.

47 Black and Koppes, "OWI Goes to the Movies," p. 57.

48 William B. Lewis, Excerpts from speech—Radio Goes to War (delivered before Summer Radio Institute of the University of Chicago), 4 August 1942, Box 638, Records of OWI.

49 Ibid.; Report on Radio, Domestic Radio Bureau, 15 April 1943, Box 613, Records of OWI; Robert J. Landry, "The Impact of OWI on Broadcasting," pp. 113–14.

50 Lewis, Excerpts from speech—Radio Goes to War, 4 August 1942, Box 638, Records of OWI; William B. Lewis to H. V. Kaltenborn, 19 August 1942, Box 599, Records of OWI; Betty W. Carter to Allen Campbell, 15 July 1943, Box 685, Records of OWI; Betty W. Carter to Arthur Marquette, 13 May 1944, Box 685, Records of OWI.

51 Script of Jack Benny on the "Victory Parade," 23 August 1942, Box 610, Records of OWI.

52 Script of Fibber McGee and Molly, 16 August 1943, Box 704, Records of OWI.

53 Summary of Radio Campaign: Use More Eggs Now, 27 March–14 May 1944 and 12–18 June 1944, Box 707, Records of OWI; Summary of Radio Campaign: Black Markets in Meat, 12 April–9 May 1943, Box 707, Records of OWI.

54 Feller, "OWI on the Home Front," p. 64; Malcolm Cowley, "The Sorrows of Elmer Davis," pp. 592–93; Polenberg, *War and Society*, pp. 52–53; Weinberg, "What to Tell America," p. 80; Catton, *The War Lords of Washington*, pp. 188–89.

55 Weinberg, "What to Tell America," pp. 81–84; Weinberg, "Wartime Propaganda," p. 256.

56 Weinberg, "What to Tell America," pp. 84–85; Cowley, "The Sorrows of Elmer Davis," pp. 591, 593.

57 "Publishers, Writers Quit OWI," *Publishers' Weekly*, 17 April 1943, p. 1576; Weinberg, "What to Tell America," pp. 84–85; Burlingame, *Don't Let Them Scare You*, p. 192.

58 "Struggle in the OWI," *The New Republic*, 26 April 1943, p. 551; Cowley, "The Sorrows of Elmer Davis," p. 592; Weinberg, "What to Tell America," pp. 86–87.

59 Weinberg, "What to Tell America," p. 86; MacLeish to Hopkins, 9 April 1943, MacLeish Papers.

60 Statement for the Press, MacLeish Papers.

61 Cowley, "The Sorrows of Elmer Davis," p. 591; Weinberg, "What to Tell America," pp. 87–88; "Davis on the Griddle," *Life*, 3 May 1943, p. 25; "Struggle in the OWI," p. 551.

62 Polenberg, *War and Society*, pp. 73–74, 79–84, 184, 187–90, 192–93; Richard Norman Chapman, "Contours of Public Policy, 1939–1945" (Ph.D. diss., Yale University, 1976).

63 Burlingame, *Don't Let Them Scare You*, p. 218; *Christian Science Monitor*, 28 April 1943.

64 "Roosevelt of America," *Victory*, vol. 1, no. 1, copy in Franklin D. Roosevelt Library; "Congress Blast Against OWI Portends Assault on New Deal," *Newsweek*, 22 February 1943, p. 25; *New York Times*, 11 February 1943.

65 "Congress Blast Against OWI," p. 26; *New York Times,* 11 February 1943; U.S., Congress, House, Subcommittee of the Committee on Appropriations, *Hearings, National War Agencies Appropriation Bill for 1944,* 78th Cong., 1st sess., 1943, p. 746.

66 "Report of Elmer Davis," pp. 239–40; Safianow, "The Office of War Information," pp. 45–46, 51–52; U.S., Congress, Senate, Subcommittee of the Committee on Appropriations, *Hearings, National War Agencies Appropriation Bill for 1944,* 78th Cong., 1st sess., 1943, p. 199; U.S., Congress, House, Subcommittee of the Committee on Appropriations, *Hearings, National War Agencies Appropriation Bill for 1944,* 78th Cong., 1st sess., 1943, p. 1311.

67 *New York Times,* 17 June 1943; I. F. Stone, "Bureaucrat Bites Press," p. 6; "Davis the Gadfly," *Newsweek,* 28 June 1943, p. 84.

68 Gaddis Smith, *American Diplomacy during the Second World War,* pp. 8, 10; Raymond G. O'Connor, *Diplomacy for Victory: FDR and Unconditional Surrender,* pp. 33–34; Robert A. Divine, *Roosevelt and World War II,* pp. 57–58; Robert A. Divine, *Second Chance: The Triumph of Internationalism in America During World War II,* pp. 49, 83–84, 185; Gabriel Kolko, *The Politics of War: The World and United States Foreign Policy, 1943–1945,* pp. 4, 167, 242.

69 Schlesinger, *Coming of the New Deal,* pp. 534–36; Leuchtenburg, *Franklin D. Roosevelt,* pp. 328–29; Arthur M. Schlesinger, Jr., *A Thousand Days: John F. Kennedy in the White House,* p. 686; Raymond F. Moley, *After Seven Years: A Political Analysis of the New Deal,* p. 10; Donald M. Nelson, *Arsenal of Democracy: The Story of American War Production,* pp. 112–15; Eleanor Roosevelt, *This I Remember,* p. 2; Marriner S. Eccles, *Beckoning Frontiers: Public and Personal Recollections,* pp. 243–44, 327–30.

70 Blum, *From the Morgenthau Diaries: Years of War,* pp. 75–77.

71 Weinberg, "What to Tell America," p. 83.

72 U.S., Congress, House, Committee on Appropriations, *National War Agencies Appropriation Bill, 1944,* H. Rept. 556, 78th Cong., 1st sess., 1943, p. 22 [Serial no. 10762]; *Congressional*

Record, 78th Cong., 1st sess., vol. 89, pt. 5, 5983, 5985, 5990, 5992, 6021, 6103, 6133 (17 and 18 June 1943); U.S., *Statutes at Large,* vol. 57, pt. 1, "National War Agencies Appropriation Act, 1944," 12 July 1943, pp. 531–32; Davis to DeVoto, 4 July 1943, Bernard DeVoto Papers, Stanford University Library, Palo Alto, California; Weinberg, "Wartime Propaganda," pp. 296, 298–99.

73 Davis to Ludlow, 5 July 1943, Box 11, Records of OWI; Ickes to Davis, 31 August 1943, Box 1, Records of OWI.

CHAPTER 3

1 James P. Warburg, *The Long Road Home: The Autobiography of a Maverick,* pp. 12–190; Interview with Lucille Gibbons Goldsen, 19 December 1972, and supplementary interview, 11 March 1976; Interview with Leonard Doob, 6 March 1973; Memorandum, Sherwood to the President, 9 August 1943, Robert E. Sherwood Papers, in possession of Lew David Feldman, House of El Dieff, Inc., 139 East 63rd Street, New York, New York 10021.

2 The Reminiscences of Joseph Barnes, 3 February 1954, pp. 27, 37–41, 48, 70–71, 80, 97–99, 108, 120–22, 134, 138, 204, 207–08, 216, 218, 223, 227, in the Oral History Collection of Columbia University, New York, New York; *New York Times,* 2 March 1970; Supplementary interview with Lucille Gibbons Goldsen, 11 March 1976; Memorandum, Sherwood to the President, 9 August 1943, Sherwood Papers; Sherwood to Donovan, 31 July 1941, Sherwood Papers.

3 *Congressional Record,* 78th Cong., 1st sess., vol. 89, pt. 5, 5991 (17 June 1943); "Winner, Percy," *Who's Who in America, 1944–1945,* vol. 23, p. 2336; U.S., Congress, House, Subcommittee of the Committee on Appropriations, *Hearings, Second Supplemental National Defense Appropriation Bill for 1943,* 77th Cong., 2nd sess., 1942, pp. 405–06; U.S., Congress, House, Subcommittee of the Committee on Appropriations, *Hearings, National War Agencies Appropriation Bill for 1944,* 78th Cong., 1st sess., 1943, p. 844; Interview with Lucille Gibbons

Goldsen, 19 December 1972, and supplementary interview, 11 March 1976.

4 U.S., Congress, House, Subcommittee of the Committee on Appropriations, *Hearings, National War Agencies Appropriation Bill for 1944,* 78th Cong., 1st sess., 1943, p. 844; Interview with Louis G. Cowan, 23 March 1973; Supplementary interview with Lucille Gibbons Goldsen, 11 March 1976; *Congressional Record,* 78th Cong., 1st sess., vol. 89, pt. 5, 5991 (17 June 1943).

5 The Reminiscences of Joseph Barnes, p. 208, Oral History Collection of Columbia University; U.S., Congress, Senate, Subcommittee of the Committee on Appropriations, *Hearings, National War Agencies Appropriation Bill for 1944,* 78th Cong., 1st sess., 1943, p. 331; "U.S. Is Losing the War of Words," *Life,* 22 March 1943, pp. 11–12, 14; U.S., Congress, House, Subcommittee of the Committee on Appropriations, *Hearings, Second Supplemental National Defense Appropriation Bill for 1943,* 77th Cong., 2nd sess., 1942, p. 427; U.S., Congress, House, Subcommittee of the Committee on Appropriations, *Hearings, National War Agencies Appropriation Bill for 1944,* 78th Cong., 1st sess., 1943, p. 708; Lerner, *Sykewar,* p. 194; Joseph Barnes, "Fighting With Information: OWI Overseas," p. 35; Notes on staff meeting of Bureau of Overseas Intelligence, 15 September 1944, Box 835, Records of OWI.

6 Thomson, *Overseas Information Service,* p. 21; Gosnell, "Organization of Information Activities," p. 324; "Report of Elmer Davis," p. 222; Interview with Lucille Gibbons Goldsen, 19 December 1972.

7 [Lilly], "Developing Overseas Operations," pp. 37–38, 56; Burlingame, *Don't Let Them Scare You,* pp. 192, 236; Warburg, *Long Road Home,* p. 190; Interview with Lucille Gibbons Goldsen, 19 December 1972; Meserve, *Robert E. Sherwood,* p. 176; Burlingame, *Don't Let Them Scare You,* p. 192; Davis, Account of Specimen Day in Washington, 5 January 1943, Davis Papers.

8 U.S., Congress, House, Subcommittee of the Committee on Appropriations, *Hearings, National War Agencies Appropriation*

Bill for 1944, 78th Cong., 1st sess., 1943, p. 768; "Beamed to Europe: OWI's Propaganda Paves the Way for Military Advances," *Newsweek,* 27 September 1943, p. 73; Statement of purposes and activities of the Eastern Press and Radio Bureau of the Overseas Operations Branch, n.d., Box 18, Records of OWI.

9 [Lilly], "Developing Overseas Operations," p. 33; "U.S. Propaganda," *Time,* 12 October 1942, p. 44; U.S., Congress, Senate, Subcommittee of the Committee on Appropriations, *Hearings, National War Agencies Appropriation Bill for 1944,* 78th Cong., 1st sess., 1943, p. 332; Thomson, *Overseas Information Service,* pp. 58–59; *San Francisco News,* 12 April 1944.

10 Richard H. S. Crossman, "Supplementary Essay," p. 341; G. E. Hughes, "History of Communications Operations" (unpublished report), n.d., pp. 15, 18–19, Box 63, Records of OWI; "U.S. Arsenal of Words," *Fortune,* March 1943, p. 85; Wallace Carroll, *Persuade or Perish,* pp. 126–27; U.S., Congress, House, Subcommittee of the Committee on Appropriations, *Hearings, National War Agencies Appropriation Bill for 1945,* 78th Cong., 2nd sess., 1944, p. 69; Memorandum, Barbara Soule to John K. Lageman, 29 March 1944, Box 18, Records of OWI; Moscrip Miller, "Talking Them out of It," p. 72; *Outpost News,* November 1944, copy in Box 3106, Records of OWI; "ABSIE" (unpublished report), n.d., Box 24, Records of OWI; "OWI's ABSIE," *Time,* 16 July 1945, p. 69; U.S., Congress, House, Subcommittee of the Committee on Appropriations, *Hearings, National War Agencies Appropriation Bill for 1946,* 79th Cong., 1st sess., 1945, p. 883.

11 Samples of the various items are available in the Records of OWI. There are copies of *The Century of the Common Man* and *The Life of Franklin D. Roosevelt* in the library of the United States Information Agency in Washington, D.C. The Franklin D. Roosevelt Library at Hyde Park, New York, has a full run of *Victory.* See also Carroll, *Persuade or Perish,* pp. 116, 124; "Truth & Trouble," *Time,* 15 March 1943, p. 13; U.S., Congress, Senate, Subcommittee of the Committee on Ap-

propriations, *Hearings, National War Agencies Appropriation Bill for 1945,* 78th Cong., 2nd sess., 1944, p. 24; "OWI's New Victory," *Newsweek,* 2 November 1942, p. 81.

12 U.S., Congress, House, Subcommittee of the Committee on Appropriations, *Hearings, National War Agencies Appropriation Bill for 1945,* 78th Cong., 2nd sess., 1944, p. 166; A. H. Feller to Edward R. Stettinius, Jr., 10 March 1943, Box 27, Records of OWI. For descriptions of the specialty items see W. H. Mullen to C. D. Jackson, 19 April 1943, Box 21, Records of OWI; *New York Herald Tribune,* 13 March 1943. For the pin cushion see the sample attached to a letter from Jo Stauffer to the Adjutant General of the Army, 29 May 1943, OPD 000.24, Sect. 1, Case 34 (noted in OPD 334.8 OWI), RG 165, Operations Division, Records of the War Department General and Special Staff, The National Archives, Washington, D.C.

13 [Edward P. Lilly], "Outposts" (Chapter 7 of official OWI history), pp. 2, 57, Box 64, Records of OWI; U.S., Congress, House, Subcommittee of the Committee on Appropriations, *Hearings, National War Agencies Appropriation Bill for 1945,* 78th Cong., 2nd sess., 1944, p. 211; Carroll, *Persuade or Perish,* pp. 136–37; *OWI-ETO: A Report on the Activities of the Office of War Information in the European Theatre of Operations, January 1944–January 1945* (London: The Reproduction Unit of OWI, n.d.), copy in the Library, The National Archives; Linebarger, *Psychological Warfare,* pp. 179, 182.

14 Memorandum, Ridge Harlan to Charles Siepmann, 24 January 1944, Box 3109, Records of OWI; Long Range Policy Directive for Japan, 2 March 1945, Box 827, Records of OWI; Central Directive, 30 May–6 June 1945, Box 819, Records of OWI; Central Directive, 27 August–3 September 1943, Box 818, Records of OWI.

15 Interim Policy Directive for France, No. 15, n.d., Box 817, Records of OWI; FIS Directive—France VII, No. 43, 20 April 1942, Box 817, Records of OWI; FIS Directive—France X, No. 64, week of 16 May 1942 and after, Box 817, Records of OWI; FIS Directive—France XV, No. 96, 24 June 1942, Box

817, Records of OWI; Central Directive, 30 May–6 June 1944, Box 818, Records of OWI; Central Directive, 6–13 June 1944, Box 818, Records of OWI; Corrected Copy of Special Guidance on the FCNL, 31 August 1944, Box 107, Records of OWI.

16 Robert A. Divine, *The Reluctant Belligerent: American Entry into World War II,* pp. 4, 39–40, 80; Gaddis Smith, *American Diplomacy,* pp. 90–98.

17 Oliver Griswold, Report on Office of War Information Participation in Psychological Warfare by Leaflets in China, 3 May 1945, Box 66, Records of OWI; Richard Watts, Jr., Informal Report for February, 5 March 1944, Box 3100, Records of OWI; Central Directive, 14–21 March 1945, Box 819, Records of OWI; Long Range Policy Directive for China, 15 January 1945, Box 827, Records of OWI; see also "Report of Elmer Davis," pp. 248–49.

18 Gaddis Smith, *American Diplomacy,* p. 82; Draft of Addendum to Minutes of Meeting of So-Called Inter-Governmental Committee, 11 August 1942, Box 5, Records of OWI.

19 Minutes of the Committee on War Information Policy— Meeting No. 2, 12 August 1942, Box 3, Records of OWI; Ralph Block to Ferdinand Kuhn, 28 December 1944, Box 67, Records of OWI; Ralph Block, Notes on OWI Operations in India, 8 June 1943, Box 67, Records of OWI.

20 State Department Comments on OWI Material, August 1942–January 1943, L:U.S. 8.5.1, Box 360/12, Records of OWI; Memorandum, Adrian Berwick to Ferdinand Kuhn, 23 February 1944, Box 67, Records of OWI; [Lilly], "Outposts," p. 7.

21 Memorandum, MacLeish to Davis, 10 November 1942, MacLeish Papers.

22 William L. Langer, *Our Vichy Gamble,* pp. 54, 136.

23 Hoyle, *A World in Flames,* pp. 166–67; William Hardy McNeill, *America, Britain, and Russia: Their Co-operation and Conflict, 1941–1946,* pp. 204–09, 245–52; Robert Murphy, *Diplomat Among Warriors,* pp. 126–41; Robert E. Sherwood, *Roosevelt and Hopkins: An Intimate History,* pp. 648–51; [Morris Jano-

witz] M.J. and [William E. Daugherty] W.E.D., "The Darlan Story," pp. 293–95.

24 Sherwood, *Roosevelt and Hopkins,* p. 655.

25 Warburg to Davis, 27 November 1942, Box 4, Records of OWI; Warburg to Sherwood, 2 January 1943, Box 43, Records of OWI; Cable #07182, Carroll to Sherwood and William D. Whitney, 7 December 1942, Box 107, Records of OWI; Carroll, *Persuade or Perish,* pp. 50–51.

26 Minutes of the Board of War Information Meeting, 16 November 1942, Box 41, Records of OWI; Sherwood, *Roosevelt and Hopkins,* pp. 653–54; Central Directive, 20–27 November 1942, Box 818, Records of OWI.

27 [Edward P. Lilly], "Words and Bullets in Battle: The Beginnings of PWB" (Chapter 5 of official OWI history), pp. 15–16, 19–20, 22, Box 64, Records of OWI; [Edward P. Lilly], "PWB Comes of Age" (Chapter 6 of official OWI history), pp. 45–46, 51, Box 64, Records of OWI; Weinberg, "Wartime Propaganda," pp. 369, 376–77; Carroll, *Persuade or Perish,* pp. 61–62; Memorandum of conversation with Peter C. Rhodes, 17 March 1943, Box 75, Records of OWI; [C. D. Jackson], Report on propaganda in the North African campaign, 1 March 1945, Box 75, Records of OWI; [Morris Janowitz] M.J. and [William E. Daugherty] W.E.D., "The Darlan Story," p. 297; [Wallace], *The Price of Vision,* p. 162.

28 Carroll, *Persuade or Perish,* p. 27; Diary of Henry L. Stimson, vol. 41, 22 December 1942, p. 108.

29 Carroll, *Persuade or Perish,* p. 80; Weinberg, "Wartime Propaganda," p. 379; Interview with Wallace Carroll, 14 March 1973; [Wallace], *The Price of Vision,* p. 161; [Lilly], "Words and Bullets in Battle," pp. 22–23.

30 Minutes of the Board of War Information Meeting, 26 January 1943, Box 41, Records of OWI; Harry L. Coles and Albert K. Weinberg, *United States Army in World War II—Civil Affairs: Soldiers Become Governors,* p. 49; Murphy, *Diplomat Among Warriors,* pp. 158–59; Hull, *Memoirs of Cordell Hull,* 2:1201; Sherwood, *Roosevelt and Hopkins,* pp. 675–77; Carroll, *Persuade or Perish,* pp. 84–85.

31 Memorandum, Winner to Sherwood, 19 July 1943, Box 43, Records of OWI.

32 Winston S. Churchill, *Closing the Ring*, pp. 45–46; Memorandum, Winner to Sherwood, 19 July 1943, Box 43, Records of OWI.

33 Memorandum, Winner to Sherwood, 19 July 1943, Box 43, Records of OWI.

34 McNeill, *America, Britain, and Russia*, p. 269; Memorandum, Roosevelt to Marshall, 21 May 1943, CCS 385 (3–1–43), Box 369, Records of the United States Joint Chiefs of Staff; Churchill, *Closing the Ring*, pp. 45–46.

35 A. Russell Buchanan, *The United States and World War II*, 1:170; Paul Kecskemeti, *Strategic Surrender: The Politics of Victory and Defeat*, pp. 73–74.

36 [James P. Warburg], Statement to Planning Board on the Incident of July 25, 1943, n.d., Box 817, Records of OWI.

37 Warburg, *Long Road Home*, pp. 201–02; Sherwood, *Roosevelt and Hopkins*, pp. 742–43; Model Story on Mussolini's Resignation (lc/No. 4), 25 July 1943, Box 817, Records of OWI; [Warburg], Statement to Planning Board on the Incident of July 25, 1943, n.d., Box 817, Records of OWI; Carroll, *Persuade or Perish*, p. 179.

38 [Warburg], Statement to Planning Board on the Incident of July 25, 1943, n.d., Box 817, Records of OWI; *New York World-Telegram*, 29 July 1943.

39 Model Stories on Mussolini's Resignation (lb & lc/No. 4), 25 July 1943, Box 817, Records of OWI; Statement of Commentator John Durfee, [25 July 1943], Box 817, Records of OWI; Statement of Samuel Grafton, 25 July 1943, Box 817, Records of OWI; James P. Warburg, *Unwritten Treaty*, p. 108.

40 [Warburg], Statement to Planning Board on the Incident of July 25, 1943, n.d., Box 817, Records of OWI; Warburg, *Unwritten Treaty*, p. 109.

41 *New York Times*, 27 July 1943; [Warburg], Statement to Planning Board on the Incident of July 25, 1943, n.d., Box 817, Records of OWI; Ted Olson, "The Short Unhappy Life of John Durfee," p. 39.

42 Press and Radio Conference #911, 27 July 1943, in Press
    Conferences, vol. 22, 1 July–31 December 1943, p. 036, in
    Franklin D. Roosevelt Library; *New York Times,* 28 July and 1
    August 1943; *New York Journal-American,* 2 August 1943;
    Washington Post, 12 August 1943.
43 *New York Times,* 1 August 1943; *New York World-Telegram,* 29
    July 1943; "The Strange Case of John Durfee," *Life,* 9 Au-
    gust 1943, p. 31; *New York Journal-American,* 2 August 1943;
    [Warburg], Statement to Planning Board on the Incident of
    July 25, 1943, n.d., Box 817, Records of OWI.
44 Kecskemeti, *Strategic Surrender,* p. 74.
45 Churchill, *Closing the Ring,* pp. 55–58; McNeill, *America, Brit-
    ain, and Russia,* p. 288.
46 McNeill, *America, Britain, and Russia,* p. 288; Press Conference
    #912, 30 July 1943, in Press Conferences, vol. 22, 1 July–31
    December 1943, p. 049, in Franklin D. Roosevelt Library;
    Churchill, *Closing the Ring,* pp. 58, 64.
47 [Warburg], Statement to Planning Board on the Incident of
    July 25, 1943, n.d., Box 817, Records of OWI; Warburg,
    Unwritten Treaty, p. 110; Memorandum, Sherwood to Milton
    Eisenhower, 7 August 1943, Warburg Papers; Statement by
    Robert E. Sherwood to the Overseas Planning Board, n.d.,
    Box 44, Records of OWI; Joseph Barnes to Earl Thacker, 24
    August 1943, reprinted in a Memorandum for circulation, 27
    August 1943, Box 3102, Records of OWI; *New York Times,* 29
    July 1943.
48 Buchanan, *United States and World War II,* 1:170–71; McNeill,
    America, Britain, and Russia, p. 298; Kecskemeti, *Strategic Sur-
    render,* p. 74.
49 Weinberg, "Wartime Propaganda," p. 412; Memorandum,
    Warburg to Davis, Sherwood, 11 August 1943, Box 21, Rec-
    ords of OWI.
50 McNeill, *America, Britain, and Russia,* pp. 300, 308; O'Connor,
    Diplomacy for Victory, pp. 59–60, 110–12; Memorandum, H. C.
    Train to Director of OWI, 31 August 1943, OPD 000.7 Secu-
    rity Sect. I, Case 3, Records of the War Department General
    and Special Staff; Central Directives, 10–17 September 1943,

25 September–2 October 1943, 8–15 October 1943, 22–29 October 1943, 25 April–1 May 1944, Box 818, Records of OWI.

51 Diary of Henry L. Stimson, vol. 41, 5 January 1943, p. 142, 22 January 1943, p. 174, vol. 42, 4 February 1943, pp. 23–24, 5 February 1943, p. 25, vol. 45, 20 December 1943, pp. 134–35.

52 Diary of Henry L. Stimson, vol. 42, 16 February 1943, p. 55; Minutes of the Board of War Information Meeting, 5 March 1943, Box 41, Records of OWI.

53 Interview with John Houseman, 12 June 1973; Calvin Hoover, *Memoirs of Capitalism, Communism, and Nazism,* p. 210; Minutes of the Board of War Information Meeting, 26 January 1943, Box 41, Records of OWI; Minutes of the Board of War Information Meeting, 10 February 1943, Box 41, Records of OWI; John Houseman, *Run-through,* p. 74; Memorandum, John Herrick to Davis, 15 February 1943, Box 45, Records of OWI; Minutes of the Board of War Information Meeting, 8 March 1943, Box 41, Records of OWI.

54 Minutes of the Board of War Information Meeting, 26 January 1943, Box 41, Records of OWI; Minutes of the Board of War Information Meeting, 6 April 1943, Box 41, Records of OWI; James Linen to Joseph Barnes, 22 August 1942, Joseph Barnes Papers, in possession of Mrs. Elizabeth Barnes, New York, New York; Interview with Lucille Gibbons Goldsen, 19 December 1972.

55 Memorandum, Milton Eisenhower to Stephen Early, 2 August 1943, Box 64, Records of OWI; Draft of letter to Elmer Davis, n.d., attached to Memorandum, Davis to the President, 11 August 1943, OF 5015, Roosevelt Papers; Sherwood to Grace Tully, 18 August 1943, PSF (OWI folder), Roosevelt Papers. The draft of the letter that Davis presented for the president to sign has "Not sent" written across the top; Harold D. Smith, Notes on Luncheon with Elmer Davis, 25 August 1943, Daily Record 1943 (#7), Harold D. Smith Papers, Franklin D. Roosevelt Library, Hyde Park, New York; *New York Times,* 26 August 1943.

56 Memorandum, Davis to the President, 14 July 1943, Box 64, Records of OWI; Memorandum, Davis to the President, 30 August 1943, Box 64, Records of OWI.

57 Roosevelt to the Secretary of State, 1 September 1943, Box 64, Records of OWI; Roosevelt to the Secretary of War, 1 September 1943, Box 64, Records of OWI; Roosevelt to the Secretary of the Navy, 1 September 1943, Box 64, Records of OWI.

58 Gosnell, "Overhead Organization of the Office of War Information," pp. 14–15.

59 Ibid., pp. 15–17; Harold F. Gosnell, "Relationship between Planning and Intelligence in Overseas Propaganda," Series 41.3, Unit 171, pp. 40–42, Records of the Bureau of the Budget; Memorandum on a conversation with Herman Kehrli and Charles Hulten and on a conference with Elmer Davis, Robert Sherwood, and Philip Hamblet, Gosnell to Pendleton Herring, 16 December 1942, Series 41.3, Unit 153d, Records of the Bureau of the Budget; *New York Herald Tribune*, 23 February 1943.

60 Gosnell, "Overhead Organization of the Office of War Information," pp. 18–19; Memorandum, Douglas Auchincloss to Sherwood, 29 November 1943, Box 835, Records of OWI; Memorandum, Davis to Sherwood, 7 December 1943, Box 835, Records of OWI.

61 "Tongue-tied," *Time,* 7 February 1944, p. 11; *PM,* 8 February 1944; *New York World-Telegram,* 28 January 1944; *New York Post,* 27 January 1944.

62 Bureau of the Budget, *United States at War,* p. 232; Burlingame, *Don't Let Them Scare You,* p. 73; Interview with Edward W. Barrett, 23 March 1973.

63 *New York Herald Tribune,* 8 February 1944; Interview with Charles A. H. Thomson, 22 August 1972, and supplemented with written comments, 11 January 1973.

64 Carroll, *Persuade or Perish,* p. 191; Interview with Wallace Carroll, 14 March 1973; *New York Times,* 10 December 1943; Cable, Opnav to Alusna, London (Davis to Ambassador Winant), 15 December 1943, MR 14, Roosevelt Papers.

65 Sherwood to Warburg, 18 December 1943, Warburg Papers.
66 Draft of Staff Order for Reorganization of the Overseas Branch, 4 January 1944, Box 4, Records of OWI.
67 Memorandum, Warburg to Sherwood, 3 January 1944, Warburg Papers; Davis to the President, 4 January 1944, Box 4, Records of OWI.
68 Roosevelt to Davis, 8 January 1944, Davis Papers; Davis to the President, 8 January 1944, PSF (OWI folder), Roosevelt Papers.
69 Warburg to Sherwood, 8 January 1944, Warburg Papers; Replies from Robert Sherwood to Charges brought by Elmer Davis, n.d., attached to a letter from Sherwood to the President, 13 January 1944, PSF (OWI folder), Roosevelt Papers.
70 Davis to the President, 18 January 1944, PSF (OWI folder), Roosevelt Papers; Memorandum, Sherwood to Grace Tully, 19 January 1944, PSF (OWI folder), Roosevelt Papers. See the *New York Times*, 29 January 1944, for one example of press comment.
71 [Davis], Notes on a Conversation with the President, 2 February 1944, Davis Papers; Davis and Sherwood, [Statement of Agreement], 5 February 1944, Davis Papers.
72 Interview with Wallace Carroll, 14 March 1973; Memorandum (containing statement to the press), Davis to All Employees, 7 February 1944, Warburg Papers; Dexter Teed, "A Warrior of Words"; "Barrett, Edward W.," *Who's Who in America, 1944–1945*, vol. 23, p. 109; Memorandum, Sherwood to Barrett, 9 February 1944, Box 74, Records of OWI; Sherwood to Davis, 22 September 1944, OF 5015-C, Roosevelt Papers; Bureau of the Budget, *United States at War*, p. 232.
73 *New York Times*, 8 February 1944; *New York Herald Tribune*, 8, 11, 13 February 1944; Memorandum (containing statement to the press), Davis to All Employees, 7 February 1944, Warburg Papers; U.S., Congress, House, Subcommittee of the Committee on Appropriations, *Hearings, National War Agencies Appropriation Bill for 1945*, 78th Cong., 2nd sess., 1944, p. 11.

74 Sherwood to Warburg, 9 February 1944, Warburg Papers; *New York Times,* 8 February 1944; *New York Herald Tribune,* 8 February 1944.
75 Teed, "A Warrior of Words."

CHAPTER 4

1 Thomson, *Overseas Information Service,* p. 95; [Lilly], "Words and Bullets in Battle," pp. 4–5; Gosnell, "Relationship between Planning and Intelligence," p. 37; Memorandum on an interview with Charles Thomson, Harold F. Gosnell to Pendleton Herring, 20 July 1943, Series 41.3, Unit 153d, Records of the Bureau of the Budget; Memorandum on an interview with Major General George V. Strong, Gosnell to Herring, 22 June 1943, Series 41.3, Unit 153a, Records of the Bureau of the Budget; Memorandum on an interview with Robert Sherwood, Gosnell to Herring, 26 May 1943, Series 41.3, Unit 153d, Records of the Bureau of the Budget; Memorandum on a telephone conversation with Allen Edwards, Gosnell to Herring, 16 June 1943, Series 41.3, Unit 153a, Records of the Bureau of the Budget; Memorandum on an interview with Charles Thomson, Gosnell to Herring, 11 January 1943, Series 41.3, Unit 153d, Records of the Bureau of the Budget.
2 [Lilly], "Outposts," pp. 20–22; [Lilly], "Words and Bullets in Battle," p. 6; Robert Lee Bishop, "The Overseas Branch of the Office of War Information" (Ph.D. diss., The University of Wisconsin, 1966), pp. 123–24; Carroll, *Persuade or Perish,* p. 12; Weinberg, "Wartime Propaganda," pp. 357–58; Interview with Archibald MacLeish, 4 November 1974.
3 Carroll, *Persuade or Perish,* pp. 27–29, 31; [Lilly], "Words and Bullets in Battle," pp. 8–9.
4 [C. D. Jackson], Report on propaganda in the North African campaign, 1 March 1945, Box 75, Records of OWI; Donald F. Hall, Psychological Warfare in the Mediterranean Theater: A Report to the War Department, Part I, n.d., Box 61, Records of OWI.

5 Frederick C. Painton, "Fighting with 'Confetti,' " p. 100; [C. D. Jackson], Report on propaganda in the North African campaign, 1 March 1945, Box 75, Records of OWI; [Lilly], "Words and Bullets in Battle," pp. 12–13; James Morris Erdmann, "U.S.A.A.F. Leaflet Operations in the ETO during the Second World War" (Ph.D. diss., The University of Colorado, 1970), pp. 119–20; Carroll, *Persuade or Perish*, p. 30.

6 [Lilly], "Words and Bullets in Battle," pp. 1–2, 11, 17.

7 Ibid., pp. 1, 17–18; [Lilly], "PWB Comes of Age," pp. 57–65; Ernie Pyle, *Here Is Your War*, p. 52; Milton Eisenhower, Speech—Psychological Warfare (delivered to Kansas Bankers' Association), 22 May 1943, Box 10, Records of OWI.

8 [Lilly], "Words and Bullets in Battle," pp. 15–16, 19; [Lilly], "PWB Comes of Age," p. 45; Weinberg, "Wartime Propaganda," p. 369.

9 [Lilly], "PWB Comes of Age," pp. 45–46; [Lilly], "Words and Bullets in Battle," pp. 22–26; Carroll, *Persuade or Perish*, p. 62; Donald F. Hall, Psychological Warfare in the Mediterranean Theater: A Report to the War Department, Part I, n.d., Box 61, Records of OWI; [C. D. Jackson], Report on propaganda in the North African campaign, 1 March 1945, Box 75, Records of OWI; [Edward Barrett] to Edward P. Lilly, n.d., Box 64, Records of OWI.

10 U.S., Congress, Senate, Subcommittee of the Committee on Appropriations, *Hearings, National War Agencies Appropriation Bill for 1944*, 78th Cong., 1st sess., 1943, p. 173; [Lilly], "PWB Comes of Age," pp. 52–54; Moscrip Miller, "Talking Them out of It," p. 23; *New York Times*, 30 April 1943; Hoyle, *A World in Flames*, p. 170; Erdmann, "U.S.A.A.F. Leaflet Operations," p. 142.

11 Erdmann, "U.S.A.A.F. Leaflet Operations," pp. 467–69; Memorandum, Brigadier General J. E. Hull to Colonel O. L. Nelson, 12 August 1943, OPD 000.24, Sect. 1, Case 37, Records of the War Department General and Special Staff.

12 Henry F. Pringle, "The 'Baloney Barrage' Pays Off," p. 79; [Lilly], "PWB Comes of Age," p. 77.

13 U.S., Congress, Senate, Subcommittee of the Committee on Appropriations, *Hearings, National War Agencies Appropriation Bill for 1945,* 78th Cong., 2nd sess., 1944, p. 57; Davis to Representative Robert Hale, 10 May 1944, Box 8, Records of OWI; Carroll, *Persuade or Perish,* pp. 156–57.

14 [Lilly], "PWB Comes of Age," pp. 77–85; Carroll, *Persuade or Perish,* pp. 165–66; Churchill, *Closing the Ring,* pp. 45–46; Moscrip Miller, "Talking Them out of It," p. 72.

15 [Lilly], "PWB Comes of Age," p. 81; Selden C. Menefee, "Propaganda Wins Battles," p. 185; Pringle, " 'Baloney Barrage' Pays Off," p. 78.

16 [Lilly], "PWB Comes of Age," p. 91; Crossman, "Supplementary Essay," pp. 327–28; Erdmann, "U.S.A.A.F. Leaflet Operations," pp. 183–84.

17 Carroll, *Persuade or Perish,* p. 174; [Lilly], "PWB Comes of Age," pp. 92–93; Menefee, "Propaganda Wins Battles," p. 184; Kecskemeti, *Strategic Surrender,* pp. 104–13.

18 [Lilly], "PWB Comes of Age," pp. 102–04; Pringle, " 'Baloney Barrage' Pays Off," pp. 18–19; Bill Mauldin, *Up Front,* pp. 95–97.

19 Menefee, "Propaganda Wins Battles," p. 185; U.S., Congress, House, Subcommittee of the Committee on Appropriations, *Hearings, National War Agencies Appropriation Bill for 1945,* 78th Cong., 2nd sess., 1944, pp. 66–67; Christopher Lewis, "The Voice of America," p. 866; James M. Minifie, "At an Alarming Rate," pp. 9–10.

20 [Lilly], "Words and Bullets in Battle," p. 2; Report on Activities of Overseas Branch in the North African Campaign, n.d., Box 64, Records of OWI; Report on North Africa prepared by R. E. Sherwood, n.d., Box 75, Records of OWI; Central Directive "A," 7 November 1942, Box 818, Records of OWI; OWI Special Guidance, 9 November 1942, Box 828, Records of OWI; Central Directive, 13–20 November 1942, Box 818, Records of OWI.

21 FIS Directive—Italy VIII, No. 56, 5–12 May 1942, Box 817, Records of OWI; FIS Directive—Italy X, No. 70, 19–26 May 1942, Box 817, Records of OWI; Eisenhower, Speech—Psy-

chological Warfare (delivered to Kansas Bankers' Association), 22 May 1943, Box 10, Records of OWI; U.S., Congress, House, Subcommittee of the Committee on Appropriations, *Hearings, National War Agencies Appropriation Bill for 1944*, 78th Cong., 1st sess., 1943, pp. 777–78; Memorandum, H. C. Train to Director of OWI, 31 August 1943, OPD 000.7 Security Sect. I, Case 3, Records of the War Department General and Special Staff; Central Directives, 21–28 May 1943, 30 July–6 August 1943, 10–17 September 1943, 25 September–2 October 1943, 8–15 October 1943, 22–29 October 1943, Box 818, Records of OWI.

22 Military Order: Office of Strategic Services, 13 June 1942, *Federal Register* 7, no. 117 (16 June 1942), pp. 4469–70.

23 Gosnell, "Organization of Information Activities," pp. 350–52.

24 Donovan to Davis, 27 June 1942, Box 2, Records of OWI; J.C.S. 155/1/D: Joint Chiefs of Staff—Functions of the Office of Strategic Services, 7 December 1942, Box 64, Records of OWI; Memorandum, MacLeish to Davis, 14 December 1942, Box 12, Records of OWI; Davis to Harry L. Hopkins, 15 December 1942, Box 12, Records of OWI.

25 Memorandum, William D. Whitney to Davis, 23 December 1942, Box 12, Records of OWI; [Lilly], "Words and Bullets in Battle," p. 32; Davis, Account of Specimen Day in Washington, 5 January 1943, Davis Papers.

26 Stimson to the President, 17 February 1943, OF 5015, Roosevelt Papers.

27 Eisenhower to Lieutenant General Joseph T. McNarney, 20 February 1943, Box 12, Records of OWI; Minutes of the Board of War Information Meeting, 23 February 1943, Box 41, Records of OWI; Memorandum, William D. Leahy to the President, 23 February 1943, CCS 334 OWI (6–13–42) I, Records of the United States Joint Chiefs of Staff; Leahy to the President, 24 February 1943, CCS 334 OWI (6–13–42) I, Records of the United States Joint Chiefs of Staff; Executive Order 9312, Defining the Foreign Information Activities

of the Office of War Information, 9 March 1943, *Federal Register* 8, no. 50 (12 March 1943), p. 3021.

28 "Report of Elmer Davis," p. 243.

29 Memorandum, Percy Winner to Sherwood, 28 December 1943, Box 43, Records of OWI; Central Directive, 20–27 January 1944, Box 818, Records of OWI.

30 *The Psychological Warfare Division, Supreme Headquarters, Allied Expeditionary Force: An Account of its Operations in the Western European Campaign 1944–1945* (Bad Homburg, Germany: Psychological Warfare Division, Supreme Headquarters, Allied Expeditionary Force, [1945]), pp. 15, 19, copy in Office, Chief of Military History, Washington, D.C.; [Richard Hollander], "A Brief Account of the Activities of the European Theater of Operations Division, United States Office of War Information" (unpublished manuscript), p. 144, Box 64, Records of OWI; Memorandum on Differences in Interpretation of Functions of PWD and OWI, no name, n.d., Box 835, Records of OWI; "Report of Elmer Davis," p. 250.

31 Anthony Cave Brown, *Bodyguard of Lies,* pp. 434–35; *The Psychological Warfare Division,* pp. 17, 106–23; Erdmann, "U.S.A.A.F. Leaflet Operations," pp. 272, 308–09, 326, 343; Carroll, *Persuade or Perish,* p. 265.

32 Pringle, " 'Baloney Barrage' Pays Off," p. 18; Frederick Sondern, Jr., "General McClure's Newsboys," p. 235; Carroll, *Persuade or Perish,* pp. 352–53, 356; Safe-Conduct Pass, in Current Combat Leaflets, Supreme Headquarters, Allied Expeditionary Force, Psychological Warfare Division, Geog M 091.412 SHAEF, in Office, Chief of Military History; Erdmann, "U.S.A.A.F. Leaflet Operations," p. 266.

33 Lerner, *Sykewar,* pp. 23, 239; William Harlan Hale, "Big Noise in Little Luxembourg," p. 377; Robert T. Colwell, "Radio Luxembourg: It Uses Jokes as Propaganda against the Nazis," p. 17.

34 Hale, "Big Noise in Little Luxembourg," pp. 379–80; Carroll, *Persuade or Perish,* pp. 302–03; Colwell, "Radio Luxembourg," pp. 17–18.

35 "Operation Annie," *Time,* 25 February 1946, pp. 68, 70;

H. H. Burger, "Operation Annie: Now It Can Be Told," pp. 12–13, 48, 50; Brewster Morgan, "Operation Annie," pp. 18–19.

36 Erdmann, "U.S.A.A.F. Leaflet Operations," p. 351; Sondern, "General McClure's Newsboys," p. 235; H. H. Burger, "Episode on the Western Front: The Amazing Story of a Psychological Unit Which Talked a Group of Nazis into Our Lines," p. 5; Carroll, *Persuade or Perish,* pp. 266, 294 n. 1.

37 FIS Directive—Germany XVII, No. 85, 8 June 1942, Box 817, Records of OWI; Summary of FIS Directives for Germany—From March to June 1942, 18 June 1942, Box 817, Records of OWI; OWI Directive—Germany XXIII, No. 109, 27 July 1942, Box 817, Records of OWI; Lerner, *Sykewar,* p. 183; Overlord: P.W.E./O.W.I. Outline Plan for Political Warfare, Annex I: Propaganda Objectives and Themes from Now until D-Day, 5 October 1943, CCS 385 (4–3–44), Sect. I, Box 367, Records of the United States Joint Chiefs of Staff; Carroll, *Persuade or Perish,* p. 203.

38 Office of the Chief of Naval Operations, Office of Naval Intelligence, "Special Activities (Z Branch)," Part 7, and "Special Warfare (W Branch)," Part 14, of "United States Naval Administration in World War II," pp. 884, 1339–40, 1348, 1379–81; Samuel Eliot Morison, *The Battle of the Atlantic, September 1939–May 1943,* pp. 403, 409; Ladislas Farago, *Burn after Reading: The Espionage History of World War II,* pp. 279–82; Ladislas Farago, *War of Wits: The Anatomy of Espionage and Intelligence,* p. 330; Maria Wilhelm, *The Man Who Watched the Rising Sun: The Story of Admiral Ellis M. Zacharias,* pp. 145–49; Ellis M. Zacharias, *Secret Missions: The Story of an Intelligence Officer,* pp. 307–11.

39 Carroll, *Persuade or Perish,* pp. 216–31; Special Directive—The Daylight Air Assault on Germany, 28 March 1944, Box 828, Records of OWI; Central Directive, 25 April–1 May 1944, Box 818, Records of OWI.

40 Carroll, *Persuade or Perish,* pp. 239–42; Central Directive, 9–16 May 1944, Box 818, Records of OWI.

41 Memorandum on Initial Allied Invasion Communiqué, John

B. Stanley and J. S. Phillips to Director of OWI and Coordinator of Inter-American Affairs, 26 May 1944, Box 113, Records of OWI; Memorandum on Statements to be Broadcast on "D" Day, Stanley and Phillips to Director of OWI and Coordinator of Inter-American Affairs, 26 May 1944, Box 113, Records of OWI; Central Directives, 20–27 June 1944, 27 June–4 July 1944, Box 818, Records of OWI; Central Directive, 11–18 July 1944, Box 819, Records of OWI; Carroll, *Persuade or Perish*, pp. 261–62.

42 Carroll, *Persuade or Perish*, pp. 270, 284; Central Directives, 11–18 July 1944, 15–22 August 1944, 22–29 August 1944, Box 819, Records of OWI.

43 Carroll, *Persuade or Perish*, pp. 272–82, 342–48; Central Directives, 5–12 December 1944, 27 December 1944–3 January 1945, 3–10 January 1945, Box 819, Records of OWI.

44 Special Information from the State Department, 15 July 1944, Box 115, Records of OWI; Special Information from the State Department, 13 July 1944, Box 115, Records of OWI; Principal Objectives of Propaganda to European Neutral Countries, 27 July 1944, Box 115, Records of OWI; Carroll, *Persuade or Perish*, p. 285; Davis to the Secretary of State, 30 September 1944, 840.48 REFUGEES/9–3044, Records of the Department of State.

45 McNeill, *America, Britain, and Russia*, pp. 269–70; Herbert Feis, *Churchill, Roosevelt, Stalin: The War They Waged and the Peace They Sought*, p. 109; Carroll, *Persuade or Perish*, pp. 309–10.

46 Warburg, *Long Road Home*, p. 192; Memorandum, Warburg to Davis, 4 May 1943, Warburg Papers; Memorandum on Anglo-American Propaganda, n.d., attached to letter from Wallace Carroll to H. Freeman Matthews, 25 March 1944, 811.20200/3–2544, Records of the Department of State.

47 Sherwood, *Roosevelt and Hopkins*, p. 696; Memorandum, Roosevelt to Marshall, 21 May 1943, CCS 385 (3–1–43), Box 369, Records of the United States Joint Chiefs of Staff; Telegram, Under Secretary of State Edward R. Stettinius, Jr., to the Secretary of State, 13 April 1944, *Foreign Relations of the*

United States: Diplomatic Papers—1944, 1:507–09; Hull, *Memoirs of Cordell Hull,* 2:1578–79; Carroll, *Persuade or Perish,* p. 322; Harry C. Butcher, *My Three Years with Eisenhower,* p. 518; Forrest C. Pogue, *George C. Marshall: Organizer of Victory, 1943–1945,* pp. 34, 383.

48 Carroll, *Persuade or Perish,* p. 321, n. 1.

49 John Mortum Blum, *Roosevelt and Morgenthau,* pp. 596–97, 600–07; Carroll, *Persuade or Perish,* pp. 298–300; Gaddis Smith, *American Diplomacy,* pp. 125–26.

50 Carroll, *Persuade or Perish,* pp. 330–32; Central Directive, 19–27 December 1944, Box 819, Records of OWI.

51 Carroll, *Persuade or Perish,* pp. 295, 338; Central Directives, 26 September–3 October 1944, 5–12 December 1944, 19–27 December 1944, Box 819, Records of OWI.

52 Weekly Propaganda Directive—Germany, 2 March 1945, Box 824, Records of OWI; Central Directive, 21–28 March 1945, Box 819, Records of OWI.

53 Carroll, *Persuade or Perish,* pp. 114, 268; Elsa Wardell, Audience Survey of Germany, 15 August 1944, Box 108, Records of OWI; U.S., Congress, House, Subcommittee of the Committee on Appropriations, *Hearings, National War Agencies Appropriation Bill for 1945,* 78th Cong., 2nd sess., 1944, p. 85; *PM,* 19 June 1945.

54 Buchanan, *United States and World War II,* 2:460–63; Kecskemeti, *Strategic Surrender,* pp. 141–42, 144–46, 149.

55 Gaddis Smith, *American Diplomacy,* p. 24.

56 U.S., Congress, House, Subcommittee of the Committee on Appropriations, *Hearings, National War Agencies Appropriation Bill for 1945,* 78th Cong., 2nd sess., 1944, p. 7.

57 Memorandum, Lieut. Col. Ben Stern to Director of OWI and Director of Overseas Branch, OWI, 27 March 1943, Box 4, Records of OWI.

58 "Overseas Branch, Pacific Operations" (unpublished report), n.d., pp. 9–10, Box 62, Records of OWI; Robert Sherwood to Stephen Early, 6 February 1942, OF 4733, Roosevelt Papers; Memorandum, Pat Frank to Davis and Sherwood, 27 August 1943, Box 64, Records of OWI.

59 "Report of Elmer Davis," p. 249; U.S., Congress, Senate, Subcommittee of the Committee on Appropriations, *Hearings, National War Agencies Appropriation Bill for 1946,* 79th Cong., 1st sess., 1945, p. 116; Burlingame, *Don't Let Them Scare You,* pp. 246–47.

60 Louis Berg, "Hog Callers In Action," p. 4; "OWI Propaganda against Japan: A Summary," *Leaflet News Letter,* vol. 1, no. 11, 1 September 1945, pp. 10–11, Box 39, Records of OWI; *Chicago Sun,* 26 November 1944; U.S., Congress, House, Subcommittee of the Committee on Appropriations, *Hearings, National War Agencies Appropriation Bill for 1946,* 79th Cong., 1st sess., 1945, pp. 884–85.

61 General Policy Outline for Propaganda as Psychological or Political Warfare Directed against Japan and into Japanese-Occupied Territories, 7 September 1942, Box 110, Records of OWI.

62 Central Directives, 4–11 July 1944, 28 November–5 December 1944, 9–16 May 1945, Box 819, Records of OWI.

63 Edwin O. Reischauer, *The United States and Japan,* pp. 108–13, 197; Takeshi Ishida, *Japanese Society,* pp. 11–12; Memorandum, Owen Lattimore to Robert Sherwood, 3 December 1943, (SC) A7–1/EF37, Folder: Secret 1943, Naval History Division; Edgar L. Jones, "Fighting with Words: Psychological Warfare in the Pacific," p. 51; Central Directive, 5–12 December 1944, Box 819, Records of OWI; Memorandum, Ruth Benedict to Leonard Doob, n.d. (attached to a cover memorandum dated 28 October 1944), Box 110, Records of OWI.

64 Edgar L. Jones, "Fighting with Words," p. 51; Central Directives, 15–22 August 1944, 4–11 July 1945, Box 819, Records of OWI; Carroll, *Persuade or Perish,* p. 262, n. 1.

65 Prisoners' suggestion quoted in "2604" (unpublished report of HQ-USAFPOA, A.C. of S., G-2), file #Geog O MidPac 314.76 (1944 Pacific War), p. 59, in Office, Chief of Military History; Leaflet, Serial No. 522, in a document entitled Psychological Warfare, Propaganda Material, Part Two, CINC-PAC-CINCPOA, December 1944, in Naval History Division;

Memorandum, George Taylor to Myrl S. Myers, 12 August 1943, 711.94114/14, Records of the Department of State; Edgar L. Jones, "Fighting with Words," p. 51.

66 Buchanan, *United States and World War II*, 2:559–67; Edgar L. Jones, "Fighting with Words," pp. 47–50; Report on Psychological Warfare Activities—Pacific Ocean Areas, n.d., Cinpac File, Naval History Division.

67 Cable Chwaa 29834, Fisher to Taylor, Fairbank, 20 January 1945, Box 110, Records of OWI.

68 Robert J. C. Butow, *Japan's Decision to Surrender,* pp. 2, 139, 141; Kecskemeti, *Strategic Surrender,* p. 163; Memorandum, Walter Wilgus to Joseph Barnes, 24 August 1942, Barnes Papers; Central Directive, 6–13 January 1943, Box 818, Records of OWI; Special Directive on Propaganda Treatment of Emperor, 3 June 1944, Box 818, Records of OWI; Annex on Treatment of Japanese Emperor, 28 November–5 December 1944, Box 819, Records of OWI; [James Forrestal], *The Forrestal Diaries,* p. 66; Brian L. Villa, "The U.S. Army, Unconditional Surrender, and the Potsdam Proclamation," pp. 76–77.

69 Zacharias, *Secret Missions,* pp. 3–70; Ellis M. Zacharias, "Eighteen Words That Bagged Japan," pp. 17, 117; Bill Davidson, "He Talked to Japan," pp. 55–56.

70 Notes on Conference with Captain Waldo Drake, 19 May 1945, Box 25, Records of OWI; Zacharias, *Secret Missions,* pp. 326–36.

71 Zacharias, *Secret Missions,* pp. 336–40, 342–45.

72 Edward Klauber to the Secretary of the Navy, 28 March 1945, Box 12, Records of OWI; Klauber to Captain John S. Phillips, 5 April 1945, Box 12, Records of OWI; Klauber to the Secretary of the Navy, 20 April 1945, Box 12, Records of OWI; Edward W. Barrett to John J. McCloy, 16 April 1945, OPD 000.24, Sect. III, Case 70, Records of the War Department General and Special Staff; Summary Note by Major General Clayton Bissell, 21 April 1945, OPD 000.24, Sect. III, Case 70, Records of the War Department General and Special Staff; Zacharias, *Secret Missions,* pp. 345–49.

73 Zacharias, *Secret Missions,* pp. 349–50, 399–401.

74 Ibid., p. 403.

75 Ibid., pp. 357–59, 406–10, 420–21.

76 Ibid., pp. 370–71.

77 Potsdam Proclamation, 26 July 1945, United States Department of State, *Foreign Relations of the United States: Diplomatic Papers—The Conference of Berlin (The Potsdam Conference), 1945,* 2:1474–76; Butow, *Japan's Decision to Surrender,* p. 140; Zacharias, *Secret Missions,* p. 421.

78 "OWI Propaganda against Japan: A Summary," *Leaflet News Letter,* vol. 1, no. 11, 1 September 1945, pp. 3–5, 13, 19, Box 39, Records of OWI; The Japanese Domestic Radio Audience—Report No. 16 from Bureau of Overseas Intelligence, Foreign Morale Analysis Division (OWI), 15 March 1945, Box 110, Records of OWI; U.S., Congress, Senate, Subcommittee of the Committee on Appropriations, *Hearings, National War Agencies Appropriation Bill for 1946,* 79th Cong., 1st sess., 1945, p. 34; *Christian Science Monitor,* 3 July 1945.

79 "OWI Propaganda against Japan: A Summary," *Leaflet News Letter,* vol. 1, no. 11, 1 September 1945, pp. 19–24, Box 39, Records of OWI; "Report of Elmer Davis," p. 249.

Epilogue

1 *New York Times,* 1 September 1945; Executive Order 9608, Providing for the Termination of the Office of War Information, and for the Disposition of Its Functions and of Certain Functions of the Office of Inter-American Affairs, 31 August 1945, *Federal Register* 10, no. 173 (1 September 1945), p. 11223.

2 Lasswell, *Propaganda Technique,* pp. 220, 222; Marks, "Idea of Propaganda," pp. xi, 64, 69, 95–96, 106, 122; see also Harold D. Lasswell, Ralph D. Casey, and Bruce Lannes Smith, *Propaganda and Promotional Activities: An Annotated Bibliography;* Harold D. Lasswell and Dorothy Blumenstock, *World Revolutionary Propaganda;* Leonard W. Doob, *Propaganda: Its Psychology and Technique.*

3 The Reminiscences of Joseph Barnes, pp. 224, 232, Oral History Collection of Columbia University; Sherman H. Dryer, *Radio in Wartime*, pp. 79, 99, 102.

4 Gordon Wright, *The Ordeal of Total War, 1939–1945*, pp. 66–72, 76–77; Peter de Mendelssohn, *Japan's Political Warfare*, pp. 10–11, 20–22, 128–33; L. D. Meo, *Japan's Radio War on Australia, 1941–1945*, pp. 1, 19–32; Frederick C. Barghoorn, *Soviet Foreign Propaganda*, pp. 7–28; Howland H. Sargeant, "Soviet Propaganda," pp. 41–44; Rhodes, *Propaganda*, pp. 18–19, 32–40, 211–12, 216–17, 224, 249, 252–53.

5 Wright, *The Ordeal of Total War*, pp. 73–76; Angus Calder, *The People's War: Britain, 1939–1945*, pp. 33–34, 503–04; R. H. Bruce Lockhart, *Comes the Reckoning*, pp. 126–27, 143, 152–55, 166, 168–71, 236, 249, 323; Rhodes, *Propaganda*, pp. 108–10, 119.

6 On war aims see Divine, *Roosevelt and World War II*, p. 58; Kolko, *Politics of War*, pp. 4, 242, 265–66.

7 *The Psychological Warfare Division*, frontispiece; Carroll, *Persuade or Perish*, p. 362.

8 "Report of Elmer Davis," p. 251.

9 Central Directive, 2–9 October 1942, Box 818, Records of OWI; FIS Directive—Italy, No. 95, 24 June 1942, Box 817, Records of OWI; *Small Town, U.S.A.*, copy in the library of the United States Information Agency; *Victory*, vol. 1, no. 2.

10 FIS General Directive—Production I, No. 63, 13 May 1942, Box 817, Records of OWI; Special OWI Guidance, 28 June 1942, Box 38, Records of OWI; Long-Range Directive, 15 January 1943, Box 43, Records of OWI; *Victory*, vol. 1, no. 1; Edward W. Barrett to Major John Boettiger, 28 September 1944, OF 5015-C, Roosevelt Papers; MacCann, *The People's Films*, pp. 144–45.

11 Jerome S. Bruner, *Mandate from the People*, p. 57; Davis, "War Information," p. 20; Transcript of a Davis speech before National Association of Broadcasters Tuesday Luncheon, n.d., Box 10, Records of OWI; U.S., Congress, House, Subcommittee of the Committee on Appropriations, *Hearings*,

National War Agencies Appropriation Bill for 1945, 78th Cong., 2nd sess., 1944, p. 6.

12 Weinberg, "Wartime Propaganda," p. 334; Draft statement —America in the World, attached to cover letter from Davis to Edward W. Barrett, 22 July 1945, Box 807, Records of OWI.

13 *Victory,* vol. 1, nos. 1, 3, 4, 5, and vol. 2, no. 3; Memorandum, Larry Rhine to Vince Mahoney, 4 September 1944, Box 3109, Records of OWI; Walter Davenport, "Free Speech— and Mr. Davis," p. 65; Interview with John Houseman, 12 June 1973; "OWI History (1942–1945) 'ONAF [Overseas News and Features] Sections' " (unpublished report), n.d., p. 76, Box 64, Records of OWI; Central Directives, 6–13 November 1942, 30 April–7 May 1943, 5–12 November 1943, Box 818, Records of OWI; Special Directive on Treatment of Negro and Other Minority Problems, 9 October 1944, Box 3107, Records of OWI.

14 MacCann, *The People's Films,* pp. 155–58; Fox, "Advertising and the Second World War," pp. 32, 290–92, 295, 297, 298– 99, 312–13; Blum, *V Was for Victory,* pp. 64–70; John M. Blum, "Where Have All the Heroes Gone?" p. 21; John Hersey, *Into the Valley: A Skirmish of the Marines,* pp. 73–75.

Bibliographical Essay

Manuscripts and archival materials were the most important sources for the study of American propaganda in World War II. Most helpful were the records of the Office of War Information, which were available at the National Archives annex in the Federal Records Center in Suitland, Maryland. While the several thousand boxes were not particularly well processed, it was possible to find the items that related to the development of OWI policy during the war. Office memoranda, letters, samples of propaganda items, and newspaper clippings were all useful. Less extensive but nonetheless indispensable were the papers of Franklin D. Roosevelt in Hyde Park, New York. I used material from the Official File (OF), the President's Personal File (PPF), the President's Secretary's File (PSF), and the Map Room collection (MR). Those records dealt with many of the problems the agency faced in the competitive atmosphere of wartime Washington. The full run of the OWI magazine *Victory* that I found at the Roosevelt Library helped reveal the image of America the agency developed. The personal papers of Elmer Davis and Archibald MacLeish in the Library of Congress, those of James P. Warburg in the John F. Kennedy Library in Waltham, Massachusetts, and those of Robert E. Sherwood in the possession of Lew David Feldman in New York recorded the reactions of top OWI policy makers to the troubles they encountered. The Diary of Henry L. Stimson at Yale University was instrumental in outlining the War Department's position toward OWI. The records of the War Department and the Joint Chiefs of Staff in the National Archives supplemented Stimson's observations. The records of the State Department in the National Archives, although lacking many references to OWI, added occasional useful bits of information.

The congressional hearings on the annual appropriation measures provided helpful material. Attempting to justify their role,

OWI's top officials spoke at length about what they were trying to do and what they were accomplishing. The hearings also revealed the barbed criticisms that members of OWI faced whenever they approached Capitol Hill.

Newspapers and general periodicals gave me a better sense of the pressures on OWI. I found numerous clippings from newspapers around the country in the records of OWI and in the papers of James P. Warburg. *Newsweek, Time, The Saturday Review of Literature,* and similar magazines followed OWI's activities closely and reported on the fortunes of the agency. One very useful source of information was the spring 1943 issue of *The Public Opinion Quarterly* which was devoted almost entirely to the Office of War Information. Articles by Elmer Davis, Joseph Barnes, and a number of scholars and public officials described the various efforts and activities of the organization in its first year of operation.

Several projects begun during the war provided important material about the Office of War Information. Edward P. Lilly became the official historian of OWI before the war ended. In that capacity, he assembled records, conducted interviews, and wrote several chapters, now in the OWI records, of an unpublished history of the agency. The sections dealing with the "Formulation of the OWI Charter" and "Words and Bullets in Battle" were particularly helpful. While Lilly was assessing the propaganda effort, the Bureau of the Budget was engaged in a study of its own. Hoping to record the activities of home front agencies in support of the war, one part of the project focused on American information policy. Harold F. Gosnell, assigned to that phase of the study, interviewed numerous individuals in OWI and related offices. His notes and unpublished essays, located in the records of the Bureau of the Budget in the National Archives, were very useful in revealing the personality conflicts that lay behind OWI's struggles in Washington.

Elmer Davis's report to the president gave me one more contemporary overview of the work of OWI. That report, in typescript in the Davis papers and records of OWI, was more readily accessible in printed form as Exhibit III in U.S., Congress, House, Foreign Operations and Government Information Subcommittee of the Committee on Government Operations, *Hearings, Government Information Plans and Policies, Part 2,* 88th Cong., 1st sess., 1963. Writing dispassionately, Davis discussed the numerous activities of his organization at home and abroad, and with his dry wit, managed to convey the frustrations he endured throughout his tenure. While he did not dwell on the personal quirks of his friends and enemies, his allusions were nonetheless revealing.

Although I was wary at first, I soon found that my interviews with people who had worked for OWI added another dimension to the picture revealed by the documentary record. Lucille Gibbons Goldsen, who served as Robert Sherwood's secretary until 1944, conveyed Sherwood's mannerisms and also the sense of loyalty he inspired in his subordinates. Wallace Carroll, on the other side of some of the bureaucratic struggles, developed further the themes he had used in his book *Persuade or Perish.* Archibald MacLeish expressed verbally the same convictions that marked his writing throughout the period. John Houseman described a number of OWI's problems, particularly those involving the State Department. Edward W. Barrett, almost thirty years after the end of the war, still appeared as the likable, well-organized executive who helped bring OWI under control in 1944. Charles A. H. Thomson, whose own work, *Overseas Information Service of the United States Government,* provided a starting point as I began my study, was most helpful. In his book he deliberately avoided dealing in personal terms with the people he had known well in the agency. In conversation he spoke freely and helped me understand what was really going on.

While I found the secondary literature about the Office of War Information somewhat limited, there were a number of useful studies. John Morton Blum's *V Was for Victory: Politics and American Culture During World War II* was suggestive, particularly about OWI at home. Charles Thomson's book laid out the structural organization of the agency. Sydney Stahl Weinberg's dissertation "Wartime Propaganda in a Democracy: America's Twentieth Century Information Agencies" was occasionally helpful but generally unexciting. I found her account of propaganda at home—

an amplification of her article "What to Tell America: The Writers' Quarrel in the Office of War Information"—more incisive than her description of the overseas work. Allen Irving Safianow's thesis "The Office of War Information" was similarly more helpful on the domestic side of the agency. David Lloyd Jones, in his dissertation "The U.S. Office of War Information and American Public Opinion during World War II, 1939–1945," dealt almost entirely with domestic affairs and gave a reasonable overview of the various information programs throughout the period. The only other work on OWI at home—LaMar Seal Mackay's dissertation "Domestic Operations of the Office of War Information in World War II"—was done for a degree in journalism, and aside from providing a useful detail here and there, was not much help. Robert Lee Bishop's "The Overseas Branch of the Office of War Information" was also done for a journalism Ph.D. It gave a broad overview but proved more descriptive than analytical. In considering combat propaganda I relied in part on Daniel Lerner's *Sykewar: Psychological Warfare against Germany, D-Day to VE-Day.* Anthony Rhodes, in *Propaganda: The Art of Persuasion: World War II,* provided commentary and pictures, not only about the American effort, but about propaganda activity in other nations as well.

To fit OWI into the broader wartime picture, both John Morton Blum's *V Was for Victory* and Richard Polenberg's *War and Society: The United States, 1941–1945* were important. For the diplomatic framework, William Hardy McNeill's *America, Britain, and Russia: Their Co-operation and Conflict, 1941–1946* provided a starting point in the voluminous literature. Gaddis Smith's shorter and more recent *American Diplomacy during the Second World War, 1941–1945* gave me a good overview of the period. Paul Kecskemeti's *Strategic Surrender: The Politics of Victory and Defeat* offered some interesting insights into the surrenders of Italy, Germany, and Japan. More useful for the Japanese case was Robert J. C. Butow's revealing account of *Japan's Decision to Surrender.*

Bibliography

Manuscripts and Archival Records

Barnes, Joseph. Papers, in possession of Mrs. Elizabeth Barnes, New York, New York.

Davis, Elmer. Papers, Library of Congress, Washington, D.C.

DeVoto, Bernard. Papers, Stanford University Library, Palo Alto, California. (Correspondence with Elmer Davis provided by mail.)

Hopkins, Harry. Papers, Franklin D. Roosevelt Library, Hyde Park, New York.

Hull, Cordell. Papers, Library of Congress, Washington, D.C.

MacLeish, Archibald. Papers, Library of Congress, Washington, D.C.

Naval History Division. Records, Washington, D.C.

Office, Chief of Military History. Records, Washington, D.C.

Office of War Information. Records, RG 208, National Archives Annex, Federal Records Center, Suitland, Maryland.

Roosevelt, Franklin D. Papers, Franklin D. Roosevelt Library, Hyde Park, New York.

Sherwood, Robert E. Papers, in possession of Lew David Feldman, House of El Dieff, Inc., 139 East 63rd Street, New York, New York 10021.

Smith, Harold D. Papers, Franklin D. Roosevelt Library, Hyde Park, New York.

Stimson, Henry L. Papers, Yale University Library, New Haven, Connecticut.

United States Bureau of the Budget. Records, RG 51, National Archives, Washington, D.C.

United States Department of State. Records, RG 59, National Archives, Washington, D.C.

United States Information Agency. Records, Washington, D.C.

United States Joint Chiefs of Staff. Records, RG 218, National Archives, Washington, D.C.

United States War Department General and Special Staff. Records, RG 165, National Archives, Washington, D.C.

Warburg, James P. Papers, John F. Kennedy Library, Waltham, Massachusetts.

PUBLIC DOCUMENTS

U.S. Department of State. *Executive Agreement Series,* no. 236.
———. *Foreign Relations of the United States: Diplomatic Papers—1944.* Washington, D.C.: Government Printing Office, 1966.
———. *Foreign Relations of the United States: Diplomatic Papers—The Conferences at Cairo and Tehran, 1943.* Washington, D.C.: Government Printing Office, 1961.
———. *Foreign Relations of the United States: Diplomatic Papers—The Conference of Berlin (The Potsdam Conference), 1945.* Washington, D.C.: Government Printing Office, 1960.
U.S. Congress, House. Committee on Appropriations. *National War Agencies Appropriation Bill, 1944.* H. Rept. 556. 78th Cong., 1st sess., 1943. [Serial no. 10762.]
———. Committee on Appropriations. *National War Agencies Appropriation Bill, 1946.* H. Rept. 653. 79th Cong., 1st sess., 1945. [Serial no. 10933.]
———. Foreign Operations and Government Information Subcommittee of the Committee on Government Operations. *Hearings, Government Information Plans and Policies, Part 2.* Exhibit III: "Report of Elmer Davis to the President on the Office of War Information." 88th Cong., 1st sess., 1963.
———. Subcommittee of the Committee on Appropriations. *Hearings, National War Agencies Appropriation Bill for 1944.* 78th Cong., 1st sess., 1943.
———. Subcommittee of the Committee on Appropriations. *Hearings, National War Agencies Appropriation Bill for 1945.* 78th Cong., 2nd sess., 1944.
———. Subcommittee of the Committee on Appropriations. *Hearings, National War Agencies Appropriation Bill for 1946.* 79th Cong., 1st sess., 1945.
———. Subcommittee of the Committee on Appropriations. *Hearings, Second Supplemental National Defense Appropriation Bill for 1943.* 77th Cong., 2nd sess., 1942.
U.S. Congress, Senate. Committee on Appropriations. *National War Agencies Appropriation Bill, 1946.* S. Rept. 380. 79th Cong., 1st sess., 1945. [Serial no. 10926.]
———. Subcommittee of the Committee on Appropriations. *Hearings,*

National War Agencies Appropriation Bill for 1944. 78th Cong., 1st sess., 1943.

————. Subcommittee of the Committee on Appropriations. *Hearings, National War Agencies Appropriation Bill for 1945.* 78th Cong., 2nd sess., 1944.

————. Subcommittee of the Committee on Appropriations. *Hearings, National War Agencies Appropriation Bill for 1946.* 79th Cong., 1st sess., 1945.

U.S. *Congressional Record.* 78th Cong., 1st and 2nd sess.; 79th Cong., 1st sess.

U.S. *Federal Register.* Volumes 7–10. 1942–45.

U.S. *Statutes at Large.* Volumes 57–59. 1943–45.

OWI PAMPHLETS AND PUBLICATIONS CITED

Battle Stations for All. Records of OWI.

The Century of the Common Man. Library, USIA.

Divide and Conquer. Records of OWI.

How to Raise $16 Billion. Records of OWI.

Information Guide of the Domestic Branch, Office of War Information: The Enemy. Library, National Archives.

Leaflet News Letter. Records of OWI.

The Life of Franklin D. Roosevelt. Library, USIA.

Negroes and the War. Records of OWI and Franklin D. Roosevelt Library.

Outpost News. Records of OWI.

OWI–ETO: A Report on the Activities of the Office of War Information in the European Theater of Operations, January 1944–January 1945. London: The Reproduction Unit of OWI, n.d. Copy in the Library, National Archives.

Small Town, U.S.A. Library, USIA.

The Thousand Million. Records of OWI.

The Unconquered People. Records of OWI.

Victory. Franklin D. Roosevelt Library.

NEWSPAPERS

Chicago Sun.
Christian Science Monitor.
New York Daily News.
New York Herald Tribune.
New York Journal-American.
New York Post.

New York Times.
New York World-Telegram.
Philadelphia Record.
PM.
San Francisco News.
Washington Post.

PERSONAL INTERVIEWS

Barrett, Edward W. 23 March 1973.
Carroll, Wallace. 14 March 1973.
Cowan, Louis G. 23 March 1973.
Doob, Leonard W. 6 March 1973.
Eisenhower, Milton S. 9 January 1973.
Goldsen, Lucille Gibbons. 19 December 1972, and supplementary inter-
    view 11 March 1976.
Houseman, John. 12 June 1973.
Kuhn, Ferdinand. 24 August 1972.
Linen, James A. 9 March 1973.
MacLeish, Archibald. 4 November 1974.
Thomson, Charles A. H. 22 August 1972, and supplemented with writ-
    ten comments 11 January 1973.

ORAL HISTORY COLLECTIONS

The Reminiscences of Joseph Barnes. In the Oral History Collection of
    Columbia University, New York, New York.

UNPUBLISHED MATERIALS

"2604." Report of HQ-USAFPOA, A.C. of S., G-2. Office, Chief of
    Military History.
"ABSIE." Report. Records of OWI.
Bean, Walton E. "George Creel and His Critics: A Study of the Attacks
    on the Committee on Public Information, 1917–1919." Ph.D. disser-
    tation, Graduate Division of the University of California, 1941.
Bishop, Robert Lee. "The Overseas Branch of the Office of War Infor-
    mation." Ph.D. dissertation, The University of Wisconsin, 1966.
Chapman, Richard Norman. "Contours of Public Policy, 1939–1945."
    Ph.D. dissertation, Yale University, 1976.
Ensley, Philip Chalfant. "The Political and Social Thought of Elmer
    Davis." Ph.D. dissertation, The Ohio State University, 1965.
Erdmann, James Morris. "U.S.A.A.F. Leaflet Operations in the ETO
    during the Second World War." Ph.D. dissertation, The University of
    Colorado, 1970.
Fox, Frank W. "Advertising and the Second World War: A Study in
    Private Propaganda." Ph.D. dissertation, Stanford University, 1973.
Gosnell, Harold F. "The Framing of the Office of War Information

Executive Order." Series 41.3, Unit 160. Records of the Bureau of the Budget.

————. "Organization of Information Activities for Defense and War, 1940–1942." Series 41.3, Unit 169. Records of the Bureau of the Budget.

————. "Overhead Organization of the Office of War Information." Series 41.3, Unit 170. Records of the Bureau of the Budget.

————. "Relationship between Planning and Intelligence in Overseas Propaganda." Series 41.3, Unit 171. Records of the Bureau of the Budget.

"History of the Radio Program Bureau for the Overseas Branch of the Office of War Information." Records of OWI.

[Hollander, Richard]. "A Brief Account of the Activities of the European Theater of Operations Division, United States Office of War Information." Records of OWI.

Hughes, G. E. "History of Communications Operations." Records of OWI.

Jones, David Lloyd. "The U.S. Office of War Information and American Public Opinion during World War II, 1939–1945." Ph.D. dissertation, State University of New York at Binghamton, 1976.

[Lilly, Edward P.]. "Developing Overseas Operations." Chapter 4 of OWI History. Records of OWI.

————. "Formulation of OWI Charter." Chapter 2 of OWI History. Records of OWI.

————. "Government Information before June, 1942: 'Confusion Confused.'" Chapter 1 of OWI History. Records of OWI.

————. "Outposts." Chapter 7 of OWI History. Records of OWI.

————. "PWB Comes of Age." Chapter 6 of OWI History. Records of OWI.

————. "Words and Bullets in Battle: The Beginnings of PWB." Chapter 5 of OWI History. Records of OWI.

Mackay, LaMar Seal. "Domestic Operations of the Office of War Information." Ph.D. dissertation, The University of Wisconsin, 1966.

Marks, Barry Alan. "The Idea of Propaganda in America." Ph.D. dissertation, University of Minnesota, 1957.

Office of the Chief of Naval Operations, Office of Naval Intelligence. "United States Naval Administration in World War II." Naval History Division.

"Overseas Branch, Pacific Operations." Report. Records of OWI.

"OWI History (1942–1945) 'ONAF Sections.'" Records of OWI.

Press Conferences. Typescript. Franklin D. Roosevelt Library.

Safianow, Allen Irving. "The Office of War Information." Master's thesis, Cornell University, 1968.

Sage, Peter. "From Poetry to Prose: Archibald MacLeish and the Defense of Democracy." Yale Misc. Mss. 70. Manuscripts and Archives. Yale University Library. New Haven, Connecticut.

Weinberg, Sydney Stahl. "Wartime Propaganda in a Democracy: America's Twentieth Century Information Agencies." Ph.D. dissertation, Columbia University, 1969.

BOOKS

Acheson, Dean. *Present at the Creation: My Years in the State Department.* New York: New American Library, 1970.

Barghoorn, Frederick C. *Soviet Foreign Propaganda.* Princeton, New Jersey: Princeton University Press, 1964.

Barrett, Edward W. *Truth Is Our Weapon.* New York: Funk & Wagnalls Company, 1953.

Blum, John Morton. *From the Morgenthau Diaries: Years of War, 1941–1945.* Boston: Houghton Mifflin Company, 1967.

———. *The Promise of America: An Historical Inquiry.* Baltimore: Penguin Books Inc., 1967.

———. *Roosevelt and Morgenthau.* Boston: Houghton Mifflin Company, 1970.

———. *V Was for Victory: Politics and American Culture During World War II.* New York: Harcourt Brace Jovanovich, 1976.

Boelcke, Willi A., ed. *The Secret Conferences of Dr. Goebbels: The Nazi War Propaganda, 1939–1943.* New York: E. P. Dutton & Co., Inc., 1970.

Brown, John Mason. *The Ordeal of a Playwright: Robert E. Sherwood and the Challenge of War.* New York: Harper & Row, Publishers, 1970.

———. *The Worlds of Robert E. Sherwood: Mirror to His Times, 1896–1939.* New York: Harper & Row, Publishers, 1965.

Bruner, Jerome S. *Mandate from the People.* New York: Duell, Sloan and Pearce, 1944.

Buchanan, A. Russell. *The United States and World War II.* 2 vols. New York: Harper & Row, Publishers, 1964.

Burlingame, Roger. *Don't Let Them Scare You: The Life and Times of Elmer Davis.* New York: J. B. Lippincott Company, 1961.

Butcher, Harry C. *My Three Years with Eisenhower.* New York: Simon and Schuster, 1946.

Butow, Robert J. C. *Japan's Decision to Surrender.* Stanford, California: Stanford University Press, 1954.

Calder, Angus. *The People's War: Britain, 1939–1945.* New York: Pantheon Books, A Division of Random House, 1969.

Carroll, Wallace. *Persuade or Perish.* Boston: Houghton Mifflin Company, 1948.

Catton, Bruce. *The War Lords of Washington.* New York: Harcourt, Brace and Company, 1948.

Cave Brown, Anthony. *Bodyguard of Lies.* New York: Harper & Row, Publishers, 1975.

Churchill, Winston S. *Closing the Ring.* Boston: Houghton Mifflin Company, 1951.

Clark, Delbert. *Washington Dateline.* New York: Frederick A. Stokes Company, 1941.

Coles, Harry L., and Weinberg, Albert K. *United States Army in World War II—Civil Affairs: Soldiers Become Governors.* Washington, D.C.: Office of the Chief of Military History, Department of the Army, 1964.

Creel, George. *How We Advertised America.* New York: Harper & Brothers Publishers, 1920.

Culbert, David Holbrook. *News for Everyman: Radio and Foreign Affairs in Thirties America.* Westport, Connecticut: Greenwood Press, 1976.

Current, Richard N. *Secretary Stimson: A Study in Statecraft.* New Brunswick, New Jersey: Rutgers University Press, 1954.

Daugherty, William E., in collaboration with Janowitz, Morris, eds. *A Psychological Warfare Casebook.* Baltimore: The Johns Hopkins University Press, 1958.

Davis, Elmer, and Price, Byron. *War Information and Censorship.* Washington, D.C.: American Council on Public Affairs, n.d.

de Mendelssohn, Peter. *Japan's Political Warfare.* London: George Allen & Unwin Ltd., 1944.

Divine, Robert A. *The Reluctant Belligerent: American Entry into World War II.* New York: John Wiley & Sons, Inc., 1965.

_____. *Roosevelt and World War II.* Baltimore: Penguin Books Inc., 1970.

_____. *Second Chance: The Triumph of Internationalism in America During World War II.* New York: Atheneum, 1971.

Doob, Leonard W. *Propaganda: Its Psychology and Technique.* New York: Henry Holt and Company, 1935.

Dryer, Sherman H. *Radio in Wartime.* New York: Greenberg, Publisher, 1942.

Eccles, Marriner S. *Beckoning Frontiers: Public and Personal Recollections.*
    Edited by Sidney Hyman. New York: Alfred A. Knopf, 1951.
Eisenhower, Milton S. *The President Is Calling.* Garden City, New York:
    Doubleday & Company, Inc., 1974.
Emery, Edwin, and Smith, Henry Ladd. *The Press and America.* New York:
    Prentice-Hall, Inc., 1954.
Falk, Signi Lenea. *Archibald MacLeish.* New York: Twayne Publishers,
    Inc., 1965.
Farago, Ladislas. *Burn after Reading: The Espionage History of World War II.*
    New York: Walker and Co., 1961.
————. *War of Wits: The Anatomy of Espionage and Intelligence.* New York:
    Funk & Wagnalls Company, 1954.
Feis, Herbert. *Churchill, Roosevelt, Stalin: The War They Waged and the Peace
    They Sought.* Princeton, New Jersey: Princeton University Press, 1967.
Ford, Corey. *Donovan of OSS.* Boston: Little, Brown and Company, 1970.
[Forrestal, James]. *The Forrestal Diaries.* Edited by Walter Millis, with the
    collaboration of E. S. Duffield. New York: The Viking Press, 1951.
Graebner, Norman A., ed. *An Uncertain Tradition: American Secretaries of
    State in the Twentieth Century.* New York: McGraw Hill Book Company,
    Inc., 1961.
Hersey, John. *Into the Valley: A Skirmish of the Marines.* New York: Alfred
    A. Knopf, 1970.
Hitler, Adolf. *Mein Kampf.* New York: Stackpole Sons Publishers, 1939.
Hoover, Calvin. *Memoirs of Capitalism, Communism, and Nazism.* Durham,
    North Carolina: Duke University Press, 1965.
Houseman, John. *Run-through.* New York: Curtis Books, 1972.
Hoyle, Martha Byrd. *A World in Flames: A History of World War II.* New
    York: Atheneum, 1970.
Hull, Cordell. *The Memoirs of Cordell Hull.* 2 vols. New York: The Macmil-
    lan Company, 1948.
Ishida, Takeshi. *Japanese Society.* New York: Random House, Inc., 1971.
Jones, Alfred Haworth. *Roosevelt's Image Brokers: Poets, Playwrights, and the
    Use of the Lincoln Symbol.* Port Washington, New York: Kennikat Press,
    1974.
Kecskemeti, Paul. *Strategic Surrender: The Politics of Victory and Defeat.* New
    York: Atheneum, 1964.
Kirkpatrick, Lyman B., Jr., and Sargeant, Howland H. *Soviet Political
    Warfare Techniques: Espionage and Propaganda in the 1970s.* New York:
    National Strategy Information Center, Inc., 1972.
Kolko, Gabriel. *The Politics of War: The World and United States Foreign Policy,*

1943–1945. New York: Vintage Books, Random House, Inc., 1970.

Langer, William L. *Our Vichy Gamble*. New York: W. W. Norton & Company, Inc., 1966.

Lasswell, Harold D. *Propaganda Technique in the World War*. New York: Alfred A. Knopf, 1927.

Lasswell, Harold D., and Blumenstock, Dorothy. *World Revolutionary Propaganda*. New York: Alfred A. Knopf, 1939.

Lasswell, Harold D., Casey, Ralph D., and Smith, Bruce Lannes. *Propaganda and Promotional Activities: An Annotated Bibliography*. Minneapolis: The University of Minnesota Press, 1935.

Leopold, Richard W. *The Growth of American Foreign Policy: A History*. New York: Alfred A. Knopf, Inc., 1962.

Lerner, Daniel. *Sykewar: Psychological Warfare against Germany, D-Day to VE-Day*. New York: George W. Stewart, Publisher, Inc., 1949.

Leuchtenburg, William E. *Franklin D. Roosevelt and the New Deal, 1932–1940*. New York: Harper & Row, Publishers, 1963.

———. *The Perils of Prosperity, 1914–1932*. Chicago: The University of Chicago Press, 1958.

Linebarger, Paul M. A. *Psychological Warfare*. Washington, D.C.: Infantry Journal Press, 1948.

Lingeman, Richard R. *Don't You Know There's a War On? The American Home Front, 1941–1945*. New York: G. P. Putnam's Sons, 1970.

Lockhart, Robert H. Bruce. *Comes the Reckoning*. London: Putnam, 1947.

Long, Breckinridge. *The War Diary of Breckinridge Long: Selections from the Years 1939–1944*. Edited by Fred L. Israel. Lincoln: University of Nebraska Press, 1966.

MacCann, Richard Dyer. *The People's Films: A Political History of U.S. Government Motion Pictures*. New York: Hastings House, Publishers, 1973.

MacLeish, Archibald. *American Opinion and the War: The Rede Lecture Delivered before the University of Cambridge on 30 July 1942*. New York: The Macmillan Company, 1942.

———. *A Time to Act: Selected Addresses*. Boston: Houghton Mifflin Company, 1943.

———. *A Time to Speak: The Selected Prose of Archibald MacLeish*. Boston: Houghton Mifflin Company, 1941.

McNeill, William Hardy. *America, Britain, and Russia: Their Co-operation and Conflict, 1941–1946*. New York: Johnson Reprint Corporation, 1970.

Manvell, Roger, and Fraenkel, Heinrich. *Dr. Goebbels: His Life and Death*. New York: Simon & Schuster, 1960.

Mauldin, Bill. *Up Front*. New York: Henry Holt and Company, 1945.

Meo, L. D. *Japan's Radio War on Australia, 1941–1945.* Carlton, Victoria: Melbourne University Press, 1968.

Meserve, Walter J. *Robert E. Sherwood: Reluctant Moralist.* New York: Pegasus, 1970.

Miller, Francis Pickens. *Man from the Valley: Memoirs of a 20th Century Virginian.* Chapel Hill: The University of North Carolina Press, 1971.

Mock, James R., and Larson, Cedric. *Words that Won the War: The Story of the Committee on Public Information, 1917–1919.* Princeton, New Jersey: Princeton University Press, 1939.

Moley, Raymond F. *After Seven Years: A Political Analysis of the New Deal.* Lincoln: University of Nebraska Press, Bison Book edition, 1971.

Morison, Elting E. *Turmoil and Tradition: A Study of the Life and Times of Henry L. Stimson.* New York: Atheneum, 1964.

Morison, Samuel Eliot. *The Battle of the Atlantic, September 1939–May 1943.* Boston: Little, Brown and Company, 1947.

Murphy, Robert. *Diplomat Among Warriors.* Garden City, New York: Doubleday & Company, Inc., 1964.

Nelson, Donald M. *Arsenal of Democracy: The Story of American War Production.* New York: Harcourt, Brace and Company, 1946.

O'Connor, Raymond G. *Diplomacy for Victory: FDR and Unconditional Surrender.* New York: W. W. Norton & Company, Inc., 1971.

Pease, Otis. *The Responsibilities of American Advertising.* New Haven, Connecticut: Yale University Press, 1958.

Pells, Richard H. *Radical Visions and American Dreams: Culture and Social Thought in the Depression Years.* New York: Harper & Row, Publishers, 1973.

Perrett, Geoffrey. *Days of Sadness, Years of Triumph: The American People, 1939–1945.* New York: Coward, McCann & Geohegan, Inc., 1973.

Peterson, H. C. *Propaganda for War: The Campaign against American Neutrality, 1914–1917.* Norman: University of Oklahoma Press, 1939.

Phillips, William. *Ventures in Diplomacy.* Boston: Beacon, 1953.

Pogue, Forrest C. *George C. Marshall: Organizer of Victory, 1943–1945.* New York: The Viking Press, 1973.

Polenberg, Richard. *War and Society: The United States, 1941–1945.* New York: J. B. Lippincott Company, 1972.

The Psychological Warfare Division, Supreme Headquarters, Allied Expeditionary Force: An Account of its Operations in the Western European Campaign, 1944–1945. Bad Homburg, Germany: Psychological Warfare Division, Supreme Headquarters, Allied Expeditionary Force, [1945].

Pyle, Ernie. *Here Is Your War.* New York: Lancer Books, Inc., 1971.

Reischauer, Edwin O. *The United States and Japan*. 3rd ed. Cambridge: Harvard University Press, 1965.

Rhodes, Anthony. *Propaganda: The Art of Persuasion: World War II*. New York: Chelsea House Publishers, 1976.

Roosevelt, Eleanor. *This I Remember*. New York: Harper & Brothers, 1949.

Rosenau, James N., ed. *The Roosevelt Treasury*. Garden City, New York: Doubleday & Company, Inc., 1951.

Schlesinger, Arthur M., Jr. *The Age of Roosevelt: The Coming of the New Deal*. Sentry Edition. Boston: Houghton Mifflin Company, 1958.

————. *A Thousand Days: John F. Kennedy in the White House*. Boston: Houghton Mifflin Company, 1965.

Sherwood, Robert Emmet. *Abe Lincoln in Illinois*. New York: Charles Scribner's Sons, 1939.

————. *Idiot's Delight*. New York: Charles Scribner's Sons, 1936.

————. *Roosevelt and Hopkins: An Intimate History*. New York: Harper and Brothers, 1948.

————. *There Shall Be No Night*. New York: Charles Scribner's Sons, 1940.

Shirer, William L. *The Rise and Fall of the Third Reich: A History of Nazi Germany*. New York: Simon and Schuster, 1960.

Shuman, R. Baird. *Robert E. Sherwood*. New York: Twayne Publishers, Inc., 1964.

Small, William J. *Political Power and the Press*. New York: W. W. Norton & Company, Inc., 1972.

Smith, Gaddis. *American Diplomacy during the Second World War, 1941–1945*. New York: John Wiley and Sons, Inc., 1965.

Smith, Grover. *Archibald MacLeish*. Minneapolis: University of Minnesota Press, 1971.

Smith, R. Harris. *OSS: The Secret History of America's First Central Intelligence Agency*. Berkeley: University of California Press, 1972.

Squires, James Duane. *British Propaganda at Home and in the United States, From 1914 to 1917*. Cambridge: Harvard University Press, 1935.

Thomson, Charles A. H. *Overseas Information Service of the United States Government*. Washington, D.C.: The Brookings Institution, 1948.

United States Bureau of the Budget. *The United States at War: Development and Administration of the War Program by the Federal Government*. Washington, D.C.: Government Printing Office, 1946.

[Wallace, Henry A.]. *The Price of Vision: The Diary of Henry A. Wallace, 1942–1946*. Edited by John Morton Blum. Boston: Houghton Mifflin Company, 1973.

Warburg, James P. *The Long Road Home: The Autobiography of a Maverick.* Garden City, New York: Doubleday & Company, Inc., 1964.

———. *Unwritten Treaty.* New York: Harcourt, Brace and Company, 1946.

Wilhelm, Maria. *The Man Who Watched the Rising Sun: The Story of Admiral Ellis M. Zacharias.* New York: A Giniger Book, published in association with Franklin Watts, Inc., 1967.

Wright, Gordon. *The Ordeal of Total War, 1939–1945.* New York: Harper & Row, Publishers, 1968.

Zacharias, Ellis M. *Secret Missions: The Story of an Intelligence Officer.* New York: G. P. Putnam's Sons, 1946.

ARTICLES

Barnes, Joseph. "Fighting with Information: OWI Overseas." *The Public Opinion Quarterly* 7 (1943): 34–45.

"Barrage on OWI." *Newsweek,* 3 May 1943, p. 36.

"Barrett, Edward Ware." *Who's Who in America, 1944–1945,* vol. 23, p. 109. Chicago: The A. N. Marquis Company, 1944.

"Beamed to Europe: OWI's Propaganda Paves the Way for Military Advances." *Newsweek,* 27 September 1943, pp. 73–74.

Behrman, S. N. "Old Monotonous—I." *The New Yorker,* 1 June 1940, pp. 33–36, 38, 40.

———. "Old Monotonous—II." *The New Yorker,* 8 June 1940, pp. 23–26, 28, 30, 33–34, 36.

Berg, Louis. "Hog Callers in Action." *This Week Magazine, New York Herald Tribune,* 27 May 1945, pp. 4–5.

Black, Gregory D., and Koppes, Clayton R. "OWI Goes to the Movies: The Bureau of Intelligence's Criticism of Hollywood, 1942–1943." *Prologue* 6 (1974): 44–59.

Blum, John Morton. "Where Have All the Heroes Gone?" *Harvard Bulletin,* 21 September 1971, pp. 19–24.

Boelcke, Willi A. "Editor's Introduction." In *The Secret Conferences of Dr. Goebbels: The Nazi War Propaganda, 1939–1943,* pp. vii–xxii. New York: E. P. Dutton & Co., Inc., 1970.

Brock, H. I. "Uncle Sam Hires a Reporter." *The New York Times Magazine,* 21 June 1942, p. 8.

Bruner, Jerome S. "OWI and the American Public." *The Public Opinion Quarterly* 7 (1943): 125–33.

Burger, H. H. "Episode on the Western Front: The Amazing Story of a Psychological Unit Which Talked a Group of Nazis into Our Lines." *The New York Times Magazine,* 26 November 1944, pp. 5, 52.

————. "Operation Annie: Now It Can Be Told." *The New York Times Magazine,* 17 February 1946, pp. 12–13, 48, 50.

Colwell, Robert T. "Radio Luxembourg: It Uses Jokes as Propaganda against the Nazis." *Life,* 5 March 1945, pp. 17–18.

"Congress Blast Against OWI Portends Assault on New Deal." *Newsweek,* 22 February 1943, pp. 25–26, 29.

[Cousins, Norman] N.C. "Abolish the OWI?" *The Saturday Review of Literature,* 26 May 1945, p. 18.

————. "Elmer Davis, Director, Office of War Information." *The Saturday Review of Literature,* 20 June 1942, p. 8.

"Cowles, Gardner, Jr." *Current Biography: Who's News and Why, 1943.* Edited by Maxine Block, pp. 145–48. New York: The H. W. Wilson Company, 1944.

Cowley, Malcolm. "The Sorrows of Elmer Davis." *The New Republic,* 3 May 1943, pp. 591–93.

Crossman, Richard H. S. "Supplementary Essay." In *Sykewar: Psychological Warfare against Germany, D-Day to VE-Day,* by Daniel Lerner, pp. 323–46. New York: George W. Stewart, Publisher, Inc., 1949.

Darrock, Michael, and Dorn, Joseph P. "Davis and Goliath: The OWI and Its Gigantic Assignment." *Harper's Magazine,* February 1943, pp. 225–37.

[Daugherty, William E.] W.E.D. "Unconditional Surrender." In *A Psychological Warfare Casebook,* by William E. Daugherty in collaboration with Morris Janowitz, pp. 273–79. Baltimore: The Johns Hopkins University Press, 1958.

————. "U.S. Psychological Warfare Organizations in World War II." In *A Psychological Warfare Casebook,* by William E. Daugherty in collaboration with Morris Janowitz, pp. 126–36. Baltimore: The Johns Hopkins University Press, 1958.

Davenport, Walter. "Free Speech—and Mr. Davis." *Collier's,* 3 June 1944, pp. 11, 62, 65.

Davidson, Bill. "He Talked to Japan." *Collier's,* 13 October 1945, pp. 15, 54–56.

Davis, Elmer. "America and the War." *The Saturday Review of Literature,* 18 May 1940, pp. 5, 11–12.

————. "Broadcasting the Outbreak of War." *Harper's Magazine,* November 1939, pp. 579–88.

————. "Is England Worth Fighting For?" *The New Republic,* 15 February 1939, pp. 35–37.

————. "OWI Has a Job." *The Public Opinion Quarterly* 7 (1943): 5–14.

————. "The Road from Munich." *Harper's Magazine*, December 1938, pp. 40–48.

————. "Roosevelt: The Rich Man's Alibi." *Harper's Magazine*, October 1939, pp. 460–68.

————. "The War and America." *Harper's Magazine*, April 1940, pp. 449–62.

————. "War Information." In *War Information and Censorship*, by Elmer Davis and Byron Price. Washington, D.C.: American Council on Public Affairs, n.d.

————. "We Lose the Next War." *Harper's Magazine*, March 1938, pp. 337–48.

————. "What the OWI Is Doing." *The Saturday Review of Literature*, 5 December 1942, pp. 7–9, 59.

"Davis on the Griddle." *Life*, 3 May 1943, pp. 24–25.

"Davis the Gadfly." *Newsweek*, 28 June 1943, pp. 84, 86.

Davison, W. Phillips. "Policy Coordination in OWI." In *A Psychological Warfare Casebook*, by William E. Daugherty in collaboration with Morris Janowitz, pp. 303–09. Baltimore: The Johns Hopkins University Press, 1958.

"Donovan Strategy." *Newsweek*, 17 November 1941, p. 21.

Drummond, Donald F. "Cordell Hull, 1933–1944." In *An Uncertain Tradition: American Secretaries of State in the Twentieth Century*, edited by Norman A. Graebner, pp. 184–209. New York: McGraw Hill Book Company, Inc., 1961.

"Dynasty in Radio." *Business Week*, 4 November 1944, pp. 81–84.

"Eisenhower, Milton Stover." *The National Cyclopaedia of American Biography*. Vol. I, pp. 332–33. New York: James T. White & Company, 1960.

"End of a Strenuous Life." *Time*, 8 May 1944, p. 14.

Feller, A. H. "OWI on the Home Front." *The Public Opinion Quarterly* 7 (1943): 55–65.

"First Time Up for Elmer." *The New Republic*, 20 July 1942, p. 83.

Gassner, John. "Robert Emmet Sherwood." *The Atlantic Monthly*, January 1942, pp. 26–33.

Hale, William Harlan. "Big Noise in Little Luxembourg." *Harper's Magazine*, April 1946, pp. 377–84.

Hawkins, Lester G., Jr., and Pettee, George S. "OWI—Organization and Problems." *The Public Opinion Quarterly* 7 (1943): 15–33.

"In Line of Duty." *Newsweek*, 8 May 1944, pp. 31–32, 35.

[Janowitz, Morris] M.J., and [Daugherty, William E.] W.E.D. "The Darlan Story." In *A Psychological Warfare Casebook*, by William E. Daugherty in collaboration with Morris Janowitz, pp. 291–98. Baltimore: The Johns Hopkins University Press, 1958.

"A Job for Elmer Davis." *The New Republic,* 22 June 1942, pp. 847–48.

Jones, Alfred Haworth. "The Making of an Interventionist on the Air: Elmer Davis and CBS News." *Pacific Historical Review* 43 (1973): 74–93.

Jones, Dorothy B. "The Hollywood War Film: 1942–1944." *Hollywood Quarterly* 1 (1945–1946): 1–19.

Jones, Edgar L. "Fighting with Words: Psychological Warfare in the Pacific." *The Atlantic Monthly,* August 1945, pp. 47–51.

"King, Ernest Joseph." *Current Biography: Who's News and Why, 1942.* Edited by Maxine Block, pp. 458–60. New York: The H. W. Wilson Company, 1942.

"Knox, [William] Frank[lin]." *The National Cyclopaedia of American Biography.* Vol. F, pp. 25–26. New York: James T. White & Company, 1942.

Koppes, Clayton R., and Black, Gregory D. "What to Show the World: The Office of War Information and Hollywood, 1942–1945." *The Journal of American History* 64 (1977): 87–105.

Landry, Robert J. "The Impact of OWI on Broadcasting." *The Public Opinion Quarterly* 7 (1943): 111–15.

Lauterbach, Richard. "Elmer Davis and the News." *Liberty,* 23 October 1943, pp. 13, 55–58.

Lewis, Christopher. "The Voice of America." *The New Republic,* 25 June 1945, pp. 864–67.

Lindley, Ernest K. "Marshall and King." *Newsweek,* 3 January 1944, p. 37.

McCormick, Robert. "King of the Navy." *Collier's,* 16 January 1943, pp. 18–20.

MacLeish, Archibald. "The Affirmation." In *A Time to Speak: The Selected Prose of Archibald MacLeish,* by Archibald MacLeish, pp. 8–16. Boston: Houghton Mifflin Company, 1941.

_____. "The American Cause." In *A Time to Act: Selected Addresses,* by Archibald MacLeish, pp. 105–16. Boston: Houghton Mifflin Company, 1943.

_____. "The Attack on the Scholar's World." *The Saturday Review of Literature,* 18 July 1942, pp. 3–6.

_____. "The Irresponsibles." In *A Time to Speak: The Selected Prose of Archibald MacLeish,* by Archibald MacLeish, pp. 103–21. Boston: Houghton Mifflin Company, 1941.

_____. "Look to the Spirit Within You." *The Reader's Digest,* February 1941, pp. 21–23.

_____. "We Cannot Escape History." In *A Time to Act: Selected Addresses,* by Archibald MacLeish, pp. 35–42. Boston: Houghton Mifflin Company, 1943.

————. "Words Are Not Enough." *The Nation*, 13 March 1943, pp. 368–72.

"MacLeish, Archibald." *The National Cyclopaedia of American Biography.* Vol. F, pp. 39–41. New York: James T. White & Company, 1942.

"Man of Sense." *Time*, 22 June 1942, p. 21.

Matthiessen, F. O. "The Quality of a Poet." *The Yale Literary Magazine* 106, no. 5 (February 1941): 7–9.

Menefee, Selden C. "Propaganda Wins Battles." *The Nation*, 12 February 1944, pp. 184–86.

Miller, Moscrip. "Talking Them out of It." *Collier's*, 19 August 1944, pp. 23, 72–73.

Minifie, James M. "At an Alarming Rate." *The Saturday Review of Literature*, 19 October 1946, pp. 9–11, 37–41.

Morgan, Brewster. "Operation Annie." *The Saturday Evening Post*, 9 March 1946, pp. 18–19, 121–24.

"Nickelling." In "The Talk of the Town." *The New Yorker*, 28 April 1945, pp. 16–17.

"Notes and Comment." In "The Talk of the Town." *The New Yorker*, 14 March 1942, pp. 13–17.

Olson, Ted. "The Short Unhappy Life of John Durfee." *Foreign Service Journal*, October 1962, pp. 36–39, 42–44.

"Once More, Where's Elmer?" *Newsweek*, 7 February 1944, pp. 53–54.

"One Year of War." *Time*, 7 December 1942, pp. 30–34.

"Operation Annie." *Time*, 25 February 1946, pp. 68, 70.

"Out of Office." *Newsweek*, 27 August 1945, pp. 78–80.

"OWI's ABSIE." *Time*, 16 July 1945, p. 69.

"OWI's New Victory." *Newsweek*, 2 November 1942, pp. 81–82.

Painton, Frederick C. "Fighting with 'Confetti.' " *The Reader's Digest*, December 1943, pp. 99–101.

Pringle, Henry F. "The 'Baloney Barrage' Pays Off." *The Saturday Evening Post*, 31 March 1945, pp. 18–19, 78–80.

"Publishers, Writers Quit OWI." *The Publishers' Weekly*, 17 April 1943, p. 1576.

R.G. "The Author." *The Saturday Review of Literature*, 23 October 1948, p. 8.

"Rockefeller, Nelson Aldrich." *The National Cyclopaedia of American Biography.* Vol. I, pp. 196–97. New York: James T. White & Company, 1960.

"Running the War." *Time*, 7 September 1942, pp. 24–26.

Sargeant, Howland H. "Soviet Propaganda." In *Soviet Political Warfare Techniques: Espionage and Propaganda in the 1970s*, by Lyman B. Kirkpat-

rick, Jr., and Howland H. Sargeant. New York: National Strategy
Information Center, Inc., 1972.

Sherwood, Robert E. "The Front Line Is in Our Hearts." *Ladies' Home Journal*, August 1941, pp. 21, 103–04.

———. "The Power of Truth." *Vital Speeches of the Day*, 1 November 1942, pp. 61–62.

———. "Rush All Possible Aid to Britain!" *The Reader's Digest*, September 1940, pp. 12–17.

Soderbergh, Peter A. "The Grand Illusion: Hollywood and World War II, 1930–1945." *University of Dayton Review* (1968–1969): 13–21.

Sondern, Frederic, Jr. "General McClure's Newsboys." *The American Mercury*, February 1945, pp. 232–36.

Spivack, Robert G. "The New Anti-Alien Drive." *The New Republic*, 29 November 1943, pp. 740–41.

Steele, Richard W. "Preparing the Public for War: Efforts to Establish a National Propaganda Agency, 1940–1941." *The American Historical Review* 75 (1970): 1640–53.

Stone, I. F. "Bureaucrat Bites Press." *The Nation*, 3 July 1943, pp. 6–8.

"The Strange Case of John Durfee." *Life*, 9 August 1943, p. 31.

"Struggle in the OWI." *The New Republic*, 26 April 1943, pp. 551–52.

Teed, Dexter. "A Warrior of Words." *Post, Weekly Picture Magazine, New York Post*, 19 February 1944.

"Tongue-tied." *Time*, 7 February 1944, pp. 11–12.

"Truth and Trouble." *Time*, 15 March 1943, pp. 13–15.

"U.S. Arsenal of Words." *Fortune*, March 1943, pp. 83–85, 169–70, 172, 174, 176.

"U.S. Is Losing the War of Words." *Life*, 22 March 1943, pp. 11–15.

"U.S. Propaganda." *Time*, 12 October 1942, pp. 44, 46.

Villa, Brian L. "The U.S. Army, Unconditional Surrender, and the Potsdam Proclamation." *The Journal of American History* 63 (1976): 66–92.

Wanger, Walter. "OWI and Motion Pictures." *The Public Opinion Quarterly* 7 (1943): 100–10.

" 'We Could Lose this War'—A Communiqué From the OWI." *Newsweek*, 17 August 1942, p. 30.

Weinberg, Sydney. "What to Tell America: The Writers' Quarrel in the Office of War Information." *The Journal of American History* 55 (1968): 73–89.

"Winner, Percy." *Who's Who in America, 1944–1945*. Vol. 23, p. 2336. Chicago: The A. N. Marquis Company, 1944.

Zacharias, Ellis M. "Eighteen Words That Bagged Japan." *The Saturday Evening Post*, 17 November 1945, pp. 17, 117–20.

Index